THE FULL BATTERY CODEBOOK

Developments in Clinical Psychology

Glenn R. Caddy, series editor
Nova University

MMPI-168 Codebook, by Ken R. Vincent, Iliana Castillo, Robert I. Hauser, H. James Stuart, Javier A. Zapata, Cal K. Cohn, and Gregory O'Shanick, 1984

Integrated Clinical and Fiscal Management in Mental Health: A Guidebook, by Fred Newman and James Sorensen, 1985

The Professional Practice of Psychology, edited by Georgiana Shick Tryon, 1986

Clinical Applications of Hypnosis, edited by Frank A. DePiano and Herman C. Salzberg, 1986

Full Battery Codebook, by Ken R. Vincent, 1987

In Preparation:

The Behavioral Management of the Cardiac Patient, by D. G. Byrne

Advances in the Treatment of Addictive Behaviors, edited by Ted D. Nirenberg

Language and Psychopathology, by Stephen Schwartz

THE FULL BATTERY CODEBOOK: A HANDBOOK OF PSYCHOLOGICAL TEST INTERPRETATION for Clinical, Counseling, Rehabilitation, and School Psychology

Ken R. Vincent
UNIVERSITY OF HOUSTON

ABLEX PUBLISHING CORPORATION
NORWOOD, NEW JERSEY

Printed in the United States of America.

Library of Congress Cataloging-in-Publication Data
Vincent, Ken R.
The full battery codebook.
(Developments in clinical psychology)
Includes bibliographies and index.
1. Psychological tests—Interpretation—Handbooks, manuals, etc. I. Title. II. Series. [DNLM:
1. Personality Assessment—instrumentation. 2. Psychological Tests—instrumentation. BF 176 V772f]
BF176.V56 1987 150'.28'7 87-1759
ISBN 0-89391-3952-2

Ablex Publishing Corporation
355 Chestnut Street
Norwood, New Jersey 07648

P

In order to keep this title in print and available to the academic community, this edition was produced using digital reprint technology in a relatively short print run. This would not have been attainable using traditional methods. Although the cover has been changed from its original appearance, the text remains the same and all materials and methods used still conform to the highest book-making standards.

CONTENTS

TO MY FAMILY

Preface

Since its development in the late 1970s, the author's Semi Automated Full Battery system of using word processor and codified statements to write psychological test reports and do psychological test analysis has been expanded considerably. The result is the Full Battery Code Book. The Full Battery Code Book is unique in that it is a carefully codified actuarial system for psychological test interpretation, coupled with ready-to-go narrative statements that can be blended into psychological test reports. It is midway between mathematical formulas for test analysis and fully automated computerized psychological test interpretations. The full battery code book is a collection of works that originated from the Semi Automated Full Battery, and has been expanded to include, not only additional tests, but stepped-down versions of computer programs.

The Full Battery Code Book should be useful to practicing clinicians, some of whom may wish to use it as is without modification, and some of whom may wish to modify it to their own phraseology. The Full Battery Code Book can also serve as a springboard for writing additional semi-automated code statements on other tests, as no code book on psychological testing interpretation would ever be complete enough to satisfy all clinicians unless it had virtually all published and unpublished instruments in its contents.

The Full Battery Code Book may also be used as a training tool for test interpretation. The author has used it both in his cognitive testing courses and advanced personality assessment courses as a tool to train psychologists in test analysis and interpretation. Given the option, students seem to fall into three approximately equal categories; namely, those who use it in a straightforward mechanical manner, those who modify the statements to fit their own phraseology, and those who use it solely as a guide to creating their own unique reports.

The Full Battery Code Book for the first time includes rules and statements for several current computer programs. This will give the reader a first-time look at the inner workings of these programs and allow the reader to use them when making decisions on tests that have been administered via paper and pencil and are being analyzed by the individual clinician. These have been included because the author strongly feels that full disclosure in computerized psychological testing is essential for the continued advancement of the science of psychology, and for the professional to be better able to use computerized testing with individuals. The recent trend of computer companies to hide their formulas and statements under the guise of trade secrets and smart business practice reduces us to accepting the validity of their statements solely on the reputation of their creators. This is regression to medieval reliance on authority and not science.

This Full Battery Code Book is an organized approach to test interpretation. Each test is thoroughly analyzed, and rules are given for the statements about what the test profiles mean for different age groups, populations, and settings. Educational and neuropsychological tests are examined, as well as tests of personality and interests.

The following provides a brief overview of the book. Chapter 1 is an introduction and history of the development of semi-automated full battery, and outlines the uses of the book. Chapter 2 details the methodology for using the Full Battery Code Book as is, in a straightforward, objective manner. Sample formats are given in the various subsections of psychological test interpretations, and overviewed. Chapter 3 provides standard formats and worksheets for psychological reports. Chapter 4 begins the interpretive section with statement of the examiner's impressions and comments about the examinee. Chapter 5 provides interpretative statements for the interview section. This section includes statements for a structured social history, the Vincent Biographical Inventory. However, its statements can be used for any social history. Chapter 6 outlines interpretation of cognitive testing, and includes the Wechsler Scales as well as brief IQ tests. Interpretation guides are provided for the neuropsychological, psychoeducational, and vocational interpretation of IQ tests. Chapter 7 outlines the Achievement portion of the Cognitive section and gives detailed interpretative statements for the Wide Range Achievement Test and Peabody Individual Achievement Test. Global functioning, psychoeducational functioning, and vocational functioning are provided, as well as a prediction of how the individual will do on the High School Equivalency Diploma tests. Chapter 8 outlines neuropsychological tests and includes the Wechsler Memory Scale, Trail Making Test, Reitan-Indiana Aphasia Screening Test, Abbreviated Halsted-Reitan Neuropsychological Test Battery, the Bender Gestalt, Memory for Designs Test, and Pfeiffer (SPMSQ) Scale.

Chapter 9 provides interpretative statements for Rorschach, and includes analysis of perceptual factors as well as content analysis. Chapter 10 focuses on Holtzman Inkblot Technique. Chapter 11 provides interpretative statements for Sentence Completion Tests, and includes global ego development rating statements for the Loevinger Ego Development rating method using sentence completion. Chapter 12 provides interpretative statements for the MMPI. Chapter 13 provides interpretative statements for the Diagnostic Inventory of Personality and Symptoms (DIPS). Chapter 14 covers interpretative statements for the Personality Inventory for Children (PIC). Chapter 15 provides interpretative statements for the Vineland Scales, both the original Vineland Social Maturity Scale and the

Vineland Adaptive Behavior Scales. Chapter 16 provides interpretative statements for the assessment of stress, and includes the Social Readjustment Rating Scale and Schedule of Recent Experience as well as the Life Event Scale for Children and the Life Event Scale for Adolescents. Chapter 17 provides statements for the Beck Depression Inventory. Chapter 18 provides interpretative statements for the Vocational Preference Inventory. Chapter 19 covers the Diagnostic Impression section as well as the Summary section.

Acknowledgements

The author wishes to express his appreciation and thanks to Dr. Bruce Duthie, who is a friend, colleague, and also publisher, for his permission to publish the author's previous works which are sold through his computer company, Pacific Psychological. Additionally, Dr. Duthie provided some of the interpretative statements used in the Rorschach section of the book. These were done in collaboration with the author in a previous handbook entitled *Semi-Automated System, Vol. III.* The author, additionally, wishes to thank Dr. Wayne Holtzman for permission to quote from his article, "New Developments on the Holtzman Inkblot Technique." The author also thanks Dr. Thomas Holmes for his permission to reproduce parts of the Social Readjustment Rating Scale and Survey of Recent Experience. Additionally, the author thanks Dr. R. Dean Coddington for his permission to reproduce parts of the Life Event Scale for Adolescents and Life Event Scale for Children. Also due thanks are Linn and Judy Wilson, who worked with me on computerizing some of the tests in the present battery, for their permission. Finally, the author acknowledges the permission of the University of Washington Press and the *Journal of Psychosomatic Research* for their permissions, and the kind permission of Jossey-Bass, who allow all authors to quote up to 1,000 words from their books on psychology.

CHAPTER ONE

Introduction

In the 7 years since its development, the Full Battery Code Book, which was originally developed as a Semi-Automated Full Battery (Vincent, 1980a,b,c, 1981, 1983a,b), has been expanded and enlarged, but the process remains the same. It is quite simply a series of objective rules and narrative statements for psychological test interpretation. The system is one step beyond a mathematical formula and the series of descriptors that go with a formula, and one step below a fully automated psychological test interpretation system.

Though the system was designed for use on a word processor, it can be used without a word processor. The psychologist can dictate the statements verbatim for his or her secretary to type, or the secretary may be provided a copy of the statements and can look up the call numbers and type them. The way it was developed, however, is the most expeditious way of getting a psychological report typed quickly and accurately, in that the prestored statements in the word processor can be called forth and assembled quickly. However, getting a report typed quickly is not the main impetus of this semi-automated full battery. Its main advantage is that it allows the psychologist to have access to codified information which he or she can then quickly sort through and assemble in a coherent interpretation of psychological testing. The system was born from the author's own frustration of time after time taking out copies of articles, books, and notes on tests, sorting them out, looking at each one as it was appropriate to the test data currently being analyzed, dictating statements about the test data, putting all the notes and references in order, and then beginning all over with the next case of test data to be analyzed. In addition to Meehl's classic mandate for good cookbooks (Meehl, 1954), the author takes much of his inspiration for the work from Jerry Wiggins. Wiggins (1973, p. 216) notes: "The clinician's best efforts on his or her best day when codified in an objective form will always be superior to his or her efforts at dynamic interpretation on any other day." This statement is the cornerstone and rationale for the Full Battery Code Book. The developed rules used in this book are a careful analysis of the literature on each test in question. The pre-coded statements are the author's synthesis in narrative form on the same literature. This type of system naturally takes the form of test-by-test interpretation rather than dynamic synthesis of the test data. In addition to the fact that it makes the battery usable verbatim, the author strongly recommends test-by-test interpretation; for when, as has been shown by research (Wiggins, 1973), the psychologist becomes overwhelmed by the data in question and makes the wrong diagnosis, the psychologist can still go back and learn which test or tests in the battery in question may have been right, even though the psychologist's analysis of the whole testing battery was wrong. In test-by-test reporting, each test stands alone and may be analyzed or re-analyzed in its own right and on its own merit. The codified interpretative statements and rules reduce test analysis time by approximately half. In compiling the report, the psychologist first scores the tests up to the interpretation stage. Then he or she looks up the test in question and searches the rule statements for those rules which fit the test profile patterns. The psychologist then either writes the code number of the narrative statement to be used, or dictates it or modifies it to suit his or her own writing style.

The author has used this system for the past 7 years and has analyzed the test results of approximately 3,000 individuals with the method. The recipients of the reports have been over a dozen psychiatrists, several neurologists, and half a dozen rehabilitation counselors. In retrospect, an advantage of this method is that the mechanical aspect of test analysis and report writing is invisible to the examinee and the recipient of the report. Because the tests are still administered in a standard way, the examinee gets personalized service, and, because the report is set up to be done on a word processor with the narrative statements merged into coherent paragraphs, the recipient of the report gets a product that is personalized and looks professional.

Probably one of the most useful functions of the Full Battery Code Book is in training psychologists, counselors, and educational diagnosticians in the business of psychological test interpretation. The author has used the handbooks and preliminary drafts of the Full Battery Code Book in teaching psychological test interpretation. In the author's experience, when allowed to use the code book statements in any way they choose, students tend to fall into three, approximately equal, groups: approximately one-third opt to use it in a straight forward mechanical manner, one third modify the statements to fit their own phraseology, and one third use it solely as a guide to creating their own unique reports. The Full Battery Code Book is, in a very real sense, "training wheels" for psychological test interpretation. Regardless of what manner in which the code book is used, there will always be low-frequency statements which need to be written into a report in addition to codified statements. However, when the Full Battery Code Book is used in the standard manner, the author's experience is that five additional sentences or less are all that is needed for a three- to four-page report. The author has attempted to include virtually all possible contingencies for psychological test interpretation, and has attempted to provide statements for a variety of test situations, including special considerations regarding age (such as children or geriatrics), race, culture, and educational factors that influence psychological test interpretation. The book is meant for the general practitioner of psychology, and practitioners who work in highly specialized settings, such as in an Institute for the Blind, are apt to find it helpful but incomplete for their special group. Neuropsychologists will wish for more interpretation than the screening test provided in the neuropsychology section. Educators wish for more and different types of achievement measures than are provided in that section, and counseling and clinical psychologists probably wish that various other tests were included in the personality and interest section than are included there. Nevertheless, in the day-to-day work in the general practice of psychology, whether in a private practice setting, a mental health center, a college counseling center, or hospital, the code book should encompass most all of the basic tests most frequently used by psychologists. It also provides a ready guide for psychologists to build their own statements on those tests that they use in addition to the tests listed in the code book.

The tests in the Full Battery Code Book are, with few exceptions, objective psychological test instruments. The Rorschach and Holtzman Inkblot Tests are projective instruments, but lend themselves to objective analysis and so are included here. A Sentence Completion Test Section is included, and it is unique among the other tests in the code book. Global statements are provided for Loevinger's objective rating of ego development using the sentence completion method, but psychosocial interpretative statements are also provided. The psychosocial interpretative statements are the author's own adaptation of objective attempts to codify projective information. While the sentence completion method has been found to be the most valid of all projective tests (Goldberg, 1965), its interpretation is essentially unstructured. While other psychologists, such as Forer (1957), have built elaborate structural summaries for analyzing Sentence Completion tests, this book goes beyond that, couples the analysis with the interpretation, and still provides ready-to-go statements, so that, if the overall rating by the psychologist of the person's Sentence Completion test performance is that they were depressed, the psychologist can choose the statement "the affective tone of the patient's responses was one of depression." This method fuses the interpretation check list and the narrative statement into one process. The Full Battery Code Book is the grandchild of the mandate for a more actuarial approach to testing (Meehl, 1954). Its method and basic application has been made possible by the advent of low cost computers. When all of the literature on a test is reviewed and the codification done at one time, the resulting statements are more inclusive than the clinician's hit and miss note review, book review, article review method of data analysis. The ready-to-go format saves time, not only in test analysis, but also by facilitating the sending of the report to the test-user before the test report is old news. All too often, before the report is received, the examinee has had to wait patiently for a decision on services to be made, or the decision was made in haste without the benefit of the highly beneficial test data. The *Full Battery Code Book* is an individualized approach to test interpretation that combines a thorough review of the literature and some automation with the human element, and also leaves the psychologist in control.

CHAPTER TWO

Using the Full Scale Battery Code Book

Any psychologist, counselor, or diagnostician using the Full Battery Code Book should first of all be thoroughly familiar with the basic principles of psychological testing. Though the Full Battery Code Book is a sophisticated system, it is no substitute for careful administration of the test to be analyzed and the examiner's notes and observations, because all psychological testing is, in a very real sense, two dimensional, and it only becomes real, accurate, usable information when it is integrated with a good history and additional test data. Even highly accurate instruments cannot stand alone and allow us to make cavalier judgements on individuals without more data, either from more tests or from the person's history.

When using the Full Battery Code Book, all psychologist test data must first be scored up to the interpretation stage. Then the examiner looks up the statements appropriate to the test in question and checks the rules for using the interpretative statement. The statements may be either written down on a worksheet for the examiner's secretary to call up on the word processor and type out, or dictated verbatim, or modified and integrated into a personalized report. Most of the time, the examiner will need to add one to five sentences to the standard format which relate to low-frequency behavior, and these can be written on the worksheet, as well as the call numbers for the statements which are then integrated into the full report by the secretary. Table 1 shows a sample worksheet with call numbers and low frequency statements written in, and Table 2 is an example of the finished report.

The user of the Full Battery Code Book may refer to the sample worksheet and report, and look back into the various sections of the book which were used to construct the report and see how to use the book in its standard manner. Each chapter is represented by a letter, and the number after the letter relates to the different call numbers and statements in the system.

The report follows the standard progression of identifying information, date, referral source, and instruments used. Next is the impression and comments section. (This section includes how the person looked, was dressed, and his or her presentation of self, as well as noteworthy comments made by the person being examined.) The next major section is the cognitive section, which includes

Table 1.

FORMAT # 1

NAME: Jane Doe REFERRAL: Dr. Smith

RACE: White AGE: 36

MARITAL STATUS: Married EDUCATION: H.S.

DATE: 1-9-86 DATE OF EXAMINATION: 1-9-86

PLACE OF EXAMINATION: Memorial Hospital

IMPRESSION:

C2, C17, C21, C28, C34, C55,

C79, C80

VINCENT BIOGRAPHICAL INVENTORY:

Q3, 6 yr. old son Q22 a 22 yr. old adopted son, Q31,

Q59, Q63, Q71, Q74, Q99, Q119, Q130, Q133;

72 of cancer., Q134, Q136: her mother: Q157:

neck pain, Q162, Q167: "neck pain, shoulder pain

and numbness in my right hand."

TEST RESULTS:

Intellectual Assessment:

I-1 IQ: Verbal: 108 Performance: Deferred Full Scale: 108

I-29, I-53, N-57

Personality Assessment:

RORSCHACH INKBLOT TECHNIQUE: R1, R9, R17, R36, R46, R83

LOEVINGER SENTENCE COMPLETION BLANK:

S-150, S-24, S-27, S-31, S-35, S-45, S-69, S-82, S-91,

S-92, S-109, S-145, "my health"

continued

Table 1. *(continued)*

DIPS or LESA: E-3, E-16, E-27, E-33

MMPI:
MVO, MVJ, M13, M13(e)

OTHER:

DSM II:
AXIS I: Psychological Factors Affecting Physical Condition (316.00)

AXIS II: Dependent Personality (301.60)
AXIS III: No data
AXIS IV: Psycho-Social Stressors for Past Year:
Health and other interpersonal: Severity: moderate

AXIS V: Highest Level of Adaptive Functioning for Past Year: Good
SUMMARY AND COMMENTS:
Z-14, Z-49, Z-60, psychogenic pain, Z-62, Z-92,
Z-101, Z-113, Z-122.

intellectual achievement and neuropsychological tests. This is followed by the personality statement section, which can include projective and objective assessment of personality, and, additionally, interest testing. This is followed by diagnostic impressions and summary comments sections.

The following is a walk-through of the different chapters of the book and how the sections and the different chapters are used.

Chapter 3 is the standard format section of the code book. It provides samples with ready-to-go formats used by the author. These can be modified and adapted as seen fit by the codebook users. The advantage of using a standard format is the saving in secretarial time, as commonly used formats can be brought up instantly and the requisite information, such as name, age, race, sex, and so on, quickly entered. Also, when one or two additional tests are used and added to the standard format, the standard format can readily be modified to accommodate these.

Table 2.

PSYCHOLOGICAL REPORT

NAME: JANE DOE
RACE: WHITE
AGE: 36
MARITAL STATUS: MARRIED
EDUCATION: HIGH SCHOOL
Date: 1-9-86
Date of Examination: 1-9-86
Place of Examination: MEMORIAL HOSPITAL

Referral: J.B. Jones, M.D.
Hospital/Clinic Name
Street Address
City, State, Zip Code

INSTRUMENTS USED:

Wechsler Adult Intelligence Scale
Pfeiffer (SPMSQ) Scale
Rorschach Inkblot Technique
Loevinger Sentence Completion Blank
MMPI
Social Readjustment Rating Scale
Vincent Biographical Inventory
Psychological Interview
Summary and Comments

IMPRESSION:

The person is a woman of medium build and stout. The person was attired in bedclothes. The person had blonde hair, which was dyed. The person wore glasses. The person was pleasant and cooperative during the evaluation.

BIOGRAPHICAL INVENTORY:

The person currently lives with her husband and 6 year old son. Additionally, she has grown children, a 22 year old adopted son. She reports her marriage is satisfactory. The person states that she is currently a housewife. She is happy in her work.

Developmentally, the individual reports being the oldest child. She has one brother. The individual reports having frequent crying spells and easily becoming upset as a child. She reports no significant educational problems.

Regarding the person's family of origin, she reports that her father died at age 72 of cancer. The person reports her mother is still living. The individual reports a history of alcoholism in her family of origin and states that drinking problems were evidenced in her mother. The individual reports she has a chronic health problem in the form of neck pain. She reports a previous psychiatric hospitalization for depression. The individual reports the reason for seeking present hospitalization as "neck pain, shoulder pain and numbness in my right hand."

INTELLECTUAL ASSESSMENT:

On the Wechsler Adult Intelligence Scale the person scored as follows:

Verbal IQ: 108; Performance IQ Deferred; Full Scale IQ: 108

continued

Table 2, Continued

The performance section of the WECHSLER was deleted because of the person's IV.

On the WECHSLER the person's overall performance was indicative of an individual whose intellectual ability was in the range of average to bright-normal intelligence.

On the Pfeiffer (SPMSQ) Scale the person's overall performance was negative regarding organic impairment.

PERSONALITY ASSESSMENT:

On the Rorschach Inkblot Technique the following is indicated: Restriction and stagnation of thought processes is likely. Significant dependency features are likely. Anxiety and tension are present; emotional lability and excitability are likely. Greater than normal somatic concern is indicated. Psychomatic symptoms are likely. The person feels insecure.

On the LOEVINGER SENTENCE COMPLETION BLANK the person's overall performance depicts an individual whose ego development is at the conformity level, which is the level of the majority of the general population. Emphasis is on conformity to external rules, law, order and authority. The person's outlook is traditional and in line with the values and mores of the polite middle class. Social acceptability and fitting in with one's peers and social group are emphasized. Individual differences are seen only in general terms. The person is passive, dependent, and insecure. The person is quite preoccupied with health concerns. The person is beset with anxiety. The person is quite preoccupied with weight problems. The individual is quite desirous of attention, support, and affection from others. The person is rigid and quite traditional in outlook regarding male-female sex roles. The individual appears close to her mother. The individual was close to her father and mourns his loss. The person appears close to and highly dependent on the spouse for emotional support. The individual is quite concerned about their children and worries about being a good parent. The individual sees her main problem as: "my health."

On the SOCIAL READJUSTMENT RATING SCALE the person's overall performance is indicative of an individual who has incurred a moderate amount of stress in the past year, the most significant of which are: Major personal injury or illness and son or daughter leaving home.

The 168 short form was administered orally because of the problems encountered in having the individual complete the standard form:

On the MMPI the person produced a valid profile and the person's validity scale configuration depicts an individual who responded to the test items in a defensive fashion and who is apt to be lacking in self insight, and be shy, inhibited and ill at ease socially. This profile type is most often encountered in neurotic individuals but, when attained in a seriously disturbed person, it may reflect a general lack of awareness on the person's part as to the seriousness of their condition.

Persons with this profile type are usually seen as neurotic and manifesting physical complaints. A wide variety of physical symptomatology is apt to be presented, including: back pain, headaches, gastro-intestinal difficulties, as well as occasionally numbness or tremors. These individuals are occasionally seen as depressed and anxious, but most likely convert their difficulties into functional physical complaints. These persons are usually egocentric, immature and suggestible and have longstanding and inordinate needs for sympathy, affection, attention and reassurance. Few of these patients are incapacitated by their illnesses, at least in regard to doing pleasurable activities. These individuals have a strong need to see and interpret problems in living as sociably acceptable. They typically make excessive use of the defense mechanisms of repression, denial and somatization. Secondary gain for their illnesses is apt to be operating in the form of either manipulation for the attention of close family members or avoiding responsibilities. In persons

Table 2, Continued

with back pain, this profile type is associated with poor surgery outcome. In a large well controlled study, less than 10% of these individuals obtained relief from back pain by purely medical measures alone.

These persons manifest physical problems of all sorts. This is the mean profile type for persons evidencing low back pain, early onset asthma, pseudo-neurologic conditions (including pseudo multiple sclerosis) and female urethral syndrome. In addition to the above-mentioned categories and gastro-intestinal and cardiac complaints, virtually no organ system is immune.

In a recent study of private psychiatric patients, the majority of this profile type received somatoform disorders (somatization, psychogenic pain, and hypochondriasis) or psychological factors affecting physical condition as their primary, secondary and tertiary diagnoses. Somatoform disorders or psychological factors affecting physical condition were modal, with the differential including affective disorders and adjustment disorders. The modal personality disorder cluster for patients of this profile type was anxious or fearful personality disorders; namely, compulsive, passive-aggressive or dependent.

As there is always the possibility that the person may be evidencing actual physical pathology in conjunction with functional symptomatology, the following is a breakdown of the probabilities of functional physical complaints being evidenced in any individual person and is based on studies done at the Mayo Clinic on individuals of this profile type. For individuals of this profile type who are the same age and sex as the person tested: two-thirds were seen as having primarily functional problems, one-tenth presented a mixed picture and one-fourth were seen as having primarily physical problems.

DIAGNOSTIC IMPRESSION:

Axis I: Psychological Factors Affecting Physical Condition (316.00)

Axis II: Dependent Personality (301.60)

Axis III: No data

Axis IV: Psycho-Social Stressors for Past Year: Health and other interpersonal:
Severity: Moderate

Axis V: Highest Level of Adaptive Functioning for the Past Year: Good

SUMMARY AND COMMENTS:

The person appears to be evidencing psychological factors affecting physical condition. The person is a passive, dependent individual who is easy prey for stress. While a case could be made from the test data that the person is suffering from psychogenic pain, the data favor the above impression. The person is a bright individual. The individual's overall level of ego-conscience development is good. Psychotherapeutically, the person will probably profit best from a treatment approach that emphasizes assertive training.

Sick role behavior is to be discouraged.

____

(Signature of psychologist)

Chapter 4 includes the interpretative statements for the impression and comments section. This was originally developed as an addendum to the Semi-Automated Full Battery and was entitled "Automated Interpretative Statements for Impression and Biographical Inventory and the Summary and Comments sections of a Psychological Assessment Battery" (Vincent, 1981). The Vincent Biographical Inventory will be covered later. Briefly put, the impression and comments section includes statements on appearance and test behavior. The statements for the Vincent Biographical Inventory cover all the information in a standard social history while covering the open-ended and multiple choice items that make up the Vincent Biographical Inventory. This section can be used to report any social history. The areas covered are living relationships, children, marriage, spouse abuse, affairs, previous marriages, problems with children, work, birth order, the examinee's own childhood and adolescent development, educational history, family of origin history, legal and addiction problems, health, and reason for seeking help.

The Cognitive Statements are sub-divided into statements for intelligence, achievement, and neuropsychological screening. The intelligence section begins with global functioning, interpretative statements for the Wechsler Scales as well as for a variety of brief IQ tests, including Wechsler short forms. Next comes the neuropsychological interpretation of the Wechsler Scales, and then the psychoeducational interpretation of the Wechsler Scales. This is followed by vocational interpretation statements of all deviation IQ tests. Next comes by the achievement portion of the cognitive section, which gives a detailed analysis of the Wide Range Achievement Test and the Peabody Individual Achievement Test. Global achievement functioning is covered, as well as psychoeducational functioning, vocational functioning, and prediction of how well the examinee would do if he or she took the High School Equivalency Diploma test. Finally, the cognitive section includes a variety of brief neuropsychological screening instruments, including the Wechsler Memory Scale, Trail Making Test, Reitan-Indiana Aphasia Screening Test, Abbreviated Halsted-Reitan Neurological Test Battery, the Bender Gestalt Test, Memory for Designs Test, and the Pfeiffer (short portable mental status questionnaire) Scale.

The personality statement section begins with projective assessment of personality, and this is divided into interpretative statements for the Rorschach and the Holtzman Inkblot Technique. The Rorschach section includes perceptual based statements as well as statements derived from analysis of content. The perceptual statements are, in part, the work of Duthie (Vincent & Duthie, 1983) and are augmented by the author's synthesis of what is most valid and has been replicated in the Rorschach literature. The system is not the Exner System (Exner, 1974) in its pure form, but generally follows the Exner symbols and interpretative formula. Those things that are not covered from Exner are essentially things that have not been replicated in the literature. Additionally, some of Exner's more elaborate formulas have not been covered because of the lack of validity information appearing in the literature since the development of the Exner System. The Exner system appears to be more of an inclusive amalgamation of all previous systems, whereas the Rorschach system in the Full Battery Code Book is exclusive of those things which have not been replicated. For example, in his analysis, Exner includes water as a content symbol and then goes on to state that water is sometimes indicative of dependency and sometimes indicative of alcoholism. The problem is that, since water as a content sign is unclear because of the contradictory findings in the literature, the Full Battery Code Book system does not include water as a content sign. The Holtzman Inkblot Technique statements are essentially those from the Semi-Automated Full Battery (Vincent, 1980c). Added to this Holtzman interpretation system, which was in part based on the work of Holtzman (1975), is the author's work on what was originally developed as the Holtzman Content Analysis Technique. This was a fully automated system based on content analysis which, when used as the sole form of inkblot analysis, has some demonstrated validity in and of itself (Vincent 1982a,b). The result is an expanded section of content analysis and determinants for the Holtzman system.

The next portion of the personality section is interpretative statements for Sentence Completion Test, and may be used with any sentence completion test. Additionally, global statements are given for Loevinger's system of rating ego development using the sentence completion method. Individuals wishing to use Loevinger's system rating ego development can use the interpretative paragraphs for ego levels within the report. The problem with Loevinger is the time it takes to score for global ego ratings; however, this is somewhat lessened with skill and with the fact that, at least in hospital based settings, the range of scores obtained is usually restricted (Vincent & Vincent, 1979, Vincent & Castillo, 1984a).

The MMPI statement section is a full revision of the earlier handbook by the author entitled "MMPI—Semi-Automated Interpretative Statements" (Vincent, 1980b). In addition to a thorough review of the literature relating to DSM III, the author's own work, which was based on code types derived from a private practice as opposed to state mental hospital settings, is included (Vincent et al., 1983; Vincent & Castillo, 1985). Also included are pertinent new findings on MMPI in general which have appeared since the publication of the earlier handbook by the author. Additionally, the author has devised a system for probable diagnoses on infrequent code types, using a formula that was developed for a fully automated program for the MMPI (Vincent, in press). This fully computerized system is presented in its entirety here in the Full Battery Code Book.

Excerpts on the rules developed for the infrequent code types, and developed for the system in general, are listed in Chapter 12 as a preface to the interpretative statements for the MMPI.

The next chapter provides interpretative statements for the Diagnostic Inventory for Personality and Symptoms, which is a new test developed by the author (Vincent, 1985a,b). The full rationale of the development for the Diagnostic Inventory of Personality and Symptoms is provided, as is the complete computer program narrative and rules for using the narrative statements.

This is followed by the interpretative statements for the Personality Inventory for Children. This is a unique test which obtains objective information on a child from a parent. The instrument provides a new way of knowing about children, as heretofore we have pretty much had to rely on projective information when the individual child was assessed, because objective testing of children is still in its infancy and beset with methodological difficulties.

The next chapter provides interpretative statements for the Vineland Scales. This is another method of assessing the child via interviewing the parent, and differs from the Personality Inventory for Children in that the examiner is the one who makes the objective rating based on the interview, as opposed to the parent actually taking an objective test. Interpretative statements are provided, not only for the original Vineland Social Maturity Scale but also for the new Vineland Adaptive Behavior Scales. Interpretative statements are provided for all three forms of the new Vineland Adaptive Behavior Scales, namely, the survey form, the expanded form, and classroom edition.

The next section covers the interpretative statements for the objective assessment of stressful life events, and covers not only the Social Readjustment Rating Scale, which was developed for use when the interviewer does the actual rating, but also the Survey of Recent Experience, which is the version of the Social Readjustment Rating Scale to be used when the examinee actually does the test-making. Additionally, the Life Event Scale for Children and the Life Event Scale for Adolescents, both of which were developed by R. Dean Coddington, are included in this section. The Life Event Scale for Adolescents can be taken by the adolescent, whereas the Life Event Scale for Children is given to the parent. Events that are peculiar to the life of a child are included in these latter scales. However, many authors prefer to use the Social Readjustment Rating Scale for all ages.

The next chapter provides interpretive statements for the Beck Depression Inventory, which, despite its psychometric limitations, has gained wide usage in the assessment of depression.

The personality assessment section ends with interpretative statements for The Vocational Preference Inventory, which is a paper-and-pencil test that is easily administered to individuals or can be read orally to them. The Vocation Preference Inventory was developed by Holland (1985b), and provides vocational information via the now famous RIASEC codes, which were also developed by Holland (1985a).

The final chapter has interpretative statements for the diagnostic section and summary, and includes major headings on the general distress of the person as well as statements covering neurosis, anxiety, disassociation, somatization, depression, psychosis, alcohol and drug problems, adolescent behavior problems, and character disorders. Differential diagnostic statements are also provided, as are statements detailing organic brain syndrome, learning disabilities, mental retardation, general IQ statements, and ego level. Medical psychiatric recommendations, psychotherapy recommendations, and recommendations for marriage and family therapy are included.

CHAPTER THREE

Standard Formats and Worksheet for the Full Battery Code Book

The following are examples of standard formats which can be used with the Full Battery Code Book. They are the ones most frequently used by the author. Individuals using the Full Battery Code Book may want to modify and develop their own formats, and the samples provided in Chapter 3 can be used as a guide.

Formats for the Full Battery Code Book

F-1_ PSYCHOLOGICAL REPORT

NAME:	Referral:	INSTRUMENTS USED:
RACE:		Wechsler Adult Intelligence Scale
AGE:		Pfeiffer (SPMSQ) Scale
MARITAL STATUS:		Rorschach Inkblot Technique
EDUCATION:		Loevinger Sentence Completion Blank
Date:		MMPI
Date of Examination:		Social Readjustment Rating Scale
Place of Examination:		Diagnostic Inventory of Personality and Symptoms
		Vincent Biographical Inventory
		Psychological Interview

F-2_ PSYCHOLOGICAL REPORT

NAME:	Referral:	INSTRUMENTS USED:
RACE:		Wechsler Intelligence Scale for Children—Revised
AGE:		Wide Range Achievement Test
MARITAL STATUS:		Memory-for-Designs Test
EDUCATION:		Rorschach Inkblot Technique
Date:		Sentence Completion Blank
Date of Examination:		Personality Inventory for Children
Place of Examination:		Life Event Scale for Children
		Psychological Interview

Formats for the Full Battery Code Book, Continued

F-3_ PSYCHOLOGICAL REPORT

NAME:	Referral:	INSTRUMENTS USED:
RACE:		Wechsler Adult Intelligence Scale
AGE:		Wide Range Achievement Test
MARITAL STATUS:		Pfeiffer (SPMSQ) Scale
EDUCATION:		Rorschach Inkblot Technique
Date:		Loevinger Sentence Completion Blank
Date of Examination:		MMPI
Place of Examination:		Social Readjustment Rating Scale
		Life Event Scale for Adolescents
		Psychological Interview

F-4_ PSYCHOLOGICAL REPORT

NAME:	Referral:	INSTRUMENTS USED:
RACE:		Wechsler Adult Intelligence Scale
AGE:		Memory-for-Designs Test
MARITAL STATUS:		Reitan-Indiana Aphasia Screening Test
EDUCATION:		Trail Making Test
Date:		Pfeiffer (SPMSQ) Scale
Date of Examination:		MMPI
Place of Examination:		Psychological Interview

F-5_ PSYCHOLOGICAL MMPI REPORT

PATIENT:
PSYCHIATRIST:
DATE:

WORKSHEET

FORMAT # _______

NAME: ______________________ REFERRAL: ______________________

RACE: ______________________ AGE: ______________________

MARITAL STATUS: ______________ EDUCATION: ______________

DATE: ______________________ DATE OF EXAMINATION: ________

PLACE OF EXAMINATION: ______________________________________

IMPRESSION: ____

____

____

____

continued

Formats for the Full Battery Code Book, Continued

VINCENT BIOGRAPHICAL INVENTORY: ______________________

TEST RESULTS:

INTELLECTUAL ASSESSMENT:

__: IQ: Verbal: ______ Performance: ______ Full Scale: ______

PERSONALITY ASSESSMENT:

RORSCHACH INKBLOT TECHNIQUE: ______________________

LOEVINGER SENTENCE COMPLETION BLANK: ______________________

Formats for the Full Battery Code Book, Continued

SRRS or LESA:

MMPI:

DIPS:

OTHER:

DSM II:
Axis I:

Axis II:

Axis III: no data
Axis IV: Psycho-Social Stressors for Past Year:

Axis V: Highest Level of Adaptive Functioning for Past Year:

SUMMARY AND COMMENTS:

CHAPTER FOUR

Interpretative Statements for Impression and Comments Section

Interpretative statements for the Impression and Comments section detail statements regarding the examinee's appearance, etc., and are fairly straightforward and self-explanatory. This section is one where, frequently, an additional comment or two is needed to describe unusual aspects of the examinee's behavior or unusual verbalizations by the examinee.

IMPRESSION

Appearance

C 1. The person is a man
C 2. The person is a woman
C 3. The person is an adolescent boy
C 4. The person is an adolescent girl
C 5. The person is a middle aged man
C 6. The person is a middle aged woman
C 7. The person is an elderly man
C 8. The person is an elderly woman
C 9. who was casually attired
C 10. who is petite
C 11. who is huge
C 12. of short stature
C 13. of medium height
C 14. who is tall
C 15. and emaciated.
C 16. and of thin build,
C 17. and of medium build.

C 18. and muscular build

C 19. and of chunky build.

C 20. and stocky build

C 21. and stout

C 22. and obese.

C 23. The person was well dressed and groomed.

C 24. The person was immaculately attired.

C 25. The person was formally attired.

C 26. The person was casually attired.

C 27. The person was attired in work clothes.

C 28. The person was attired in bedclothes.

C 29. The person was attired in a robe.

C 30. The person was attired in ward clothes.

C 31. The person was unkempt and slovenly attired.

C 32. The person has sandy blonde hair.

C 32a. The person had frosted hair.

C 33. The person had bleached blonde hair.

C 34. The person had blonde hair.

C 35. The person had light brown hair.

C 36. The person had brunette hair

C 37. The person had black hair.

C 38. The person had an Afro

C 39. The person had a bushy Afro

C 40. The person had reddish blonde hair

C 41. The person had bright red hair

C 42. The person had reddish brown hair

C 43. The person had streaked hair

C 44. The person had black hair.

C 45. The person had salt-and-pepper hair.

C 46. The person had a mustache.

C 47. The person had a full beard.

C 48. The person had the beginnings of a beard.

C 49. The person was unshaven.

C 50. The person had a goatee.

C 51. The person was bald.
C 52. which was thinning.
C 53. which was long.
C 54. which was laced with grey.
C 55. which was dyed.
C 56. which was a wig.
C 57. The person has a tattoo.
C 58. The person has multiple tattoos.
C 59. The person had braces on their teeth.
C 60. The person had several teeth missing.
C 61. The person had gold capped teeth.
C 62. The person walked with a limp.
C 63. The person walked with a cane.
C 64. The person walked with crutches.
C 65. The person was in a wheel chair.
C 66. The person had an obvious motor impairment.
C 67. The person's dominant arm was in a cast.
C 68. The person's non-dominant arm was in a cast.
C 69. The person's dominant arm was paralyzed.
C 70. The person's non-dominant arm was paralyzed.
C 71. The person was receiving an IV which compromised the testing somewhat.
C 72. The person stuttered.
C 73. The person's speech was slurred.
C 74. The person had an obvious speech impediment.
C 75. The person was a bit hard of hearing.
C 76. The person was hard of hearing.
C 77. The person was quite hard of hearing and this made the testing difficult.
C 78. The person wore a hearing aid.
C 79. The person wore glasses.

Test Behavior

C 80. The person was pleasant and cooperative during the evaluation.
C 81. The person was despondent during the initial phase of the evaluation but brightened as the examination progressed.

C 82. The person was despondent during the evaluation.

C 83. The person was negative and sullen during the evaluation.

C 84. The person was overtly cooperative during the evaluation.

C 85. The person was initially somewhat negative during the initial phases of the testing, but the person's mood improved as the evaluation progressed.

C 86. The person was anxious during the evaluation.

C 87. The person was somewhat anxious during the evaluation.

C 88. The person was defensive during the evaluation.

C 89. The person was generally uncooperative during the evaluation.

C 90. The person was hostile and suspicious during the evaluation.

C 91. The person was hostile during much of the evaluation.

C 92. The person was restless.

C 93. The person was distractible.

C 94. The person was agitated.

C 95. The person was restless and euphoric during the evaluation.

C 96. The person manifested a pressure of speech during the evaluation.

C 97. The person was quite verbose during the evaluation.

C 98. The person was emotionally labile during the evaluation.

C 99. The person was overdramatic and emotionally labile during the evaluation.

C 100. Overdramatization was evidenced.

C 101. The person was withdrawn during much of the evaluation.

C 102. Many of the person's verbalizations were loose, disjointed and bizarre.

C 103. Some of the person's responses were a bit unusual.

C 104. Some of the person's verbalizations seemed a bit loose.

C 105. The person alluded to feelings of paranoia.

C 106. Paranoid ideation was evidenced.

C 107. Some of the person's verbalizations appeared delusional.

C 108. Delusional content was evidenced in the person's thinking.

C 109. The person alluded to experiencing hallucinations.

C 110. The person appeared to be hallucinating during the evaluation.

C 111. Childlike behavior was evidenced.

C 112. The person was quite slow during the evaluation.

C 113. The person approached the task as if a Herculean effort was required to endure them.

C 114. The person appeared quite fatigued during the evaluation.

C 115. The person was unable to complete the evaluation in its entirety.

C 116. The person was unwilling to complete the evaluation in its entirety.

C 117. The person did not appear to be a reliable interview source.

C 118. The person's reliability as an interview source appeared somewhat questionable.

CHAPTER FIVE

Interpretative Statements for the Interview and Vincent Biographical Inventory (Social History) Section

This section contains interpretative statements that can be used with any social history. It is especially devised to be used with the Vincent Biographical Inventory, which is a brief interview sheet that may be used to structure the interview and be filled out by the examiner, or it can be filled out by the examinee and followed up with an interview. The author prefers to ask the questions and record the statements himself, and this format was used in the development of the *MMPI Code Book* (Vincent et al., 1984). The *MMPI Code Book* (Vincent et al., 1984) gives an analysis of frequency for the objective portions of the Vincent Biographical Inventory on a sample of 400 private psychiatric patients. The Vincent Biographical Inventory facilitates the use of this section, but any interview, structured or unstructured, is satisfactory. A sample copy of the Vincent Biographical Inventory is presented at the end of the chapter.

INTERPRETATIVE STATEMENTS FOR VINCENT BIOGRAPHICAL INVENTORY

Living Relationship

Q 1. The person currently lives with her husband.

Q 2. The person currently lives with his wife.

Q 3. The person currently lives with her husband and

Q 4. The person currently lives with his wife and

Q 5. The person currently lives alone.

Q 6. The person currently lives in a nursing home.

Q 7. The person currently lives with ______.

Q 8. The person currently lives with her lover.

Q 9. The person currently lives with his lover.

Q 10. The person currently lives with her boy friend.

Q 11. The person currently lives with his girl friend.

Q 12. The person currently lives with the person's parents.

Q 13. The person currently lives with their parents and

Q 14. The person currently lives with their mother.

Q 15. The person currently lives with their mother and

Q 16. The person currently lives with their father.

Q 17. The person currently lives with their father and siblings ______.

Q 18. The person currently lives with their mother and step-father.

Q 19. The person currently lives with their mother, step-father and

Q 20. The person currently lives with their father and step-mother.

Q 21. The person currently lives with their father, step-mother and

Children

Q 22. Additionally, the person has grown children ______.

Q 23. The person's children are ______.

Q 24. The person has a grown son.

Q 25. The person has a grown daughter.

Q 26. The person's grown children are ______.

Q 27. The person's children currently live with the person's ex-spouse.

Q 28. The person's children currently live with ______.

Q 29. The person's son currently lives with ______.

Q 30. The person's daughter currently lives with ______.

Marriage

Q 31. The person reports their marriage is satisfactory.

Q 32. The person reports their marriage is unhappy.

Abuse

Q 33. The person reports their spouse abuses them.

Q 34. The person states their spouse abuses them physically.

Q 35. The person states their spouse abuses them emotionally.

Q 36. The person states their spouse abuses them physically and emotionally.

Affairs

Q 37. The person states they are currently having an affair.

Q 38. The person relates their spouse is currently having an affair.

Previous Marriages

Q 39. The person reports being married once previously.

Q 40. The person reports being married twice previously.

Q 41. The person reports being married three times previously.

Q 42. The person reports multiple previous marriages.

Q 43. The person has been divorced for _____.

Problems of Children

Q 44. The individual states that one of their children has a learning disability.

Q 45. The individual states that one of their children is retarded.

Q 46. The individual states that one of their children is handicapped physically and suffers from _____.

Q 47. The individual states that one of their children is handicapped emotionally and suffers from _____.

Q 48. The individual reports that one of their children is a discipline problem.

Q 49. The individual states that their child has a learning disability.

Q 50. The individual states that their child is retarded.

Q 51. The individual states their child has a physical handicap and suffers from _____.

Q 52. The individual states that their child has an emotional problem.

Q 53. The individual states their child is a discipline problem.

Q 54. The individual reports the following problems with their children _____.

Q 55. The individual states they have difficulty caring for their children because _____.

Work

Q 56. The person is currently a student and is in the _____.

Q 57. The person states they are currently employed as a _____.

Q 58. The person is a college student.

Q 59. The person states that she is currently a housewife.

Q 60. The person states they are currently unemployed.

Q 61. The person is retired.

Q 62. The person reports being unhappy in their career.

Q 63. The person is happy in their work.

Q 64. The person reports being currently on disability and receiving Social Security Disability insurance.

Q 65. The person reports being currently on company disability.

Q 66. The person reports being currently on disability and receiving Workmens Compensation.

Q 67. The person relates having a work-related lawsuit pending.

Q 68. The person reports having difficulty holding a job.

Q 69. The person is currently a student at ______.

Birth Order

Q 70. Developmentally, the individual reports being an only child.

Q 71. Developmentally, the individual reports being the oldest child.

Q 72. Developmentally, the individual reports being the youngest child.

Q 73. Developmentally, the individual reports a birth order of ______.

Q 74. The person has one brother.

Q 75. The person has two brothers.

Q 76. The person has three brothers.

Q 77. The person has four brothers.

Q 78. The person has five brothers.

Q 79. The person has one sister.

Q 80. The person has two sisters.

Q 81. The person has three sisters.

Q 82. The person has four sisters.

Q 83. The person has five sisters.

Q 84. The person has one step-brother.

Q 85. The person has two step-brothers.

Q 86. The person has three step-brothers.

Q 87. The person has one step-sister.

Q 88. The person has two step-sisters.

Q 89. The person has three step-sisters.

Q 90. The person has one half-brother.

Q 91. The person has two half-brothers.

Q 92. The person has three half-brothers.

Q 93. The person has one half-sister.

Q 94. The person has two half-sisters.

Q 95. The person has three half-sisters.

Childhood and Adolescence

Q 96. The individual relates having few friends as a child.

Q 97. The individual relates having few friends as a child and adolescent.

Q 98. The individual reports having frequent temper tanrums as a child.

Q 99. The individual reports having frequent crying spells and easily becoming upset as a child.

Q 100. The individual reports being a sickly child.

Q 101. The individual reports having few friends as a teenager.

Q 102. The individual reports not dating as a teenager.

Q 103. The individual states they are adopted.

Q 104. The individual states they are raised by ______.

Q 105. The individual reports being raised by their natural parents.

Q 106. The individual states they were raised by their mother after their parents were divorced.

Q 107. The individual states they were raised by their father after the parents were divorced.

Q 108. The individual states they were primarily raised by their grandparents.

Q 109. The individual states they were raised primarily by their grandmother.

Q 110. The individual relates being raised primarily by an aunt.

Q 111. The person reports being abused as a child.

Q 112. The person reports being emotionally abused as a child.

Q 113. The person reports being physically abused as a child.

Q 114. The person reports being sexually abused as a child.

Q 115. The person reports being abused by their mother.

Q 116. The person reports being abused by their father.

Q 117. The person reports being abused by both parents.

Q 118. The person reports no significant developmental problems.

Educational History

Q 119. The person reports no significant educational problems.

Q 120. Educationally, the person reports a learning problem in school.

Q 121. The person reports being in basic skills classes.

Q 122. The person reports being in special education classes.

Q 123. The person reports being diagnosed as hyperactive by a physician.

Q 124. The person reports being on Ritalin.

Q 125. The person reports frequent problems with the teachers at school.

Q 126. The person reports having frequent fights at school.

Q 127. The person reports having difficulty making friends at school.

Q 128. The person reports failing a grade at school.

Q 129. The person reports failing the ____.

Family History

Q 130. Regarding the person's family of origin,

Q 131. The person reports that both parents are still living.

Q 132. The person reports that their mother died at age ____, and died of ____.

Q 133. The person reports that their father died at age ____ of ____.

Q 134. The person reports their mother is still living.

Q 135. The person reports their father is still living.

Q 136. The individual reports a history of alcoholism in their family of origin and states that drinking problems were evidenced by ____.

Q 137. The individual reports a history of drug addiction in their family of origin and states that addiction problems were evidenced by ____.

Q 138. The individual reports that their family has a history of nervous breakdowns and states that mental and emotional problems requiring hospitalization were evidenced by ____.

Drug & Addiction Problems

Q 139. The person reports that they have been arrested for ____.

Q 140. The person reports they are on probation for ____.

Q 141. The person reports having been arrested for a DWI in ____.

Q 142. The person reports having been arrested for public intoxication in ____.

Q 143. The person reports having been incarcerated in prison for ____.

Q 144. The person states that they have a drinking problem and generally consume an average weekly intake of ____.

Q 145. The person reports they have had a drinking problem in the past.

Q 146. The person reports being a binge drinker.

Q 147. The person reports they attend Alcoholics Anonymous.

Q 148. The person reports having experimented with a variety of drugs, including:

Q 149. The person reports they have a drug problem.

Q 150. The person reports they had a drug problem in the past.

Q 151. The person states that they are addicted to ______.

Q 152. The person reports that they frequently use ______.

Q 153. The person reports that they have a problem with gambling.

Q 154. The person reports that they have had a problem with gambling in the past.

Q 155. The person reports currently having a lawsuit pending against ______.

Q 156. The person reports they have a history of being addicted to prescription medicines.

Health

Q 157. The individual reports they have a chronic health problem in the form of ______.

Q 158. The individual reports a history of chronic health problems, including ______.

Q 159. The individual reports currently taking the following prescription medications:

Q 160. The individual relates being in psychotherapy previously as an out patient.

Q 161. The individual reports a previous psychiatric hospitalization in ______.

Q 162. The individual reports a previous psychiatric hospitalization for depression.

Q 163. The individual reports a previous psychiatric hospitalization for drug addiction.

Q 164. The individual reports a previous psychiatric hospitalization for alcoholism.

Q 165. The individual reports a previous psychiatric hospitalization for schizophrenia.

Q 166. The individual reports being hospitalized in the past in ______.

Reason for Hospitalization

Q 167. The individual reports the reason for seeking present hospitalization as ______.

Q 168. The individual reports their reason for seeking psychiatric assistance is ______.

Q 169. The individual reports the reason they were referred is ______.

Vincent Biographical Inventory

NAME: ____________________ AGE: ____________

RACE: ____________________ MARITAL STATUS: ________

EDUCATION: ________________

MARRIAGE AND FAMILY HISTORY

I currently live with ______________________________

I have ______ children (ages & sexes) ______________________

My children currently live with ______________________

I have ______ brothers and ______ sisters.

Please check all that apply:

______ 1. My marriage is unhappy.
______ 2. My spouse abuses me.
______ 3. I am currently seeing someone else outside my marriage.
______ 4. My spouse is seeing someone else.
______ 5. I have been married before. (If Yes, ______ times).
______ 6. One of my children has a learning disability.
______ 7. One of my children is retarded.
______ 8. One of my children has a physical handicap. (If Yes, please specify)

____

______ 9. One of my children has an emotional problem. (If Yes, please specify)

____

______ 10. One of my children is a discipline problem.
______ 11. I am having difficulty caring for my children.
(If Yes, please state what your difficulties are)

____

____

OCCUPATIONAL HISTORY

______ 12. I am currently employed. (If Yes, please state occupation)

____

______ 13. I am unhappy in my career.
______ 14. I am currently on disability.
______ 15. I have a work-related lawsuit pending.
______ 16. I have trouble holding a job.

CHILDHOOD AND ADOLESCENCE

______ 17. As a child I had few friends.
______ 18. As a child I have (had) frequent temper tantrums.
______ 19. As a child I have (had) frequent crying spells and became easily upset.
______ 20. I was sick a lot as a child.

_____ 21. As a teenager I have (had) few friends.
_____ 22. As a teenager I didn't (don't) date at all.
_____ 23. I was adopted, or raised away from my parents. Please state who reared you.

____

_____ 24. I was abused as a child. (Please circle: emotionally, physically, sexually).

EDUCATIONAL HISTORY

_____ 25. I have (had) a learning problem in school.
_____ 26. I have been diagnosed as being a hyperactive.
_____ 27. I have (had) frequent problems with teachers at school.
_____ 28. I have (had) frequent fights at school.
_____ 29. I have (had) difficulty making friends at school.
_____ 30. I have failed a grade in school. (If Yes, state what grade(s) _____).

FAMILY HISTORY

_____ 31. One or both of my parents are dead. If Yes, please state:
a) Cause of death(s): Mother _____; Father _____.
b) Ages at death: Mother _____; Father _____.
_____ 32. One of my close family members (circle those who apply: father, mother, brother, sister, aunt, uncle, grandmother, grandfather) has a drinking problem.
_____ 33. One of my close family members (circle those who apply: father, mother, brother, sister, aunt, uncle, grandmother, grandfather) has a drug problem.
_____ 34. One of my close family members (circle those who apply: father, mother, brother, sister, aunt, uncle, grandfather, grandmother) has (had) a nervous breakdown.

LEGAL PROBLEMS AND ADDICTION

_____ 35. I have been arrested. (If Yes, please explain the outcome—probation, etc.).

____

_____ 36. I have (had) a drinking problem.
_____ 37. I have (had) a drug problem.
_____ 38. I have (had) a problem with gambling.

HEALTH

_____ 39. I have (had) a chronic illness, major handicap, or other health problems.

(If Yes, please describe) ______________________________

_____ 40. I am currently on the following medications: ______________________________
_____ 41. I have been in psychotherapy as an outpatient.
_____ 42. I have had a nervous breakdown or psychiatric hospitalization.

(If Yes, please describe) ______________________________

____

Please briefly describe your reason for seeking help or hospitalization:

____

____

____

CHAPTER SIX

Interpretative Statements for the Cognitive Section: Intelligence

This section of the Full Battery Code Book covers intellectual assessment and provides interpretative statements for the Wechsler Scales, as well as Wechsler short forms and brief IQ tests such as the Ammons, Slosson, Clark Vocabulary Scale, Shipley-Hartford, Peabody Picture Vocabulary Test, and Ravens Standard Progressive Matrices. Global intellect statements are provided, and are fairly self-explanatory in that they consist of brief narrative statements for all possible levels of intellect.

It is worth noting that the Wechsler short form is the most viable alternative to a full individually administered IQ test, in that most brief paper-and-pencil IQ tests correlate about .6 to .7 with the Full Scale Wechsler IQ. The vocabulary subscale of WAIS and WAIS-R correlates .8 with the Full Scale IQ, as does the information subscale. This makes these subscales the most viable, quick measure of IQ; if one wants an IQ test that correlates with Wechsler which has become the standard for IQ measurement. One should note that Finegold (1982, 1983) found that the information and/or the vocabulary subtest of the Wechsler were better predictors of job success and school success than the full Wechsler Scale. Another alternative measure for giving the Wechsler which decreases the time for individuals of average or better intelligence by 25% is the modified WAIS (Vincent, 1979). The modified WAIS has been replicated on six different populations, and essentially involves giving the Wechsler like the Stanford-Binet (Vincent, 1979). The Cognitive section also includes modification of the Wechsler Scales when they are administered to groups different from the normal sample, namely, handicapped individuals, individuals for whom English is a second language, and individuals from other cultures. The section on interpretation of the Wechsler Scales is essentially the same as that of the Semi-Automated Full Battery (Vincent 1980c), with the exception that a formula developed by Leli and Filskov (1979, 1981, 1984) has been added which provides a deterioration index based on comparison of the individual's full scale IQ with his or her educational level and occupational level ratings.

The interpretation statements for psychoeducational interpretation of the Wechsler is based primarily on the work of Kaufman (1979). Additional scores have been used, including Sattler (1982). As in keeping with the general philosophy of this book, statements based on non-cross-validated studies are not included. The psychoeducational interpretation essentially relates to the specific scales and the three factor scales that were identified by Kaufman (1979) and replicated a multiplicity of times (Kaufman, 1979). Interpretative statements for the Wechsler Verbal versus Performance IQ Differences are included, and cover such things as delinquency, under-achievement, English as a second language, motor handicaps, over-achiever, depression, and organic impairment. All are based on cross-validated, empirically derived research findings. Vocational interpretation of deviation IQs for the Wechsler, as well as other brief IQ measures, are essentially the author's own synthesis and literature, and are based primarily on information derived from the *Occupational Outlook Handbook* (United States Department of Labor, 1982) and the *Dictionary of Occupational Titles* (United States Department of Labor, 1965). Another main source are tables that can be readily found in Matarazzo's *Measurement and Appraisal of Adult Intelligence* (1972, p. 167, 178). All statements relate to standard deviation IQ unless otherwise noted.

TEST RESULTS

Intellectual Assessment

I-1 On the WECHSLER ADULT INTELLIGENCE SCALE the person scored as follows:
Verbal IQ: Performance IQ: Full Scale IQ:

I-2 On the WECHSLER ADULT INTELLIGENCE SCALE REVISED, the person scored as follows:
% Verbal IQ: Performance IQ: Full Scale IQ:

I-3 On the WECHSLER INTELLIGENCE SCALE FOR CHILDREN the person scored as follows:
Verbal IQ: Performance IQ: Full Scale IQ:

I-4 On the WECHSLER INTELLIGENCE SCALE FOR CHILDREN REVISED the person scored as follows:
Verbal IQ: Performance IQ: Full Scale IQ:

I-5 On the WAIS (short form) the person scored as follows: IQ:

I-6 On the WAIS-R (short form) the person scores as follows: IQ:

I-7 On the WISC (short form) the person scored as follows: IQ:

I-8 On the WISC-R (short form) the person scores as follows: IQ:

I-9 On the AMMONS QUICK TEST the person scored as follows: IQ:

I-10 On the SLOSSON INTELLIGENCE TEST the person scored as follows: IQ:

I-11 On the CLARK VOCABULARY TEST the person scored as follows: IQ:

I-12 On the SHIPLEY HARTFORD INTELLIGENCE TEST the person scored as follows: IQ:

I-13 On the PEABODY PICTURE VOCABULARY TEST the person scored as follows: IQ:

I-14 On the PEABODY PICTURE VOCABULARY TEST REVISED the person scored as follows: IQ:

I-15 On the PEABODY INDIVIDUAL ACHIEVEMENT TEST—GENERAL INFORMATION SUBTEST the person scored as follows: IQ:

I-16 On the RAVEN'S STANDARD OF PROGRESSIVE MATRICES the person scored as follows: IQ:

I-17 On the TEST OF NON-VERBAL INTELLIGENCE (TONI) the person scored as follows: IQ:

INTERPRETATIVE STATEMENTS FOR WHEN A BRIEF (NON-WECHSLER) IQ TEST WAS USED

I-18 IQ less than 70:

The person's overall IQ performance yields an intellectual estimate of an individual whose intellectual ability was in the range of mental retardation, and an individually administered Full Scale IQ test appears in order to verify this intellectual estimate.

I-19 IQ 70–79:

The person's overall IQ performance yields an intellectual estimate of an individual whose intellectual ability is in the range of borderline intellect; however, it would probably be well if the person was given an individually administered Full Scale IQ test in order to verify this intellectual estimate.

I-20 IQ 80–87:

The person's overall IQ test performance was indicative of an individual whose intellectual ability was in the range of normal to dull-normal intellect.

I-21 IQ 88–90:

The person's overall IQ test performance was indicative of an individual whose intellectual ability was in the range of normal to dull-normal intellect.

I-22 IQ 91–107:
The person's overall IQ test performance was indicative of an individual whose intellectual ability was in the range of average intellect.

I-23 IQ 108–110:
The person's overall IQ test performance was indicative of an individual whose intellectual ability was in the range of average to bright-normal intelligence.

I-24 IQ 111–117:
The person's overall IQ test performance was indicative of an individual whose intellectual ability was in the range of bright-normal intelligence.

I-25 IQ 118–120:
The person's overall IQ test performance was indicative of an individual whose intellectual ability was in the bright-normal to superior range.

I-26 IQ 121–127:
The person's overall IQ test performance was indicative of an individual whose intellectual ability was in the superior range.

I-27 IQ 128–130:
The person's overall IQ test performance was indicative of an individual whose intellectual ability was in the superior to very superior (or genius) range.

I-28 IQ greater than 130:
The person's overall IQ test performance was indicative of an individual whose intellectual ability was in the very superior or genius range of intelligence.

INTERPRETATIVE STATEMENTS WHEN SUBSCALES ARE DELETED FROM THE WECHSLER

Please use the appropriate statement:

I-29 The performance section of the WECHSLER was deleted because of the person's IV.

I-30 Several subscales of the WECHSLER were deleted because of the person's physical condition: consequently, the results are prorated.

I-31 Several subscales of the WECHSLER were deleted because of the person's medical condition; consequently, the results are prorated.

I-32 The verbal section of the WECHSLER was deleted because the person spoke no English.

I-33 The verbal section of the WECHSLER was deleted because of the person's handicap.

I-34 The verbal section of the WECHSLER was deleted because the person was unable to continue.

I-35 The verbal section of the WECHSLER was deleted as the person refused to do the tasks.

I-36 The performance section of the WECHSLER was deleted because of the person's handicap.

I-37 The performance section of the WECHSLER was deleted as the person was unable to continue.

I-38 The performance section of the WECHSLER was deleted because the person refused to do the tasks.

I-39 Several subscales on the WECHSLER were deleted because of the person's handicap and, consequently, the results were prorated.

I-40 Several subscales on the WECHSLER were deleted because the person was unable to continue; consequently, the results were prorated.

I-41 Several subscales on the WECHSLER were deleted because the person refused to continue; consequently, the results were prorated.

INTERPRETATIVE STATEMENTS FOR GLOBAL INTELLECT OF THE WECHSLER SCALES

I-42 IF IQ is less than 33

On the WECHSLER, the person's overall performance was indicative of an individual whose intellectual ability was in the range of severe mental retardation.

I-43 IF IQ is 33–35

On the WECHSLER, the person's overall performance was indicative of an individual whose intellectual ability was in the range of moderate-to-severe mental retardation.

I-44 IF IQ is 36–47

On the WECHSLER, the person's overall performance was indicative of an individual whose intellectual ability was in the range of moderate mental retardation.

I-45 IF IQ is 48–50

On the WECHSLER, the person's overall performance was indicative of an individual whose intellectual ability was in the range of mild-to-moderate mental retardation.

I-46 IF IQ is 51–67
On the WECHSLER, the person's overall performance was indicative of an individual whose intellectual ability was in the range of mild mental retardation.

I-47 IF IQ is 68–70
On the WECHSLER, the person's overall performance was indicative of an individual whose intellectual ability was in the range of mild mental retardation to borderline intellect.

I-48 IF IQ is 71–77
On the WECHSLER, the person's overall performance was indicative of an individual whose intellectual ability was in the range of borderline intellect.

I-49 IF IQ is 78–80
On the WECHSLER, the person's overall performance was indicative of an individual whose intellectual ability was in the range of dull-normal to borderline intellect.

I-50 IF IQ is 81–87
On the WECHSLER, the person's overall performance was indicative of an individual whose intellectual ability was in the range of dull-normal intellect.

I-51 IF IQ is 88–90
On the WECHSLER, the person's overall performance was indicative of an individual whose intellectual ability was in the range of normal to dull-normal intellect.

I-52 IF IQ is 91–107
On the WECHSLER, the person's overall performance was indicative of an individual whose intellectual ability was in the range of average intellect.

I-53 IF IQ is 108–110
On the WECHSLER, the person's overall performance was indicative of an individual whose intellectual ability was in the range of average to bright-normal intelligence.

I-54 IF IQ is 111–117
On the WECHSLER, the person's overall performance was indicative of an individual whose intellectual ability was in the range of bright-normal intelligence.

I-55 IF IQ is 118–120
On the WECHSLER, the person's overall performance was indicative of an individual whose intellectual ability was in the bright-normal to superior range.

I-56 IF IQ is 121–127

On the WECHSLER, the person's overall performance was indicative of an individual whose intellectual ability was in the superior range.

I-57 IF IQ is 128–130

On the WECHSLER, the person's overall performance was indicative of an individual whose intellectual ability was in the superior to very superior (or genius) range.

I-58 IF IQ is greater than 130

On the WECHSLER, the person's overall performance was indicative of an individual whose intellectual ability was in the very superior or genius range of intelligence.

I-59 If English is the person's second language, use the following statement after statements about deletion of scales, or, if no scales were deleted, print after the IQ narrative.

The discrepancy between the person's Verbal and Performance IQ is significant and is likely due to the person's bilingual background. The Performance IQ is probably indicative of the individual's true intellectual potential, while the Verbal IQ should be viewed as an acculturation index of the person's orientation into English-speaking American culture.

I-60 If the subscale scores are to be reported on the test report and the WAIS or WAIS-R was given, use:

(If a subscale was deleted, please type in the word "deferred")

Information-
Digit Span-
Vocabulary-
Arithmetic-
Comprehension-
Similarities-

Picture Completion-
Picture Arrangement-
Block Design-
Object Assembly-
Digit Symbol-

I-61 If the WISC/WISC-R was given, use:

(If a subscale was deleted, please type in the word "deferred").

Information-
Similarities-
Arithmetic-
Vocabulary-

Comprehension-
Digit Span-
Picture Completion-
Picture Arrangement-
Block Design-
Object Assembly-
Coding-
Mazes-

Next, with this information, obtain the average of the reported subscale scores. The denominator will vary here depending on the test used and on whether any of the scores were deleted.

I-62 If mean of the standard scores on Information, Similarities, Vocabulary, and Comprehension is 3 points or less of the mean of the total standard scores, print:

Psychoeducationally, the person's subscale configuration on the WECHSLER depicts an individual with deficits in the area of verbal comprehension.

I-63 If mean of the standard scores on the Picture Completion, Picture Arrangement, Block Design, Object Assembly, and Mazes, if given, is 3 points or less of the mean of the total standard scores, print:

Psychoeducationally, the person's subscale configuration on the WECHSLER depicts an individual with deficits in the area of perceptual organization.

I-64 If mean of the standard scores on Arithmetic, Digit Span, and Coding is 3 points or less of the mean of the total standard scores, print:

Psychoeducationally, the person's subscale configuration on the WECHSLER depicts an individual with deficits in the area of distractibility.

I-65 If statements I-62, 63, 64, 80, 81, or 84 are not used, and if Verbal IQ is 15 points less than Performance IQ, print:

The discrepancy between the person's Verbal and Performance IQ is significant, and a discrepancy in favor of the Performance IQ is commonly attained in individuals who are underachievers and/or behavior problems.

I-66 OR if statements I-62, 63, 64, 80, 81, or 84 are not used, and if Performance IQ is 15 points less than Verbal IQ, print:

The discrepancy between the person's Verbal and Performance IQ on the WECHSLER is significant, and such a discrepancy in favor of the Verbal IQ is commonly attained in individuals who are overachievers or who are significantly depressed.

If any of the following (presented by subscale) subscales are *less* than 3 points of the average of all the reported subscale scores, and below a scale score of 8, print the statement for that subscale.

I-67 For Information.
The person's performance on the WECHSLER was significantly low on the subscale relating to general information and factual knowledge.

I-68 For Comprehension.
The individual's performance on the WECHSLER was particularly deficient on the subscale relating to verbal social judgement and practical reasoning.

I-69 For Arithmetic.
The person's performance on the WECHSLER was significantly low on the subscale relating to oral arithmetic and computational skill.

I-70 For Similarities.
The individual's performance on the WECHSLER was particularly deficient on the subscale relating to divergent thinking, logical judgement, abstract thinking, and concept formation.

I-71 For Digit Span.
The person's performance on the WECHSLER was significantly low on the subscale relating to immediate memory.

I-72 For Vocabulary
The individual's performance on the WECHSLER was particularly deficient on the subscale relating to word knowledge and language development.

I-73 For Digit Symbol or Coding.
The person's performance on the WECHSLER was significantly low on the subscale relating to clerical skills and visual motor efficiency.

I-74 For Picture Completion.
The individual's performance on the WECHSLER was significantly low on the subscale relating to attention to detail.

I-75 For Block Design.
The person's performance on the WECHSLER was significantly low on the subscale relating to spatial perception and nonverbal conceptualization.

I-76 For Picture Arrangement.
The person's performance on the WECHSLER was significantly low on the subscale relating to social intelligence and planning ability.

I-77 For Object Assembly.
The person's performance on the WECHSLER was significantly low on the subscale relating to form perception and visual interrelationships.

I-78 For Mazes.

The individual's performance on the WECHSLER was particularly deficient on the subscale relating to visual patterns and sequencing ability.

WAIS-WAIS-R AND WISC-WISC-R TESTS: ORGANIC SCREENING AND INTERPRETATIVE STATEMENTS

*RULES FOR STATEMENT I-81

Note: Either A or B for WAIS or C for WISC-R. All WAIS statements refer to age-corrected scale scores.

A. WAIS/WAIS-R: Organic Impairment in Nondominant Hemisphere or Diffuse Organic Impairment

IQ less than 120 and Verbal IQ greater than Performance IQ by 15 points (10 points if IQ less than 85). Digit Symbol less than 9 points and less than 3 points of the mean of the standard scores, and (a) Similarities 3 standard scores greater than Block Design and Picture Arrangement; or (b) Block Design and Picture Arrangement less than 9 points, and less than 3 points of standard scores; or/and (c) Block Design less than or equal to a standard score of 4.

B. WAIS/WAIS-R: Organic Impairment—Dominant Hemisphere

IQ less than 120 and Verbal IQ less than Performance by 15 points (10 points if IQ less than 85). Digit Symbol less than 9 points, and less than 3 points of the mean of the standard scores; and (a) Arithmetic and Digit Span less than 3 points of the mean of the standard scores; (b) Similarities and Arithmetic less than 3 points of the mean of the standard scores; or (c) All Vocabulary 3 points or less than Picture Arrangement and Block Design.

C. WISC/WISC-R

The WISC/WISC-R is not as well researched as a test for organic impairment. About the only certain prediction of organic impairment is IQ less than 110 and 25 point drop between the present test performance and a previous testing.

I-79 WAIS IQ greater than 120, or
WAIS Arithmetic, Similarities, Digit Span, Digit Symbol, and Block Design greater than 8 on age-corrected subscales, or Rule I-81 and I-84 not met

The person's subscale configuration on the WECHSLER was generally not indicative of behavioral correlates associated with organicity.

I-80 Some (but not all) of the rules for Statement I-81 and I-84 satisfied, and the rules for Statement I-79 not satisfied.

The person's subscale performance on the WECHSLER was indeterminate with regard to organic impairment.

I-81 See above*

The person's subscale performance on the WECHSLER was generally indicative of behavioral correlates associated with organic impairment.

I-82 Verbal IQ 15 points greater than Performance IQ and Organic Statement. I-81 Used

The discrepancy between the person's Verbal and Performance IQ is significant, and depicts an individual whose organic impairment is either chronic or more localized in the nondominant hemisphere.

I-83 Verbal IQ 15 points less than Performance IQ and Organic Statement. I-81 Used

The discrepancy between the person's Verbal and Performance IQ depicts an individual whose organic impairment is more localized in the dominant hemisphere.

Using the Leli and Filskov (1979, 1981, 1984) Cross Validated Formula, which consists of using the two tables in Matarazzo (1972, pp. 166–167, 178) which relate to educational level and IQ and occupational level and IQ, Matarazzo and Herman (1984) may be a better reference for educational level when the WAIS-R is given, but this has not been tested. Assign a rating of 1 when the Wechsler Full Scale IQ is lower than would be expected from his or her educational level. A rating 2 is given when the Full Scale IQ and education level correspond. A rating of 3 is given when the Full Scale IQ is higher than would be expected for the person's education. The same procedure is used with occupational level.

The resulting data is to be used with the following formula derived from Levi and Filskov (1979, 1981, 1984):

1.1 (IQ vs. Educational Level Rating) + .6 (IQ vs. Occupational Level Rating) −

3.5 = Deterioration Index

A score of <-0.1 = Deterioration

A score of ≥-0.1 = No Deterioration

If the person's score is in the impaired range, use the following statement:

I-84 An analysis of the person's educational and occupational attainment compared to their Full Scale IQ indicates the presence of intellectual deterioration.

STATEMENTS FOR THE VOCATIONAL INTERPRETATION OF DEVIATION IQ TESTS ($\bar{x}$ = 100/S.D. = 15)

I-85 If IQ is 80–89, print:

Persons scoring in this intellectual ability range usually have the intellectual ability to complete a high school education; however, they may need some additional help with basic skills subjects. These individuals are usually found working in occupations that do not require a mastery of complex academics or higher math—occupations such as assembly line workers, service occupations such as nurse's aide, waitress, and short order cook, as well as apprenticeable trades such as cement finisher and welder. Often, life is frustrating for them, as they "almost" qualify for jobs held by the mainstream of society and are also apt to have difficulty coping with the forms and written material (such as income tax forms) required by modern society.

I-86 If IQ is 90–99, print:

Persons scoring in this intellectual ability range usually have the intellectual ability to achieve a high school degree, and may go on to achieve an associate degree at a junior college. Persons of this range of intellectual ability are apt to be found in occupations such as cosmetologist, electronics assembler, machine trades occupations, LVN, laboratory technicians, surgical technicians, and clerical occupations such as key punch operator or printer.

I-87 If IQ is 100–109, print:

Persons scoring in this intellectual ability range usually have the intellectual prowess to achieve a baccalaureate degree at a liberal arts or teachers college. Also, they are capable of executing work at the level of skilled trades, technical occupations, advanced clerical occupations, and professional occupations such as nurse or high school teacher, as well as minor management positions and proprietorships.

I-88 If IQ is 110–119, print:

Persons scoring in this intellectual ability range have the intellectual prowess to achieve a baccalaureate degree at competitive colleges, as well as go on to earn a masters degree or doctorate. At this range of intellect, virtually all occupational choices are open to the individual with regard to their intellectual ability. Individuals scoring in this IQ range are quite often found in complex occupations such as manager of a large corporation, accountant, engineer, social work, or computer programmer.

I-89 If IQ is 120–129, print:

Persons scoring in this intellectual ability are capable of achieving advanced degrees, and this is the range of intellect for the average M.D. or Ph.D.

I-90 If IQ is 130 or greater, print:
Persons in this range of intellectual ability obviously have the intellectual prowess to achieve advanced degrees and are capable of executing work, at the highest level, demanding complex problem solving and intellectual skills.

CHAPTER SEVEN

Interpretative Statements for the Cognitive Section: Achievement

Interpretative statements for the Wide-Range Achievement Test and the Peabody Individual Achievement Test integrate these tests with Wechsler data, and were derived from the Semi-Automated Full Battery (Vincent, 1980a,b). This work has been expanded into the Psychoeducational and Vocational Report Writer (Vincent, in press). What follows has been taken directly from the Manual for the Psychoeducational and Vocational Report Writer.

The Psycho-Educational Report Writer is an extension of the author's earlier work of the Semi-Automated Full Battery (Vincent, 1980a,b). The program provides a comprehensive psycho-educational and vocational analysis of the Wechsler Scales and the WRAT-WRAT-R or PIAT Achievement Test.

The educational portion of the psychoeducational portion of the Report Writer addresses whether or not a student has a learning disability according to the criteria of Federal Regulation 300.541, and the criteria of Axis-II of the DSM-III. While the Psycho-Educational and Vocational Report Writer is based on a solid foundation of research on the instruments analyzed, it is no substitute for the practicing clinician (educator, psychologist, or counselor).

An exception that would preclude the diagnosis of learning disability that is not covered by the Psycho-Educational and Vocational Report Writer is emotional disturbance, and the program assumes that organic impairment has been ruled out or, if present, that it is chronic and the Report Writer is only being used for educational analysis of the individual. The Psycho-Educational and Vocational Report Writer can be used on individuals with visual, hearing, and motor handicaps to assess their intellectual functioning, assuming the user deletes the performance section on individuals with significant visual and motor handicaps and deletes the verbal section on individuals with significant hearing handicaps. The author takes the premise that it is much better to delete entirely subscales that are not representative of the individual's functioning rather than administer subscales to individuals that are apt to be influenced by their handicap. Clinicians may wish to do this to gain some insight into ability level; however, they should be mindful that doing so is largely a subjective procedure and based upon their own clinical internal norms. The Psycho-Educational and Vocational Report Writer does attempt to deal with the educational and vocational potential functioning of individuals with visual, hearing, and motor handicaps by deleting the verbal or performance section where appropriate, and by interpreting the remaining Verbal or Performance IQ as also the full scale IQ. Also, the program does take into account cultural bias and subsequent disadvantage and also English as a second language.

The Psycho-Educational and Vocational Report Writer makes the following assumptions: A 15-point discrepancy between verbal and performance IQ or between full scale IQ and achievement standard scores is interpreted as significant. With regard to the instruments in question, this is significant at the .01 level. While it has been noted by some authors, such as Kaufman (1979), that 25% of the so-called normal population has a verbal-performance IQ discrepancy of 15 points or greater, the data from the so-called normal population is based on a general population that includes handicapped individuals, individuals with learning disabilities, and individuals for whom English is a second language. When these various clinically significant groups are added together, the 25th percentile deviance in the general population is amply met. Also, this is a standard method of interpreting differences between IQ and standard scores.

The Psycho-Educational and Vocational Report Writer analyzes the Wechsler Scale Scores, taking into account the mean of all scale scores given. This may range from as few as 8 scale scores (which is the critical minimum usually set for interpreting IQ scores without noting that the test was a short form) to the full twelve scales given on the WISC/WISC-R. This average is what is used to compare whether there are significant differences between the subscales of IQ, with 3 points being considered significant. Three points is, for all practical purposes, the .01 level of significance for the differences between the subscales, though one should be mindful of the standard error measurement on the Wechsler subscales is about 1.5 points. Other authors, such as Kaufman (1979), suggest interpreting the verbal subscales with the average of the verbal subscale IQ, and performance subscales with the average of the performance subscale IQ, so as, as Kaufman puts it, "not to suggest that all of their deficiencies are in the verbal area or the performance area." The author strongly disagrees with this practice, because, if the discrepancy of subscales clusters on either the verbal or performance side, this *is* where the individual's deficiencies are. For a subscale to be classified as deficient, it must also be a standard subscale score of 7 or less. So it is not only below the average of the individual's mean subscales scores but also significantly below that of the general population.

As stated earlier, interpretive statements are provided for deletions of the verbal or performance portions of the Wechsler IQ tests, as well as individual subscales due to the person's refusal, inability, or handicap. Full scale IQ on the Wechsler is recorded using the standard categories for intellect as outlined in the Wechsler manuals. English as the second language is dealt with by noting that a significant discrepancy between the verbal performance IQ in the favor of performance in individuals for whom English is a second language is usually due to that. Also, when achievement tests and IQ tests are compared, the person's ethnic status is considered and a discrepancy in favor of achievement versus IQ is attributed to cultural bias on the intellectual test. Individual subscales that are significantly below the individual's mean and the mean for the general population are reported as specific deficiencies. The other analysis of the Wechsler besides verbal and performance IQ differences and specific subscales is that of the three major factors that have been identified by Kaufman (1979) and replicated by many others (Kaufman, 1979). The program does not include findings that have not been replicated. The literature on educational psychology is filled with examples of theories and analysis of intellectual and achievement tests that did not replicate.

In addition to the manuals for the test in question, and the author's article "Semi-Automated Full Battery" and a handbook by the same name (Vincent, 1980a,b), the primary sources used in constructing the Psycho-Educational and Vocational Report Writer are Kaufman's book *Intelligent Testing with the WISC-R* (Kaufman, 1979) and Sattler's (1982) *Assessment of Children's Intelligence and Special Abilities*. The vocational section draws heavily on articles in the Journal of Employment Counseling regarding GED prediction by the General Aptitude Test Battery and Other Intelligence Tests, and Volume II of the *Dictionary of Occupational Titles* (U.S. Department of Labor, 1965) and the *Manual for the General Aptitude Test Battery* (U.S. Department of Labor, 1967).

Another underlying assumption of Psycho-Educational and Vocational Report Writer is that Wechsler Scales, the PIAT, and WRAT/WRAT-R are nationally well-standardized tests and, consequently, that comparisons can be made both within and between them with confidence. Also, regarding general educational functional levels in the vocational recommendations section, the assumption is made that national norm levels such as those developed by the Department of Labor can be extrapolated to these well standardized tests regarding the level of intellectual and achievement functioning required for specific educational and vocational preparation. Finally, numerous uncited sources, as well as the author's 20 years of experience as a counselor and professional psychologist, help "glue" the program together.

The Psycho-Educational and Vocational Report Writer is designed for use by the practicing educator, counselor, or psychologist. As with any test and/or test interpretation-computer program, it is not designed to be used in a vacuum. We assume that the practicing clinician will integrate and use this data in conjunction with the person's history, teacher reports, medical reports, and additional test data. When additional data does not alter the picture in a manner beyond the scope of the above mentioned exceptions (which are essentially those dictated by Federal Regulation), the report can often be shared directly with other professionals as well as patients, clients, students, or parents.

Finally, as our knowledge base is ever changing and expanding, the author welcomes user comments and suggestions for any future revised editions.

A-1 If WRAT or WRAT-R is chosen, use:

Please enter in the following scores:

Enter pre first as −1 and above 12 as 12+.
(If a test is not given, please type in "deferred.")

Reading Grade Level _____
Reading Standard Score _____
Reading Percentile _____

Spelling Grade Level _____
Spelling Standard Score _____
Spelling Percentile _____

Arithmetic Grade Level _____
Arithmetic Standard Score _____
Arithmetic Percentile _____

NOTE: If WRAT-R is chosen, interpret the following grade level suffixes as:

B = .3; for example, 3B = 3.3

M = .5; for example, 2M = 2.5

E = .8; for example, 8E = 8.8

always print out B/M/or E through.
Also −1 = should be printed as below 1, and 12+ should be printed as above 12.

NOTE: If WRAT is chosen, print out an entry of K as below 1 and any number entry of 13.0 or greater as above 12.

A-2 If the PIAT was given, use:

Please enter in the following scores:

Reading Recognition *Grade* Equivalents _____
Reading Recognition *Age* Standard Scores _____
Reading Recognition *Age* Percentile Ranks _____

Reading Comprehension *Grade* Equivalents _____
Reading Comprehension *Age* Standard Scores _____
Reading Comprehension *Age* Percentile Ranks _____

Spelling *Grade* Equivalents _____
Spelling *Age* Standard Scores _____
Spelling *Age* Percentile Ranks _____

Mathematics *Grade* Equivalents _____
Mathematics *Age* Standard Scores _____
Mathematics *Age* Percentile Ranks _____

NOTE: On the PIAT, report Grade 0.1 thru 0.9 as below 1 and 12.1 as above 12.

WRAT/WRAT-R SECTION

If the WRAT or WRAT-R is used, use the following statements where appropriate. (change WRAT to WRAT-R if WRAT-R is used.)

A-3 If Reading Standard Score is 15 Standard Score Points greater than either the Verbal or Full Scale IQ, use:

The person's oral reading score is higher than would be expected from analysis of the individual's IQ test scores. Possible reasons for this include:

1. Cultural bias; consequently, the IQ may be an underestimate of the person's true intellectual potential;
2. A better knowledge of phonics than actual word knowledge;
3. An overachiever.

A-4 If Reading Standard Score is not less than the Full Scale IQ by 10 points, and not more than 15 points above Verbal or Full Scale IQ, use:

On the WRAT, the person's overall reading achievement was consistent with the individual's attained intellect.

A-5 If Reading Standard Score is less than Full Scale IQ by 10–14 points, use:

On the WRAT, the person's overall reading achievement was somewhat below the individual's attained intellect.

A-6 If the person is *not* bilingual, Reading Standard Score is less than Full Scale IQ by 15 points, and 1 year behind grade level placement for under age 12 or 2 years behind grade level for over age 12, and reading score is not above 10.0 grade score, use:

On the WRAT, the person's overall reading achievement was significantly below the individual's attained intellect and depicts an individual with a Specific Learning Disability/Developmental Reading Disorder (DSM-III Axis II: 315.00).

A-7 If the person *is* bilingual, and Reading Standard Score is less than Full Scale IQ by 15 points, use:

On the WRAT, the person's overall reading achievement was significantly below the individual's attained intellect. This is likely due to the individual's bilingual background.

A-8 If Spelling Standard Score is not less than the Full Scale IQ by 10 points, use:

On the WRAT Test, the person's overall spelling achievement was consistent with the individual's attained intellect.

A-9 If Spelling Standard Score is less than Full Scale IQ by 10–14 points, use:

On the WRAT, the person's overall spelling achievement was somewhat below the individual's attained intellect.

A-10 If Spelling Standard Score is less than Full Scale IQ by 15 points, use:

On the WRAT, the person's overall spelling achievement was significantly below the individual's attained intellect.

A-11 If Arithmetic Standard Scores are not less than Full Scale IQ by 10 points, use:

On the WRAT arithmetic test, the person's overall performance was consistent with the individual's attained intellect.

A-12 If Arithmetic Standard Scores are less than Full Scale IQ by 10–14 points, use:

On the WRAT arithmetic test, the person's overall performance was somewhat below the individual's attained intellect.

A-13 If Arithmetic Standard Scores are less than Full Scale IQ by over 15 points, and 1 year behind in grade level placement under age 12 or 2 years over age 12, and WRAT math score is not over 10.0 grade level, use:

On the WRAT arithmetic test, the person's overall performance is significantly below the individual's attained intellect and indicates an individual with a Specific Learning Disability/Developmental Arithmetic Disorder (DSM III,Axis II: 315.10).

PIAT SECTION

If the PIAT is used, use the following statements where appropriate:

A-14 If the Reading Recognition Score is 15 Standard Score points above Reading Comprehension, use:

The person's Oral Reading Score is higher than would be expected compared to the individual's Reading Comprehension score, indicating a better knowledge of phonics than actual reading understanding.

A-15 If the Reading Comprehension is 15 Standard Score points higher than Full Scale IQ, use:

The person's reading recognition achievement is higher than would be expected compared to the individual's Full Scale IQ. Possible reasons for this include:

1. Cultural bias; consequently the IQ may be an underestimate of the person's true intellectual potential;
2. An overachiever.

A-16 If Reading Recognition Standard Score is not less than the Full Scale IQ by 10 points, and not 15 standard score points above either Full Scale IQ or Reading Recognition, use:

On the PIAT, the person's overall reading recognition achievement score was consistent with the individual's attained intellect.

A-17 If Reading Recognition Standard Score less than the Full Scale IQ by 10–14 points, use:

On the PIAT, the person's overall reading recognition achievement score was somewhat below the individual's attained intellect.

A-18 If the person is *not* bilingual, the Reading Recognition Standard Score is less than Full Scale IQ by 15 points and 1 year below the grade level attained for under 12-year-olds or 2 years below the grade level attained for 12 years and up, and Recognition Score is not over 10.0 grade, use:

On the PIAT, the person's overall Reading Recognition Achievement Score was significantly below the individual's attained intellect, and indicates a Specific Learning Disability/Developmental Reading Disorder (DSM III, Axis II, 315.00).

A-19 If the person *is* bilingual and the Reading Recognition Standard Score is less than Full Scale IQ, by 15 points, use:

On the PIAT the person's overall Reading Recognition Achievement Score was significantly below the individual's attained intellect. This is probably due to the individual's bilingual background.

A-20 If Reading Comprehension Standard Score is not less than Full Scale IQ by 10 points, use:

On the PIAT, the person's overall reading comprehension achievement was consistent with the individual's attained intellect.

A-21 If the Reading Comprehension standard score is less than the Full Scale IQ by 10–14 points, use:

On the PIAT, the person's overall reading comprehension achievement was somewhat below the individual's attained intellect.

A-22 If the person is *not* bilingual, and the Reading Comprehension Standard Score is less than Full Scale IQ by 15 points and 1 year below the grade level attained for under-12-year-olds or 2 years below the grade level attained from 12 and up, and the Reading Comprehension Score is not above 10th grade, use:

On the PIAT, the person's overall reading comprehension achievement was significantly below the attained intellect and indicates a Specific Learning Disability/Developmental Reading Disorder (DSM III, Axis II, 315.00).

A-23 If the person is bilingual and the Reading Comprehension Standard Score is less than Full Scale IQ by 15 points, use:

On the PIAT the person's overall reading comprehension score was significantly below the individual's attained intellect. This is most likely due to the individual's bilingual background.

A-24 If Spelling Standard Score is not less than the Full Scale IQ by 10 points, use:

On the PIAT, the person's overall spelling achievement was consistent with the individual's attained intellect.

A-25 If Spelling Standard Score is less than Full Scale IQ by 10–14 points, use:

On the PIAT, the person's overall spelling achievement was somewhat below the individual's attained intellect.

A-26 If Spelling Standard Score is less than Full Scale IQ by 15 points, use:

On the PIAT, the person's overall spelling achievement was significantly below the individual's attained intellect.

A-27 If Math Standard Scores are not less than Full Scale IQ by 10 points, use:

On the PIAT, the individual's overall mathematics performance was consistent with the person's attained intellect.

A-28 If Math Standard Scores are less than Full Scale IQ by 10–14 points, use:

On the PIAT, the individual's overall mathematics performance was somewhat below the person's attained intellect.

A-29 If Math Standard Scores are less than Full Scale IQ by over 15 points and grade level difference is 1 year below the grade level attained for under 12 years or 2 years below for 12 and up, and not at or above 10th grade level, use:

On the PIAT the individual's overall mathematics performance is significantly below the persons attained intellect and indicates a Specific Learning Disability/Developmental Arithmetic Disorder (DSM III, Axis II, 315.10).

ACHIEVEMENT INTERPRETATION SECTION

For the WRAT, WRAT-R or the PIAT, use the following if appropriate:

A-30 If the average of Reading Recognition grade level and Reading Comprehension on the PIAT or on the WRAT/WRAT-R Reading is greater than 8.5, use:

The individual's reading achievement depicts an individual who can understand written material at the level of an Income Tax instruction booklet and is capable of functioning adequately in everyday society.

A-31 If the average of Reading Recognition grade level and Reading Comprehension on the PIAT or Reading on the WRAT/WRAT-R is greater than 6.0 and less than 8.5 (use with 14-year-olds and older only), use:

The individual's reading achievement depicts an individual who can understand written material at the level of difficulty of *Reader's Digest* and is minimally competent to function in everyday society.

A-32 If the average of Reading Recognition grade level and Reading Comprehension on the PIAT or Reading on the WRAT/WRAT-R is greater than 4.0 and less than 6.0, (use only with 14-year-olds and older), use:

The individual's reading achievement is deficient with regard to functioning in everyday society.

A-33 If the average of Reading Recognition grade level and Reading Comprehension on the PIAT or Reading on the WRAT/WRAT-R is less than 4.0 (use only with 14-year-olds and older), use:

The individual is functionally illiterate and incompetent to deal with the written material required in everyday society.

A-34 If Spelling Score is below 5th grade (use only with 14-year-olds and older), use:

The person's overall spelling performance depicts an individual who is deficient with regard to writing simple letters in everyday society.

A-35 If Spelling Score is 5th grade or more, but less than 8th grade, use:

The person's spelling performance depicts an individual who is capable of writing basic letters and notes required for communication in everyday society.

A-36 If Spelling Score is 8th grade or more, but less than 11th grade, use:

The person's overall spelling performance depicts an individual who is capable of writing simple business letters.

A-37 If Spelling Score is 11th grade or greater, use:

The person's overall spelling performance depicts an individual who is capable of writing professional letters and/or business reports.

A-38 If Math grade level is greater than 2.0 and less than 4.0 (use only with 12-year-olds and up), use:

The person's math performance depicts an individual whose knowledge of math is limited to simple addition and substraction with whole numbers.

A-39 If Math grade level is greater than 4.0 and less than 6.0 (use only with 12-year-olds and up), use:

The person's mathematical performance depicts an individual who has knowledge of basic mathematical functions, but may have some problem with multiplication and division. The individual has no knowledge of fractions and decimals.

A-40 If Math grade level is greater than 6.0 and less than 8.5 (use only with 12-year-olds and up), use:

The person's mathematical performance depicts an individual who has a reasonable working knowledge of basic mathematics, but has not mastered fractions and decimals.

A-41 If Math grade level is greater than 8.5, use:

The person's mathematical performance depicts an individual who has a solid foundation in basic mathematics.

EDUCATIONAL RECOMMENDATION SECTION

Use the following statements on IQ, if appropriate (see above to see if bilingual).

A-42 If Verbal IQ is 15 points *lower* than Performance IQ, and the person is *not* from a bilingual background use:

This person is primarily a visual learner. Individuals with this intellectual learning style comprehend better when material is presented to them with the aid of graphics and visual aids.

A-43 If the Verbal IQ is 15 points *lower* than Performance IQ and the person *is* from a bilingual background, use:

The person is apt to be in need of either an English as a Second Language instructional program, or at least additional education in basic English.

A-44 If the Verbal IQ is 15 points *higher* than Performance IQ, then use:

This person is primarily a verbal learner. Individuals with this learning style comprehend better when material is presented to them in written or auditory form.

NOTE: Refer back to the IQ (WECHSLER SECTION) in Chapter 6 on Verbal Comprehension, Perceptual Organization, and Distractibility.

A-45 If deficits on verbal comprehension: statement I-62 was used, use:

The individual may profit from additional instruction in the areas of language development, verbal concepts, and vocabulary acquisition.

A-46 If deficits in perceptual organization: statement I-63 was used, use:

The individual may profit from additional instruction in the areas of visual-special relationships and visual planning tasks. Speeded tasks may present a special problem for this person.

A-47 If deficits in distractibility: statement I-64 was used, use:

The individual may profit from a program that breaks down instructional units into brief segments and reinforces attention and concentration skills.

NOTE: Refer to above Achievement Scores and use the following rules:

A-48 If the PIAT Reading Comprehension standard score is 15 points below the PIAT Reading Recognition standard and/or the Full Scale IQ score, and 1 year below grade level for under 12 or 2 years below grade level for 12 and up and not above a score of 10.0 grade, use:

A listening–reading comprehension skill-building program in a tension-free and anxiety reduced learning situation should be initiated.

A-49 If the PIAT Reading Recognition standard score is 15 points below the PIAT Reading Comprehension Standard Score and/or the Full Scale IQ score or the WRAT/WRAT-R Reading score is 15 points below the Full Scale IQ score, and 1 year below grade level for under 12 or 2 years below grade level for 12 and up and not over a score of 10.0 grade, use:

Utilize a conventional basis reading vocabulary building program using basic skills material aimed at the person's reading level as opposed to grade level.

A-50 If the PIAT, WRAT, or WRAT-R Spelling Standard Score is 15 points below the IQ and 1 year below grade level under 12 or 2 years below grade level over 12 and not above a score of 10.0 grade, use:

The person is in need of remediation in the area of spelling. Such a program should include emphasis on correct pronunciation, dictionary usage, and, if possible, immediate feedback.

A-51 If the PIAT, WRAT, or WRAT-R Math Standard Score is 15 points below the IQ score, and is less than 4.0, and 1 year below grade level under 12 or 2 years below grade level over 12 and not above 10th grade level, use:

Remediation in the area of math is indicated in virtually all areas of arithmetic.

A-52 If the PIAT, WRAT, or WRAT-R Math Standard Score is greater than 4.0 but less than 6.0, and 1 year below grade level under 12 or 2 years below grade level over 12 and not above 10.0 grade, use:

Remediation in the area of math is indicated. The person needs additional drill with multiplication and division. Fractions, decimals, and percentages need to be dealt with, beginning at the rudimentary level.

A-53 If the PIAT, WRAT, or WRAT-R Math Standard Score is greater than 6.0 but less than 8.5, and 1 year below grade level under 12 and 2 years below grade level over 12 and not over 10.0 grade, use:

Remediation in the area of math is indicated. The person needs help in the areas of fractions, decimals, and percentages.

VOCATIONAL RECOMMENDATION SECTION

If Vocational report is less than high school education or GED, listed above under "education," use the following heading: Vocation Section: GED Predictions.

Use the following statements as appropriate:

A-54 If the average of the PIAT Reading Recognition grade level and PIAT Reading Comprehension or the WRAT/WRAT-R Reading is greater than 8.5 and Arithmetic grade level is greater than 8.5, use:

The person's overall performance depicts an individual who should be able to obtain a high school equivalency diploma (GED) with virtually no preparation.

A-55 If the average of the PIAT Reading Recognition grade level and PIAT Reading Comprehension or the WRAT/WRAT-R Reading is greater than 6.5 and less than 8.5, and/or Arithmetic grade level is greater than 6.5 and less than 8.5, use:

The person's overall performance depicts an individual who should be able to attain a high school equivalency diploma (GED) with a very limited amount of basic education.

A-56 If the average of the PIAT Reading Recognition grade level and PIAT Reading Comprehension or WRAT/WRAT-R Reading is greater than 8.5, and Arithmetic grade level greater than 6.5 and less than 8.5, use:

The person's overall performance depicts an individual who should be able to attain a high school equivalency diploma (GED) with preparation in the area of mathematics.

A-57 If the average of the PIAT Reading Recognition grade level and Reading Comprehension or WRAT/WRAT-R Reading is less than 6.5 and greater than 5.0, and/or Arithmetic grade level less than 6.5 and greater than 5.0, use:

The person's overall performance depicts an individual who will need a significant amount of preparation in basic education to attain a high school equivalency diploma (GED).

A-58 If the average of PIAT Reading Recognition and Reading Comprehension or WRAT/WRAT-R reading is less than 5.0, or Arithmetic is less than 5.0, use:

The person's overall performance depicts an individual for whom attaining a high school equivalency (GED) would require an extensive amount of preparation in basic education and may not be a viable educational-vocational objective.

VOCATION SECTION: CURRENT ACHIEVEMENT SKILL LEVEL

Use the following where appropriate:

A-59 If IQ is 15 points below PIAT Reading Comprehension Standard Score and/or scores on the PIAT or WRAT/WRAT-R Math Standard Score, use:

The person's Achievement Scores in some areas depict a higher functioning level than their intellectual assessment. This may be due to cultural and/or language bias on the IQ test, or to the fact that the person is an overachiever. In any case, careers listed in the achievement section should be considered viable.

A-60 If IQ is 15 points above any achievement standard score on the PIAT or WRAT/WRAT-R, use:

The person's IQ Score depicts a higher ability level than the individual's current achievement skills in some areas. The individual's current achievement skill levels should be the prime consideration for immediate educational and career training and placement. However, the individual's intellectual potential should serve as an index of what can be obtained with additional basic education.

A-61 If 11.0+ for the average of PIAT Reading Comprehension and PIAT Reading Recognition or WRAT/WRAT-R Reading is scored, use:

The individual's current overall reading level is satisfactory for pursuing college work. The individual's reading level alone is sufficient for pursuing college majors that do not require extensive preparation in math, such as education and liberal arts. Other majors, such as engineering, will require scrutiny of the individual's math skills.

A-62 If 8.0 to 10.9 for the average of PIAT Reading Comprehension and PIAT Reading Recognition or WRAT/WRAT-R Reading is scored, use:

The individual's current overall reading level is satisfactory for pursuing careers requiring a High School or Community College level of education. The individual's reading level alone is sufficient for undergoing training in careers that do not require extensive preparation in math, such as typist or offset printer. Other occupations at this level, such as machinist, will require scrutiny of the individual's math skills.

A-63 If 6.0 to 7.9 for the average of PIAT Reading Comprehension and PIAT Reading Recognition or WRAT/WRAT-R reading is scored, use:

The individual's current overall reading level is satisfactory for pursuing careers requiring minimal basic reading skills, such as cook or

LVN. Other occupations at this level, such as auto mechanic, will require scrutiny of the individual's math skills.

A-64 If below 6.0 on the average of PIAT Reading Comprehension and PIAT Reading Recognition or WRAT/WRAT-R Reading is scored, use:
The individual's current overall reading ability severely limits the occupational choices available to the person. Unless the individual's math skills are significantly higher than the individual's reading skills, only low-skill level jobs, such as motel maid and laborer, are apt to be suitable.

A-65 If 11.0+ for math level is scored, use:
The individual's current overall math level is satisfactory for pursuing college work requiring a significant amount of mathematics, such as careers in accounting and computer programming.

A-66 If 8.0 to 10.9 for math level is scored, use:
The individual's current overall math level is satisfactory for pursuing careers requiring a significant but not substantial amount of mathematics. College degrees not significantly oriented toward math and math occupations at the high school or community college level of preparation, such as buyer, bank teller, chemical operation, and bookkeeper, can be attained at this math level.

A-67 If 6.0 to 7.9 for math level is scored, use:
The individual's overall math level is satisfactory for occupations requiring minimal basic math skills, as well as occupations not requiring extensive math skills. Examples of occupations at the individual's present level are: carpenter, plumber, and electronics assembler.

A-68 If below 6.0 on math level is scored, use:
The individual's current overall math level significantly restricts the level of occupations available unless the individual's reading skills offer alternatives at a higher level. Based on the individual's present math level, only occupations requiring no significant math are viable, such as truck driver, dry cleaning worker, and welder.

CHAPTER EIGHT

Interpretative Statements for the Cognitive Section: Neuropsychological Tests

The section is essentially an amplification or expansion of those tests listed in the Semi-Automated Full Battery (Vincent 1980a,c). The Pfieffer Scale has been added to the test repertoire.

The first test covered is the Wechsler Memory Scale, which details an interpretation of this instrument relating to memory deficits in general and also to statements to be made about specific subscales. It is worth noting that the Wechsler Memory Scale should be used with caution with the Wechsler Intelligence Scale-Revised. Prifitera and Barley (1985) found the Memory Quotient tended to be about 6 points on the average higher than the WAIS-R full scale IQ of psychiatric in-persons. You may want to add a 6-point consonent to the Wechsler Memory Scale to facilitate comparison with the WAIS-R.

The Trail Making test included here is a simple global screening device for organic impairment which is fairly straightforward. The chapter provides a table and age corrections for the Trail Making test which is helpful when using the test on geriatric populations.

The Reitan-Indiana Aphasia Screening test is included, and is fairly straightforward. Its descriptive statements provide global indication of deficits as well as specific statements relating to consistent deficits on particular test items.

The Abbreviated Halsted-Reitan Neuropsychological Test Battery is a brief neuropsychological test battery which was developed by Erickson, Calsyn, and Scheupbach (1978). The system utilizes the Trail Making test, the Reitan-Indiana Aphasia Screening test, and the block design and digit symbol tests from WAIS and WAIS-R. Ericksen et al. (1978) cross-validated their instrument, but it should be noted that, to the author's knowledge, the instrument has not been re-replicated to this date. Nevertheless, it is a convenient way of summarizing and analyzing a group of highly useful organic screen tests.

The Bender Gestalt Test statements could be adapted for use with any Bender Gestalt scoring system, but they were devised for the Hain Scoring System (Hain, 1964).

The scoring system for the Memory for Designs Test (Graham & Kendall,

1960) is the one used in this manual. The Memory for Designs Test is included, as, in the author's opinion, it has several advantages over the Bender Gestalt, even though it is not as well known. The advantages of the Memory for Designs Test are: it has correction scores for the intellectual ability of the subject, and takes the age of the subject into account. Additionally, the author has found the Memory for Designs Test useful in administration to impulsive teenagers, as they are not as apt to be penalized for carelessness on the Memory for Designs Test as they are on the Bender Gestalt.

The Pfeiffer (Short Portable Mental Status Questionnaire) Scale is another brief screening test for organic impairment. Unlike tests such as the Memory for Designs and Bender Gestalt, which are sensitive to global, diffuse organic impairment and impairment in the nondominant hemisphere, the Pfieffer Scale is sensitive, not only to global diffuse organic impairment, but also to impairment in the dominant hemisphere. Pfieffer developed his scale for use with geriatric persons, and it has also been shown to be viable for use with adolescents and non-geriatric adults (Vincent & Castillo, 1984b).

The user of the Full Battery Code Book should always keep in mind that the above-mentioned neurological screening tests, as well as the Wechsler, taken together, provide a reasonably viable estimate of the person's organic functioning, but are individually good screening tests for the general practitioner-psychologist and are not meant to substitute for the full neuropsychological test battery.

INTERPRETATIVE STATEMENTS FOR THE WECHSLER MEMORY SCALE

N-1 Memory Quotient less than 15 points below Full Scale IQ or Memory Quotient less than 10 points below Full Scale IQ, if IQ is less than 90.

On the WECHSLER MEMORY SCALE, the person's overall performance reveals no general or specific memory deficits.

N-2 Memory Quotient less than 20 points below Full Scale IQ or Memory Quotient 15 points below Full Scale IQ, if IQ is less than 90.

The person's performance on the WECHSLER MEMORY SCALE was significantly deficient when compared to the patient's IQ, and significant memory deficits are indicated.

N-3 Memory Quotient greater than 20 and less than 15 points below Full Scale IQ, or Memory Quotient greater than 10 or less than 15 points below Full Scale IQ, if IQ is less than 90.

On the WECHSLER MEMORY SCALE, the person's overall performance shows a tendency toward minor deficits in memory.

N-4 The individual showed particular deficits on the memory subscale relating to:

N-5 personal and current information (this is often encountered in aphasics and seniles).

N-6 orientation.

N-7 mental control (this is often deficient in patients with early organic impairment).

N-8 immediate recall of logical material.

N-9 immediate memory.

N-10 visual memory.

N-11 short-term memory.

INTERPRETATIVE STATEMENTS FOR THE TRAIL MAKING TEST

Rating Time in Seconds for Different Age Groups on the Trail Making Test (Adapted from Davies, 1968)

	Trails A		Trails B	
Age	Borderline	Critical	Borderline	Critical
40	+42	+50	+94	+129
40–49	+45	+59	+100	+151
50–59	+49	+67	+135	+177
60–69	+67	+104	+172	+282
70+	+105	+168	+292	+450

N-12 Less than the borderline time.

On the TRAIL MAKING TEST, using age-appropriate norms, the person's overall performance was negative with regard to organic impairment.

N-13 Between the borderline and critical time.

On the TRAIL MAKING TEST, using age-appropriate norms, the person's performance was borderline with regard to organic impairment.

N-14 Over the critical time.

On the TRAIL MAKING TEST, using age-appropriate norms, the person's performance was critical with regard to organic impairment.

INTERPRETATIVE STATEMENTS FOR THE REITAN-INDIANA APHASIA SCREENING TEST

N-15 0 to 4 errors.

On the REITAN-INDIANA APHASIA SCREENING TEST, the person's performance was negative with regard to organic impairment.

N-16 5–6 errors.

On the REITAN-INDIANA APHASIA SCREENING TEST, the person's overall performance was equivocal with regard to organic impairment.

N-17 7–15 errors.

On the REITAN-INDIANA APHASIA SCREENING TEST, the person's overall performance was indicative of mild organic impairment.

N-18 16–25 errors.

On the REITAN-INDIANA APHASIA SCREENING TEST, the person's overall performance was indicative of moderate organic impairment.

N-19 26–40 errors.

On the REITAN-INDIANA APHASIA SCREENING TEST, the person's overall performance was indicative of severe organic impairment.

N-20 41+ errors.

On the REITAN-INDIANA APHASIA SCREENING TEST, the person's overall performance was indicative of catastrophic organic impairment.

N-21 Specific deficits evidenced by the individual were:

N-22 construction apraxia,

N-23 anomia,

N-24 spelling apraxia,

N-25 agraphia,

N-26 letter agnosia and alexia,

N-27 number agnosia and alexia,

N-28 letter agnosia,

N-29 alexia,

N-30 central dysarthria,

N-31 auditory verbal agnosia,

N-32 acalculia,

N-33 ideo-kinetic apraxia

N-34 right-left disorientation.

INTERPRETATIVE STATEMENS FOR THE ABBREVIATED HALSTED-REITAN NEUROPSYCHOLOGICAL TEST BATTERY

The Formula for the Average Impairment Rating (AIR) is:

27.3 + 1.0 (Trails A + Trails B Russell Rating—see below)
+ (−.7 Block Design Standard Score) + 1.7 Aphasia Error Rating +
(−1.0 Digit Symbol Standard Score) divided by 12 = the Average Impairment Rating (AIR)

In the formula, the Russell Rating for Trails A are as follows:

0 = 19 seconds or less; 1 = 20–33 seconds;
2 = 34–48 seconds; 3 = 49–62 seconds;
4 = 63–86 seconds and 5 = 87 seconds or more.

The Russell Rating for Trails B is as follows:

0 = 57 seconds or less; 1 = 58–87 seconds;
2 = 88–123 seconds; 3 = 124–186 seconds;
4 = 187–275 seconds and 5 = 276 seconds or more.

The Aphasia Error Rating is as follows: A rating of 0 means a 0 raw score on the Reitan-Indiana Aphasia Screening Test; a rating of 1 equals a raw score of 1–6; a rating of 2 equals a raw score of 7–15; a rating of 3 equals a raw score of 16–25; a rating of 4 equals a raw score of 26–40; a rating of 5 equals a raw score of 41 or more.

N-35 Introductory Statement; insert the AIR score at the end.
Combining the relevant above-mentioned instruments into the ABBREVIATED HALSTED-REITAN neuropsychological screening battery, the person attained an Average Impairment Rating of:

N-36 Less than 1.5 AIR
which is negative with regard to organic impairment.

N-37 1.6–2.5 AIR
which is indicative of mild organic impairment.

N-38 2.6–3.0 AIR
which is indicative of mild to moderate organic impairment.

N-39 3.1-3.5 AIR
which is indicative of moderate organic impairment.

N-40 3.6–4.0 AIR
which is indicative of moderate to severe organic impairment.

N-41 4.0+ AIR
which is indicative of severe organic impairment.

BENDER GESTALT TEST: ORGANIC SCREENING AND INTERPRETIVE STATEMENTS

The Bender Gestalt Test statements could be adapted for use with any Bender Gestalt scoring system, but they were devised for the Hain Scoring System (Hain, 1964). The following is an outline of the Hain System. Score as 4-point errors: perseveration, rotation, reversal, or concretism. Score as 3-point errors: added angles, separation of lines, overlap, or distortion. Score as 2-point errors: embellishment and partial rotations. Score as 1-point errors: omission of a subpart, abbreviation of designs 1 and 2, separation of subparts, absence of erasers, closure difficulties, or an error of the point of contact on Figure A.

N-42 Hain error score less than 5.
The individual's performance on the BENDER GESTALT TEST was negative.

N-43 Hain error score 6 or greater.
The individual's performance on the BENDER GESTALT TEST was in the normal to borderline range.

N-44 Hain error score 8–10.
The individual's performance on the BENDER GESTALT TEST was in the borderline range, indicating possible minimal organic impairment.

N-45 Hain error score 11 or 12.
The individual's performance on the BENDER GESTALT TEST was in the borderline to critical range, indicating possible organic impairment.

N-46 Hain error score 13 or over.
The individual's performance of the BENDER GESTALT TEST was in the critical range, indicating organic impairment.

N-47 IQ less than 70.
The individual's performance on the BENDER GESTALT TEST was defective, but generally in line with other individuals of limited intellectual endowment.

N-48 Poor cooperation observed.
The individual's performance on the BENDER GESTALT TEST was defective, but this appears more likely to be due to emotional problems than organic impairment.

N-49 IQ greater than 70, plus inconsistent performance and marked gross distortion (such as concretism).
The individual's performance on the BENDER GESTALT TEST was quite defective, but this performance is more indicative of functional psychosis than organic impairment.

MEMORY FOR DESIGNS TEST: ORGANIC SCREENING INTERPRETIVE STATEMENTS

Note: See Memory for Designs Manual to compute the Memory for Designs difference score.

N-50 MFD difference score one or below.
The individual's performance on the MEMORY FOR DESIGNS TEST was negative.

N-51 MFD differences score 2.
The individual's performance on the MEMORY FOR DESIGNS TEST was in the normal to borderline range.

N-52 MFD difference score 3–5.
The person's performance on the MEMORY FOR DESIGNS TEST was in the borderline range, indicating possible minimal organic impairment.

N-53 MFD difference score 6–7.
The person's performance on the MEMORY FOR DESIGNS TEST was in the borderline to critical range, indicating possible organic impairment.

N-54 MFD difference score 8+.
The person's performance on the MEMORY FOR DESIGNS TEST was in the critical range, indicating organic impairment.

N-55 Poor cooperation observed.
The person's performance on the MEMORY FOR DESIGNS TEST was defective, but this appears more likely to be due to emotional problems than organic impairment.

N-56 IQ greater than 70 and inconsistent performance, plus marked gross distortions (such as concretism).
The person's performance on the MEMORY FOR DESIGNS TEST was quite defective, but this performance is more indicative of functional psychosis than organic impairment.

INTERPRETATIVE STATEMENTS FOR THE PFEIFFER (SPMSQ) SCALE

N-57 0 to 4 errors

On the Pfeiffer (SPMSQ) Scale, the person's overall performance was negative regarding organic impairment.

N-58 5–7 errors

On the Pfeiffer (SPMSQ) Scale, the person's overall performance is indicative of significant organic impairment.

N-59 8–10 errors

On the Pfeiffer (SPMSQ) Scale the person's overall performance is indicative of severe organic impairment.

CHAPTER NINE

Interpretative Statements for the Rorschach

The Rorschach interpretation is based primarily on the work of Bruce Duthie (Vincent & Duthie, 1983b), which was expanded by the author. The system includes data on content analysis from the author's Fully Automated Rorschach and Fully Automated Holtzman Content Analysis Technique, which have demonstrated some degree of validity (Vincent, 1982a,b). These systems were welded together and the perceptual section expanded. The system, as is, incorporates only those perceptual and content factors which have been cross-validated. The system should be usable by any experienced Rorschacher, regardless of whether he or she uses the Exner, Klopfer, or Rapport-Schafer System. Keys to the symbols which vary from system to system are provided below. The system is not totally Exner, in that Exner is an inclusive system which seems to incorporate virtually all systems. Since the publication of the Exner system, the author is not aware of a single validity study in the literature demonstrating the superiority of the Exner system over previous systems, though numerous studies have been done demonstrating the Exner system's increased reliability. Whether or not this increased reliability (as it has been with the Holtzman) is synonymous with an increase in validity has yet to be demonstrated. The system does not incorporate symbols of the Exner which are subject to a variety of interpretations. For example, Exner uses water in one of his content scales, but the literature shows that water sometimes is indicative of dependent personality features, and sometimes indicative of alcoholism. Because of the mixed data on water's interpretation as content, it is excluded from the interpretation system. The author strongly feels that individuals who use such things in the reports to mean one thing on one particular occasion, and another thing on another occasion, are primarily keying off other information from either other test data or other information. When mixed feelings have occurred regarding the interpretation of a Rorschach factor, the factor is included only when the majority of studies have found the Rorschach factor indicates something. Consequently, the following statements are the author's attempt to include only the most objective on the Rorschach factors.

Key to Rorschach Perceptual Symbols

Symbol	Name
W	whole response
D	detail response
S	space response
X+%	good form (F+)−total responses (R)
M	human movement
FM (or AM)	animal movement
m	inanimate movement
C	pure color
CF	color-form
FC	form-color
C′	pure achromatic color
C′F	achromatic color-form
FC′	form-achromatic color
T	pure texture
TF	texture-form
FT	form-texture
V	pure vista
VF	vista-form
FV	form-vista
Y	pure shading
YF	shading-form
FY	form-shading

KEY TO PATHOLOGICAL VERBALIZATIONS

CONTAMINATION (CONTAM or CT) responses occur when two separate interpretations are fused into one, or when the same area stands for two separate concepts that are fused into one. Example: The front of a bug-Ox, must be a cricket—a man—cricket shaped like crickets and men. A diamond—not a man's head—a diamond-shaped head. Except in young children (under 5) this response is almost always indicative of psychosis (95%) and schizophrenia (90%).

DEVIANT VERBALIZATIONS (Dv), also known as Queer Responses (Qr), occur when distorted language is used and/or the responses have an odd flavor. For example: It's a bat, but I was going to say a dog; another femine distribution; a cat on a platter.

AUSTIC LOGIC (Alog or Al) responses occur when the person gives a faulty or grossly illogical reasoning to explain their response. This is more significant when the explanation is given without inquiry. For example: Two dogs because they are green; a heart bleeding because it looks bitter.

FABILIZED COMBINATION (FACOM or Fc) responses occur when illogical elements are combined into one response. For example: a woman giving birth to a dog; two men with sheep's heads.

DETERIORATION COLOR (Dc) responses occur when the color associations are unreal and bizarre. For example: purple bones; red milk; yellow blood.

SELF REFERENCE (Sr) responses occur when the person draws himself or herself into responses. For example: that looks like my father; a butterfly that was in my dream last night.

ABSURD (Abs) or INCOHERENT (Ic) responses occur when they bear no relationship to the inkblot by any stretch of the imagination. For example: calling all of Card I the Empire State Building.

Key to Rorschach Content Symbols

Scale Abbreviation	Scale Name
1. A + Ad	animal and animal detail
2. Ab	all abstract responses
3. Ab+	all positive abstract responses
4. Ab−	all negative abstract responses
5. Al	alphabet, numbers, letters
6. At or An (include Xy)	anatomy
7. Bd	bridge
8. Bi	bisexual figures
9. Bl	blood
10. Cg	clothing
11. Ck	chicken
12. Cl	cloud
13. Cn	color naming
14. Cs	castration
15. Em	emblems
16. Ex	explosion
17. Ey	eyes
18. Fd	food
19. Fe	fetus
20. Fi	fire
21. Ft	fighting
22. Ge	geography, maps
23. H + Hd	human and human detail
24. Jc	Jesus, Christ, God
25. Ms	mask
26. P	popular
27. R	# of responses
28. Rj	total number of cards rejected
29. Rf	reflection
30. Rk	rocks
31. Sm	smoke
32. Sx	all sex responses
33. Th	teeth
34. Tw	twins
35. Ur	urine or feces

PERSEVERATION OF RESPONSES (Psv) occurs when the same response is given to more than one card. For example: there is that hat again; now the same people are dancing.

RORSCHACH INTERPRETIVE STATEMENTS: CONTENT AND PERCEPTUAL FACTORS

R-1 (Introductory Statement used on all reports). On the Rorschach Inkblot Technique the following is indicated:

R-2 (Ey3) Excessive sensitivity, projection, and probable paranoia is indicated.

R-3 (2Ey) A high degree of sensitivity to the opinions of others is indicated.

R-4 (2Tw) A feeling of being more than one person and a lack of self integration is present.

R-5 (Rj 5+ cards rejected). The person rejected over half of the cards; this is a passive aggressive equivalent to refusing to take the test, which is most frequently encountered in paranoid individuals. The person is apt to be hostile, defensive, impulsive, and explosive. Such individuals are apt to be quite difficult to reach via psychotherapeutic intervention.

R-6 (+Ab) The person is apt to be overexuberant, excitable, impressionable, and expressive.

R-7 (−Ab) The person is apt to be impulsive, restless, belligerent, and irreconcilable.

R-8 (Ab 2+) The person is apt to be overexuberant and emotional. Hypomania and/or marked affective instability is likely.

R-9 (At 5+) Restriction and stagnation of thought processes is likely.

R-10 (A + Ad 1 or less.) Lowered emotional control and marked autistic preoccupation is likely.

R-11 (R greater than 7 but less than 12; or, in the case of children or adolescents, R greater than 5 but less than 10) The person evidences a significant amount of blocking. Hampered intellectual ability or defensiveness is likely.

R-12 (Cn 2+) A lack of affective control is indicated.

R-13 (H+Hd is 2 or less, except in 5-year-olds.) A lack of interest in others is indicated, as is possible hostility towards others.

R-14 (H+Hd is 2 or less and A is 20% or less except in 5-year-olds.) Stereotyped thinking is indicated.

R-15 (A + Ad is 70% or greater.) The person lacks spontaneity and is apt to be inflexible, predictable, and resistant to change and has a high potential for confusion and disruption in greater than average demanding situations.

R-16 (Cg is 2+) Concern with social status and attractiveness are indicated.

R-17 (Fd is 2+) Significant dependency features are likely.

R-18 (Th is 2+) Immaturity and feelings of resentment and rejection are indicated in an individual whose dependency needs are frustrated.

R-19 (Em is 2+) The person has high prestige drives but feels inadequate in competing with others.

R-20 (Cs is 2+ and the person is female.) The person feels sexually inadequate and fears abandonment.

R-21 (Cs is 2+ and the person is male.) The person feels sexually inadequate and evidences a fear of bodily harm.

R-22 (Fe is 2+) Concern with reproduction and sexual viability is indicated.

R-23 (Sx is 2+) Probable sexual conflicts and concern regarding one's capacity to carry out sexual relations is evidenced.

R-24 (Bi is 2+) Conflicts over sexual identity and sexual orientation is likely.

R-25 (Sx is three or greater.) Conflict attributable to sexual maladjustment is indicated.

R-26 (Sx-2 or more, and B1—2 or more.) Sexual and/or aggressive acting out in a psychotic or borderline individual is likely.

R-27 (At is 6 or more +B1.) Problems with self control are indicated, as is possible sadistic and destructive impulses.

R-28 (Al) Evasiveness and anxiety are suggested.

R-29 (Bl) Deep negative emotions and serious emotional disturbance is likely. The person is apt to be anxious, phobic, emotionally labile, and hostile. Aggressive feelings, a fear of contact with others, and a need to dissociate oneself from others is probable.

R-30 (Bl is 2+) Marked problems with self control are indicated.

R-31 (Bd is 2+) Emotional insecurity is indicated. A history of disrupted parental relations is a distinct possibility.

R-32 (Ck is 2+) A history of affection deprivation is likely.

R-33 (Cl is 2+) Significant anxiety is apt to be present.

R-34 (Ex) A desire to release impulses or a fear of releasing impulses is suggested. Dynamic tension is apt to be present.

R-35 (Ft is 3+) Aggressive and hostile tendencies toward others is quite probable.

R-36 (Fi) Anxiety and tension are present; emotional lability and excitability are likely.

R-37 (Jc is 3+) Marked religious preoccupation is evidenced. Religious delusions are a distinct possibility.

R-38 (Ge) Guardedness and evasive tendencies are likely.

R-39 (Rf is 3+) Narcissistic tendencies are suggested.

R-40 (Rk) Security needs are present.

R-41 (Sm) Depressive features are likely in an anxious, apprehensive individual.

R-42 (Ur) The presence of overt psychosis or a borderline condition is likely.

R-43 (P is 2 or less, except in children under 8.) A lack of conformity and indifference to convention is likely.

R-44 (P is 12+) Guardedness and conformity is indicated. The person is apt to be fearful of making errors and quite conventional. Anxiety is present and depressive features are likely.

R-45 (R less than 17, W less than 5, M less than 2, FC less than 2, CF less than 2, C less than 1):

R45-a (If 2 met—on children under 9, if 4 meet.) Significant depression is suggested.

R45-b (If 3 met—on children under 9, if 5 meet.) The person is significantly depressed and apt to be negative toward self.

R45-c (If 4 met. Do not use on children under 9.) Very significant depression is indicated; inertia and a self-rejecting attitude is likely.

R45-d (If 5 met. Do not use on children under 9.) Major depression is indicated, as are impoverished self esteem and feelings of hopelessness.

R-46 At is 3+. Greater than normal somatic concern is indicated. Psychomatic symptoms are likely.

R-47 R 33+. Affective lability is suggested, and the person is apt to be emotionally expansive and unstable.

R-48 C2 or more (or C+Cn 2+). The person is apt to be excitable and emotionally labile.

R-49 Cf+C+Cn greater than 5+. Emotional lability and impulsiveness is likely in a person overwhelmed by feelings.

R-50 FC 5+ (do not use if C2+, Cn2+ C+Cn2+, or Cf+C+Cn5+ are used.) The person maintains a balance of controlling and releasing emotions; prognosis for psychotherapy is good.

R-51 M5+. A rich inner life is suggested.

R-52 M 0 or 1 (except in children under 10). Depressive features are likely.

R-53 Y+YF+FY3+. Passivity, emotional helplessness, and anxiety are likely.

R-54 T+TF+FT 2+. The person has high needs for emotional interpersonal contact.

R-55 V+VF+FV 2+. Feelings of inferiority and depression are likely.

R-56 C′ 2+, or C′ + C′F 3+. Pain, tension, and emotional intensity are indicated. Obsessive features are likely.

R-57 *m* 2+. Tension and discomfort are present.

R-58 FM (AM) 5+. A lack of capacity to control impulses is suggested.

R-59 CF & C are 0. Constriction of emotions are indicated. Significant depression is likely.

R-60 D 80% + of R and R less than 30. The person is apt to be obsessive and a perfectionist.

R-61 S2+ (other than eyes). Passive aggressive features are indicated. The person is apt to be oppositional and negativistic.

R-62 X+% 60% or less (all ages). Poor reality contact is present. If the person's cognitive abilities are intact, psychosis is a distinct possibility.

R-63 X+% 70% or less (all ages). Low ego strength is indicated, and the person lacks the capacity to deal with stress effectively.

R-64 (Contam or Ct) 1+. Poor reality testing is evident as is autistic thinking. Psychosis is probable. A thought disorder is likely.

R-65 Dv (Qr) 3+. Significant emotional disturbance and a partial breakdown in the reasoning process is indicated.

R-66 Alog (Al) 1+. Poor reality testing is apt to be present.

R-67 Facom (FC) 3+. Passivity and obsessive features are suggested. Depression may be present.

R-68 DC 2+. Distributed thinking is apt to be present.

R-69 SR 3+. Marked self preoccupation is likely. Depression and/or depersonalization is likely.

R-70 Abs(Ic) 1+. Rule out mental retardation.

R-71 Psv 4:. (except in children under 8). The person is intellectually rigid. Rule out organic brain syndrome or mental retardation.

R-72 Turning the card upside down without twisting it 2+ times: Passive aggressive features are indicated.

R-73 Twisting and turning of the card (in other words, turning it every which way 3+ times): anxiety and insecurity are apt to be present.

The following combinations are adopted from Duthie (Vincent & Duthie, 1983b) and require at least two of the decision criteria be met (they are for use with individuals age 9 and up).

R-74 X+%<75 / W>10 / P<4
Marked, free floating anxiety is evident.

R-75 FM>4 / M<2 X+%<75
The person is tense.

R-76 FM>4 / X+%>95 / A + Ad>49%
Anxiety may markedly cripple functioning.

R-77 M>5 / S>2
A rigid, punitive superego may be apparent.

R-78 A + Ad%>49 / X+%>95
The person is apt to feel guilt.

R-79 S>2 / P>9 / M>5
The person is filled with self doubt and is apt to be critical of self and self-depreciating.

R-80 S<1 / P>9 / M>5
Feelings of discouragement are often manifest.

R-81 M<2 / S>2
The person may often feel inadequate.

R-82 A+Ad%>49 / W<4
The individual lacks drive and has limited ambition.

R-83 X+%<75 / P>9
The person feels insecure.

R-84 M<2 / X+%<75 / FM=O
A weak ego unable to handle even moderate psychic conflict is suggested.

R-85 A+Ad%>49 / CF=O / FC<2
The individual tends to withdraw from conflict.

R-86 A+Ad%<29 / M<2 / P<4
Intellectual withdrawal and a detached attitude towards others is suggested.

R-87 FC>5 / X+%>95 / W>10
The person tends to be meticulous and a perfectionist.

R-88 FC>5 / CF=O / FM=O
Lack of spontaneity is suggested.

R-89 M<2 / X+%>95 / CF=O
The individual is cautious.

R-90 FC>5 / FM>4 / M<2
Neurotic inhibition may be manifest.

R-91 M>5 / X+%>95 / P>9
Neurotic constriction in a rigid inflexible individual is suggested.

R-92 X+%>95 / CF=O / FC<2
The person seems to lack the capacity to enjoy life.

R-93 S=0/ A+Ad%>49 / M<2
The individual feels blocked and cannot make decisions.

R-94 P>9 / FC>5 / A+Ad%>49
The person tends to be overly compliant to the wishes of others, and is often perceived as passive.

R-95 M>5 / FC<2 / A+Ad%>49
The individual is socially inhibited.

R-96 P>9 / X+%<75 / FC>5
The person is guarded, and in times of stress may become paranoid.

R-97 CF=O / FC>5
The individual is stilted, precise, and socially correct.

R-98 FC>5 / CF=O / C + Cn = 0
The person is not assertive and may have trouble coping with aggressive or hostile individuals. The individual is superficially social and may pretend to have social sophistication.

R-99 CF=0 / FC<2
The person is self-centered, egocentric, and tends to be selfish.

R-100 M>5 / S>2 / X+%<75
Suicidal potential and ideation are suggested.

R-101 M<2 / W<4 / P>9
Repression is an often used defense mechanism.

R-102 FM>4 / CF=O
This individual is apt to employ regression.

R-103 W>10 / S>2
Intellectualization may often be used.

R-104 X+%<75 / S>2
This individual is apt to displace his problems and conflicts upon others.

R-105 A+Ad%>49 / W<4 / P>9
Individuals with this type of performance are typically depressed.

R-106 CF>2 / P>9 / W<4
The person tends to be histrionic.

R-107 X+%>95 / M<2 / S>2
The individual may somaticize in times of stress.

R-108 M<2 / X+%>95 / P>9
Hypochondriacal tendencies are suggested.

R-109 S>2 / CF>2 / A+Ad%>49
Antisocial tendencies are suggested.

R-110 P<4 / S>2 / A+Ad%<29
The person tends to be rebellious.

R-111 CF>2 / S>2
The individual is oppositional and negativistic.

R-112 CF>2 / S>2 / A+Ad%>49
The person may be hostile or assaultive.

R-113 X+%>95 / M>5 / FC<2
The individual tends to be cautious, but impulsive.

R-114 C>1 / FM>4 / M<2
The person is impulsive and has a high potential to act out. Gratification is not easily delayed.

R-115 CF>2 / FC<2 / X+%<75
Emotional lability is suggested.

R-116 FC<2 / M<2 / C + CN>1
Extremely impaired emotional control is indicated.

R-117 A+Ad%<29 / CF>2 / C + CN>1
The person easily becomes excited and may be agitated.

R-118 FM>4 / M<2
The individual has an oral character style and is apt to be dominated by the pleasure principle.

R-119 FM>4 / CF>2 / A+Ad%>49
Immaturity is indicated.

R-120 FC<2 / M>5 / P<4 (all 3 criteria must be met)
Poor reality contact is indicated.

R-121 P<4 / X+%<75
Impaired reality testing may be present.

R-122 M>5 / CF=0 / FC<2 (all 3 criteria must be met)
Delusional thinking is indicated.

R-123 W<4 / M>5
The person is likely to escape into fantasy when they feel overwhelmed.

R-124 C>1 / M<2 / X+%<75
Markedly inappropriate affect is suggested.

R-125 X+%<75 / W>10
The person is apt to be expansive and grandiose.

R-126 C>1 / A+Ad%<29
Impulsive, bizarre behavior is sometimes manifest in individuals with this type of protocol.

R-127 A+Ad%<29 / X+%<75 / S>2 (all 3 criteria must be met)
Individuals with this profile may act out unexpectedly.

R-128 A+Ad%>49 / CF>2 / S>2 (all 3 criteria must be met)
The person has a tendency to be hypomanic.

R-129 (No other statement used)
The person's performance is unremarkable. Such individuals usually present with adjustment disorders or marital problems.

CHAPTER TEN

Interpretative Statements for the Holtzman Ink Blot Technique

The Holtzman Ink Blot Technique is an attempt to improve upon the Rorschach and has been demonstrated to be more reliable than the Rorachach. However, a demonstration of increased validity has yet to be forthcoming. Nevertheless, according to Aronow and Reznikoff (1976), it has become the instrument of choice for researchers, whereas the Rorschach has remained the instrument of choice to the clinician. The Holtzman Inkblot statements provided here are an expansion of the author's earlier work in the Semi-Automated Full Battery (Vincent, 1980a,b), which essentially expanded statements from New Developments in the Holtzman Inkblot Technique (Holtzman, 1975).

HOLTZMAN INKBLOT TECHNIQUE

Introductory Statement

H-1 On the HOLTZMAN INKBLOT TECHNIQUE, the following is indicated:

Introductory Statement when MR norms are used

H-2 On the HOLTZMAN INKBLOT TECHNIQUE, the following report takes into account the person's low intellect and reflects those areas in which the person differs from other retarded individuals.

H-3 FD<21 + FA<21 + V>90 (with AL or CT) + I<21 + Pn>79
Schizophrenia with disturbed thought process, marked self-absorption, and body image distortion are indicated.

H-4 FA<10 + V>79 (with AL or CT); or V>95 (with CT or AL)
Psychosis is indicated, in an individual with a thought disorder. Poor reality testing is evident, as is autistic thinking.

H-5 FA<10
Low ego strength is indicated. The person is apt to have difficulty in concentration.

H-6 FA<10 + V>95
Reality distortion and confusion is likely.

H-7 L<20 + FA<20 + P<20
Schizoid features are indicated, as is autistic thinking.

H-8 3 + Eyes (if staring at me (you))
Excessive sensitivity, projection, and probable paranoia is indicated.

H-9 3 + Eyes (without elaboration)
A high degree of sensitivity to the opinions of others is indicated.

H-10 2 + Twins
A feeling of being more than one person and a lack of self integration is present.

H-11 R>98
The person rejected over half the cards; this is a passive-aggressive equivalent of refusing to take the test, which is most frequently encountered in paranoid individuals. The individual is apt to be relatively inaccessible to therapeutic intervention, have difficulty relating to others on a one-to-one basis, and lack the capacity for insightful self-evaluation. The person is apt to lack a free fantasy life, be unable to discharge feelings via imagination, and may evidence episodic, impulsive, explosive behavior because of a lack of alternatives for coping with affect.

H-12 FA<20 + I>95 + Ab
An affective push of ideas is likely.

H-13 C>90
Unrest, a lack of emotional stability, and possible exhibitionism behavior is likely.

H-14 C>79 + M>79 + (1>79 or Ab or Sh>79)
Hypomania is likely, in an excited, restless, impulsive individual.

H-15 C>95
Probable lack of capacity to delay affective responses is indicated, in an emotionally overactive individual who is overwhelmed with feelings is suggested.

H-16 2 + Ab (with color)
The person is apt to be dominated by feelings, take chances, and act impulsively.

H-17 2 + positive Ab
The person is apt to be over-exuberant, excitable, impressionable, and expressive.

H-18 2 + negative Ab
The person is apt to be impulsive, restless, belligerent, and irreconcilable.

H-19 C>79 + Sh>79 + M>79

Marked emotional lability is indicated.

H-20 R>98; or At>98 + Pn>98; C>79 + M>79 + At>79 + Pn>79

There is evidence of disturbed thought processes.

H-21 C<21 + M<6 + H<6

This person is dull and stolid and seems to be making an inferior adjustment to life.

H-22 R>79 + L<6 + FD<6 + I<6

Little effort is made to organize experience beyond a diffuse perception.

H-23 C<6 + Sh<11 + M<6

Emotional flatness and apathy are indicated in this record.

H-24 L<21 + C<21 + Sh<21 + P<21

There is a lack of spontaneity and alertness to events in the environment.

H-25 L<6 + FD<21 + C<6 + I<6

There is a low capacity for active coping, structuring, integrating, and organizing.

H-26 C<21 + M<21 + H<6; or C<6 + M<19 + H<6 + A<6; or C<19 + M<6 + H<6 + A<6

Emotional constriction is indicated. The person cannot acknowledge impulses through imaginal processes.

H-27 FD<10

The person's affect appears feeble or overwhelmed. Weak defensive and adaptive abilities are indicated, in a tense, impulsive individual.

H-28 FD<10 + C<10 + M<10

The person's behavior may be unpredictable and uneven. A fear of contact or responsibility is indicated, in an excessively cautious, indecisive individual.

H-29 At>98

Restriction and reduction of intellectual drive are revealed.

H-30 M<11 + A<6

A lack of constitutional strength to carry out a program of self-development is indicated.

H-31 A<6

Lowered ego control or nonadaptive preoccupation with original ideas is indicated.

H-32 R>89

The person shows minor blocking of ideational activity.

H-33 H<6
The person lacks interest in other people and may have serious interpersonal problems.

H-34 L>79 + FD>79
There is an over emphasis upon accuracy, correctness, and exactitude.

H-35 L>94
This individual is interested in details for the sake of details, rather than as part of a larger scheme of things.

H-36 C<10
The presence of significant depression is likely, in a self-rejecting, rigid, inhibited, defensive individual.

H-37 C<21 + Sh<21 + P<21
Reduced involvement in external events is evidenced.

H-38 V>90 + Pn>90
Self-preoccupied, disordered thinking is indicated.

H-39 C>98 + Sh>79 + H>79
Lack of conscious control over feelings and impulses is likely. Inner unrest and lack of emotional stability are revealed.

H-40 L<20 + FA<20 + V>79 + At>79 + Hs>79 + Pn>79
The person turns hostility inward, and disintegration and depersonalization is likely.

H-41 FD>89 + C<20 + Sh<20 + M<20
The person is apt to be rigid, inflexible, and limited in feelings.

H-42 FD<21 + C<21 + Sh<21
Emotional flatness, apathy, and rigidity are present.

H-43 2 + dried blood, death and/or mutilation
The person is hostile toward self and suicidal tendencies are probable.

H-44 V>98 (with Absurd and/or DC>other V)
Rule out mental retardation.

H-45 Rt<21 + C>79 + Sh>79 + M>79 + Hs>79
The person has problems centering on a lack of self control.

H-46 3 + S
Over-concern with problems of autonomy is indicated. The person is negativistic, unbending, tenacious; and passive-aggressive or paranoid features are likely.

H-47 Rt<10
The person is apt to be impulsive, spontaneous, and have a limited capacity for concentration.

H-48 A>80 (with aggressive animals over-emphasized)
A lack of control and judgement are indicated.

H-49 Sh>79 + M>79 + H>79 + Hs>79
Aggressive and antisocial acting out is likely.

H-50 3 + color naming
Inability to control and direct the reaction of affect is indicated.

H-51 C>90 + M<20
Excessive emotional lability and acting out behavior is likely.

H-52 C>79
Sensitivity to the emotional impact of others is indicated, in a suggestible individual.

H-53 C>79 (with three C-3 responses)
Diffuse emotional lability and irritability are suggested.

H-54 Rt<21 + R>80
Inability to become involved in stimulus is indicated.

H-55 C<21 + Sh<21
Lack of involvement and insensitivity are indicated.

H-56 L<21 + I<21
Low motivation to achieve and discipline intellect is evidenced.

H-57 H<21 + P<21
Lack of interest in the motives of others, a rebellious attitude, and indifference to conventionality is present.

H-58 Br<21
Passivity and low ability to tolerate stress are evidenced.

H-59 M<21 + H<21 + A<21 + P<21
The person lacks the ability to express feelings via normal channels.

H-60 At>95 + Pn>95
Emotional conflicts with excessive bodily concern are indicated.

H-61 L>79 + FD>79 + M>79 + Ax>79
The person is obsessive and is insensitive to the emotional impact of the outer world, although aware of inner needs and feelings. Worry, in combination with increased fantasy life and decreased overt behavior, is indicated.

H-62 Rt>79 + R>79 + V>79 + Ax>79 + Pn>79
Depression and a self-punitive attitude are indicated.

H-63 L>79 + H>79 + Ax>79
The person is a rigid, compulsive, tense, indecisive individual whose major defense is that of repression.

H-64 H>94 + Ax>94; or H>79 + Ax>79 + Hs>79
Problems in interpersonal relations and a fear of people are indicated.

H-65 M>94 + Ax>94
The person is tense and alert as if facing an emergency.

H-66 I<51 + H>94 + Ax>94 + Pn>94
There is excessive reliance on inner fantasy, to the exclusion of reality.

H-67 At>94 + Ax>94 + Pn>94
Emotional conflict with excessive body concern is present; and psychosomatic symptoms are likely.

H-68 H>79 + At>79 + Ax>79 + Pn>79
Emotional immaturity and body preoccupation are indicated.

H-69 Sh>98 + Ax>98
Responses reveal an individual who has doubts, uncertainties, and intense feelings of which they are only dimly aware. The person is sensitive, fearful, and vigilant.

H-70 H<21 + Pn>94
There are feelings of personal inadequacy.

H-71 Rt>79 + R>79 + FD<21
Cognition and motor inhibition is indicated.

H-72 V>98 (with FB and/or FC> other V)
Marked emotional turmoil is indicated.

H-73 I<21 + At>79 + Pn>94
Poor ego identity and a poor sense of body boundary definiteness are indicated.

H-74 L>79 + FD>79 + Ax>79 + P>79
Fear and anxiety compel this person to cling to obvious and safe thoughts.

H-75 FD<21 + C>94 + I<6
This individual is dominated by emotional reactivity.

H-76 L>89 + FD<20 + I<20
The person is apt to be petty, meticulous, and critical.

H-77 M<10
Excessive repression is likely.

H-78 M>95
The person is preoccupied with their own ideas at the expense of being responsive to external stimuli.

H-79 C<10 + M>89
A reduction of overt activity is suggested, as is social introversion.

H-80 FA<20 + M>89
Poor social skills and poor interpersonal relations are likely.

H-81 C<20 + M<20

An overcontrol of inner life and fantasy are indicated, as is possible depression.

H-82 FD<20 + M<20

A lack of ability to express self and acknowledge impulses is indicated.

H-83 I<10

Emotional immaturity is indicated.

H-84 Sh<10

Passivity and repression in dealing with moods which evoke anxiety is likely, as is difficulty dealing with the threatening aspects of interpersonal relations.

H-85 Sh>90

Anxiety, emotional insecurity, and general oversensitivity to environmental pressure is likely.

H-86 4 + "B"

Obsessive-compulsive features are indicated. The person is apt to be insecure and fears impulsiveness in self.

H-87 P<10

Probable conscious rebellion is indicated, in an individual who is detached from the influences of practical social demands.

H-88 P>98

Guardedness and conformity are indicated, as is excessive concern with social convention.

H-89 Br<10

A low internal stability to tolerate stress is indicated, as is passivity and possible low achievement orientation and low goal direction. The person may react internally to stress via somatizations.

H-90 Br>95

The person may be excessively self-protective from the impact of threatening situations.

H-91 H<10

A lack of interest in others is indicated, as is possible hostility toward others.

H-92 H>98

The person views interpersonal relationships as threatening, and may have a fear of others and their intentions.

H-93 Ax>95

Chronic anxiety is evidenced, in an individual who is apt to be manifesting feelings of insecurity and have personality conflicts. The person is apt to be quite sensitive to pain.

H-94 Hs>95 (with overt aggression > threatening content)
Acting out behavior is likely, especially if the person is provoked.

H-95 Hs>95 (with threatening content > overt aggression) or Ax>90 and Hs>90
A fear of aggression from others is indicated, in an individual who tends to avoid threatening situations.

H-96 Pn>95
Anxiety, a low tolerance for stress, and feeling of vulnerability are indicated. Emotional immaturity and body preoccupation are likely, and the individual may view their body as disgusting or deteriorating at present.

H-97 M>90 (with aggressive content)
Oral sadistic drives are apt to be present.

H-98 M>90 (with inanimate aggression towards humans (example: machine crushing someone or crucifixion)
Disassociation of hostile, aggressive impulses is indicated.

H-99 M>90 (with frequent explosions or eruptions)
A desire to release impulses and/or a fear of releasing impulses is indicated.

H-100 H<10 + A<10
Stereotyped thinking is indicated.

H-101 H>79 + A<10
The person is apt to be intellectually introversive, but not particularly overcontrolled, possibly due to intellectual inertia or excessive conventionality.

H-102 A>95
The person lacks spontaneity, draws heavily on inner needs, is apt to be predictable and resistant to change, and has a high potential for confusion and disruption in greater-than-average demanding situations.

H-103 At>95 (delete this statement for medical professions)
Greater-than-normal somatic concern is indicated, in an individual who turns hostility inward on self and is quite self-preoccupied. A lack of emotional insight is indicated.

H-104 2 + mask (with human movement)
A tendency to misrepresent self, and appear as something which one is not, is revealed.

H-105 2 + mask (without human movement)
The person is fearful of hypocrisy in others and feels they may be presenting a facade and are not what they seem to be.

H-106 2 + separate articles of clothing
Concern with social status and attractiveness are indicated.

H-107 2 + food
Significant dependency features are likely.

H-108 2 + teeth
Immaturity and feelings of resentment and rejection are indicated, in an individual whose dependency needs are frustrated.

H-109 2 + emblems
The person has high prestige drives, but feels inadequate in competing with others.

H-110 Castration responses in female patients. (Examples: withered, stunted objects; unfinished figures; broken branches, incomplete figures).
The person feels sexually inadequate and fears abandonment.

H-111 Castration responses in males. (Examples: withered, stunted objects; unfinished figures; broken branches; incomplete figures)
The person feels sexually inadequate and evidences a fear of bodily harm.

H-112 Sx 2+ (with breasts)
An oral receptive, dependency orientation is likely, in an individual whose affection needs may be frustrated.

H-113 Sx 2+ (with ovary, uterus, womb, fetus or pregnant female)
Concern with reproduction and sexual viability is indicated.

H-114 Sx 2 (with genitalia)
Probable sexual conflicts and concern regarding one's capacity to carry out sexual relations is evidenced.

H-115 Sx 2+ (with bisexual figures)
Conflicts over sexual identity and sexual orientation is likely.

H-116 Sx raw score 5
Conflict attributable to sexual maladjustment is indicated.

H-117 2+ Sx with 2 blood responses
Sexual and/or aggressive acting out, in a psychotic or borderline individual, is likely.

H-118 At>90 + 2 blood responses
Problems with self-control are indicated, as are possible sadistic and destructive impulses.

H-119 Perseveration of responses
The person is hampered in the free use of intellect, possibly because of psychological defenses. Rule out organic brain syndrome and mental retardation.

H-120 3 + Ab
The person is apt to be overexuberant and emotional. Hypomanic and/or marked affective instability is likely.

H-121 Alphabet, numbers, punctuation & geometric figures
Evasiveness and anxiety are suggested.

H-122 Blood
Deep negative emotions and serious emotional disturbance are likely. The person is apt to be anxious, phobic, emotionally labile, and hostile. Aggressive feelings, a fear of contact with others, and a need to disassociate oneself from others is probable.

H-123 2 + Blood responses (add to Blood)
Marked problems with self control are indicated.

H-124 Mutilation
Hostility is present; aggressive behavior is likely.

H-125 Bridges
Emotional insecurity is indicated. A history of disruptive parental relations is a distinct possibility.

H-126 2 + Chicken
A history of affection deprivation is likely.

H-127 2 + Cloud
Significant anxiety is apt to be present.

H-128 Explosion
Dynamic aggression is suggested.

H-129 3 + Fighting
Aggressive and hostile tendencies toward others is quite probable.

H-130 Fire
Anxiety and tension are present; emotional lability and excitability are likely.

H-131 3 + Jesus, Christ or God
Marked religious preoccupation is evidenced. Religious delusions are a distinct possibility.

H-132 Knife
Aggressive behavior is probable.

H-133 Mummy, cadavers, deformed, and deformity.
Significant anxiety is present.

H-134 Maps and geography
Guardedness and evasive tendencies are likely.

H-135 3 plus reflection
Narcissistic tendencies are suggested.

H-136 Rocks
Security needs are present.

H-137 Smoke
Depressive features are likely, in an anxious, apprehensive individual.

H-138 Urine
The presence of overt psychosis or a borderline condition is likely.

H-139 War
Strong aggressive and hostile tendencies are likely.

H-140 No other statement used
This appears to be an essentially normal performance.

CHAPTER ELEVEN

Interpretative Statements for Sentence Completion Test

Sentence Completion tests are one of the most widely used forms of projective techniques. In contrast to the dismal validity information derived from the TAT, the Sentence Completion Test has been demonstrated to be the most valid of all projective techniques (Goldberg, 1965). The major areas for the psychosocial interpretation of Sentence Completion Tests which are included are: approach to the instrument; overall presentation itself; use of others in the environment; sex and role; attitude toward family of origin; marriage; children; achievement and career; addictions; present, past, and future.

The Full Battery Code Book statements carry the rating system of Sacks (1965) and Forer (1957) a step further, in that, in addition to providing a rating system, a narrative statement is provided at the same time. The user is instructed to first read over the Sentence Completion Test and to make notes on the content areas, either mentally or on paper, and then read over the interpretation statements, selecting those which are appropriate for the interpretation. Additionally, global statements are provided for the Loevinger Sentence Completion method for scoring and arriving at an ego development level. These statements provide an overview of the meaning of Loevinger's ego levels. Included in them are the author's recent research (Vincent & Castillo, 1984a; Vincent & Vincent, 1979) as well as that of others regarding ego development level and its relation to psychopathology. This provides an additional diagnostic tool for understanding the person's Axis II diagnosis. Examiners who are not familiar with Loevinger's method can learn it via Volumes 1 and 2 of her book *Measurement of Ego Development* (Loevinger & Wechsler, 1970; Loevinger, Wechsler, & Redmore, 1970). The ego development rating method is one that can be mastered by studying her books, as they provide a carefully detailed training program.

PSYCHOSOCIAL INTERPRETATIVE STATEMENTS

Approach to the Instrument

S-1 The person appeared threatened by the instrument.

S-2 The person blocked on many of the sentence stems.

S-3 The affective tone of the person's statements was one of depression.

S-4 Many of the person's statements were unusual and highly idiosyncratic.

S-5 Many of the person's statements were loose, disjointed, and bizarre.

S-6 Verbalizations suggestive of delusional content were evidenced in the person's responses.

S-7 The person alluded to feelings of paranoia.

S-8 The person's statements were characterized by rambling, stream-of-conscious statements.

S-9 The person appeared to rationalize excessively.

S-10 Marked emotional conflict was evidenced in many of the person's responses.

S-11 Marked religious preoccupation was indicated.

S-12 Suicidal preoccupation is evidenced.

S-13 The person appears agitated, frustrated, and rebellious.

S-14 The person appeared somewhat defensive in the approach to the instrument.

Overall Presentation of Self

S-15 The person has a childlike view of the world and self.

S-16 The person has a strong need to be seen as the epitome of moral virtue.

S-17 The person is rebellious, defiant, and egocentric.

S-18 The person is emotionally labile, overdramatic, and histrionic.

S-19 The person is a seething torrent of repressed hostility.

S-20 The person is shy, inhibited, and socially anxious.

S-21 The person is withdrawn and easily threatened.

S-22 The person is negative towards self and beset with guilt.

S-23 The person is negative towards self and appears to spend a large amount of time in subvocal self-flagellation.

S-24 The person is passive, dependent, and insecure.

S-25 The person has not yet worked through the adolescent identity crisis.

S-26 The person is sensitive and negative towards self.

S-27 The person is quite preoccupied with health concerns.

S-28 Disturbed identity formation is suggested.

S-29 The person is euphoric, overdramatic, and grandiose.

S-30 The person is preoccupied with the "shoulds," "oughts," and "musts."

S-31 The person is beset with anxiety.

S-32 The person is currently wallowing in self pity.

S-33 The person is preoccupied with finances.

S-34 The person is quite preoccupied with physical disability.

S-35 The person is quite preoccupied with weight problems.

S-36 The person feels unattractive and physically inferior.

S-37 The person is impulsive, anxious, and emotionally labile.

S-38 The person feels overwhelmed at present.

S-39 The person feels overburdened with responsibility at present.

S-40 The person appears a bit naive.

S-41 The person verbalizes depression.

View of Others and Environment

S-42 The individual views life as a cheap game.

S-43 The individual appears to have a life script of moving against people.

S-44 The individual is fearful of others and easily threatened by change.

S-45 The individual is quite desirous of attention, support, and affection from others.

S-46 The individual is extremely sensitive and fearful of rejection.

S-47 The individual is tenacious and hangs on to grudges as if they were gold.

S-48 The individual is socially extroverted and has a high need for social approval.

S-49 The individual feels put-upon and harrassed by others.

S-50 The individual lacks assertiveness and withdraws in the face of stress.

S-51 The individual is preoccupied with being accepted by peers.

S-52 The individual tends to deny social anxiety.

S-53 The individual is ill at ease with the opposite sex.

Sex and Role

S-54 The person appears not to have begun to deal with their emerging sexuality.

S-55 The person is sexually inhibited and has significant sexual conflicts.

S-56 The person feels sexually inadequate.

S-57 Possible latency conflicts are indicated.

S-58 Marked sexual conflicts are indicated.

S-59 Significant homosexual conflicts are present.

S-60 The person feels inadequate in the masculine roles.

S-61 The person is conflicted regarding what is the appropriate feminine role for her.

S-62 The person sees herself as very feminine and is quite traditional regarding male–female sex roles.

S-63 The person's masculinity appears identified, but he has feelings of inadequacy.

S-64 The person appears to compensate for underlying sexual insecurities by the adoption of a pseudo-macho stance.

S-65 The person alludes to guilt over sexual acting out.

S-66 The person manifests the adolescent preoccupation of finding oneself through a love relationship.

S-67 The person views the opposite sex as having an easier life.

S-68 The person views the opposite sex as having the upper hand in interpersonal relationships.

S-69 The person is rigid and quite traditional in outlook regarding male–female sex roles.

S-70 The person is quite sexually preoccupied.

S-71 The person is a bit sexually inhibited.

Attitude Toward Family of Origin

S-72 The individual is close to the family of origin and appears to depend on them for emotional support.

S-73 The individual was close to the family of origin and dependent on them as a source of emotional support.

S-74 The individual has marked conflicts with their family of origin.

S-75 The individual feels harassed and abused by their family of origin.

S-76 The individual appears to be estranged from their father.

S-77 The individual appears to be estranged from their mother.

S-78 The individual has ambivalent feelings toward their father.

S-79 The individual has ambivalent feelings toward their mother.

S-80 The individual has significant conflict with their mother.

S-81 The individual has significant conflict with their father.

S-82 The individual appears close to their mother.

S-83 The individual appears close to their father.

S-84 The individual appears quite concerned about their family of origin.

S-85 The individual has ambivalent feelings toward their family of origin.

S-86 The individual feels dominated and harassed by their mother.

S-87 The individual appears to be absorbing and reacting to conflicts the parents are having between themselves.

S-88 The individual appears quite concerned about their mother.

S-89 The individual appears quite concerned about their father.

S-90 The individual was close to their mother and mourns her loss.

S-91 The individual was close to their father and mourns his loss.

Marriage

S-92 The person appears close to and highly dependent on the spouse for emotional support.

S-93 The person is desirous of more support from their spouse.

S-94 Significant marital conflict is indicated.

S-95 The person and their spouse appear to interact with each other in a neurotic, symbiotic dyad.

S-96 The person is angry with spouse and sees the bulk of their problems as being caused by the spouse.

S-97 The person appears jaundiced toward men in general.

S-98 The person appears negative toward women in general.

S-99 The person feels harassed and abused by their spouse.

S-100 The person appears close to their spouse.

S-101 The person fears the loss of love and is desirous of constant reassurance from their spouse.

S-102 The person is hopeful of resolving marriage conflicts.

S-103 The person has not completely worked through and accepted their divorce.

S-104 The person's expectations of marriage appear naive and unrealistic.

S-105 The person feels dominated and/or overwhelmed by their spouse.

S-106 The person may feel a bit henpecked by his wife.

S-107 The person is ambivalent about the future of their marriage.

S-108 The person feels neglected by their spouse.

Children

S-109 The individual is quite concerned about their children and worries about being a good parent.

S-110 The individual feels unable to cope with the children and it may be that they have outgrown her emotionally.

S-111 The individual feels abandoned by their children.

S-112 The individual feels slighted by their children and is angry with them.

S-113 The individual appears overwhelmed by family responsibilities.

S-114 The individual has invested a large amount of self in being a good homemaker and now feels at a loss for a role.

S-115 The individual feels a failure as a parent.

S-116 The individual is very family-oriented and places a heavy emphasis on family responsibilities.

S-117 The individual feels ineffective as a parent.

Achievement and Career

S-118 The person is achievement-oriented and has a strong need to prove self.

S-119 The person has invested a large amount of himself in his career and now feels useless and at a loss for a role.

S-120 The person wants desperately to prove self and succeed at something, but is apt to feel inadequate in doing so.

S-121 The person feels inadequate in achieving and competing with others.

S-122 The person feels harassed and put-upon by others at work.

S-123 The person invests heavily in career concerns, which is a major source of satisfaction.

S-124 The person feels overburdened with responsibility at work.

S-125 The person has a view of being a failure vocationally.

S-126 The person is negative towards school.

S-127 The person expresses concern about not being able to work.

S-128 The person has conflicts over having a career versus being a homemaker.

S-129 The person is preoccupied with school failure.

S-130 The person is negative toward their present work situation.

S-131 The person likes their work.

Addictions

S-132 The person views drinking as the cause of all their problems.

S-133 The person sees drug abuse as the cause of all their problems.

S-134 The person views drinking and drug abuse as the cause of all their problems.

S-135 The person sees drinking as a significant problem.

S-136 The person sees drug abuse as a significant problem.

S-136 The person manifests overstated guilt over drinking.

S-137 The person manifests overstated guilt over drug abuse.

S-138 The person manifests overstated guilt over drinking and drug abuse.

S-139 The person's motivation for substance abuse treatment appears to be primarily external.

Present, Past, and Future

S-140 The individual is oriented toward the past and views life as over.

S-141 The individual feels hopeless and sees little hope for the future.

S-142 The individual is significantly upset at present but is hopeful for the future.

S-143 The individual appears naive regarding the future.

S-144 The individual is preoccupied with and worried about the future.

S-145 The individual sees her main problem as: ______.

S-146 The individual sees his main problem as: ______.

Use the following statement if Loevinger's incomplete sentence method of scoring ego development is used.

EGO LEVEL INTERPRETATIVE STATEMENTS

Impulsive Level

S-147 On the LOEVINGER SENTENCE COMPLETION BLANK, the person's overall performance depicts an individual whose ego development is at the impulsive level. The person is apt to be preoccupied with bodily impulses, especially sexual and aggressive ones, and present centered. Individuals at this level of ego development are distractible and exploitative. While this orientation is normal in preschoolers, by the third-grade only one-fourth of all children remain at this stage. This stage is rare in adults and almost always associated with mental retardation.

Self-Protection Level

S-148 On the LOEVINGER SENTENCE COMPLETION BLANK, the person's overall performance depicts an individual whose ego development is at the self-protective level. The individual is opportunistic, hedonistic, wary, manipulative, and exploitive. Individuals at this stage of ego development externalize blame and, while aware of rules, see them as obstacles to be circumvented. This level of ego development is common in young children, but only one-fourth of the middle school age children are still at this level. For adolescents, individuals at this level of ego development are almost always seen as conduct disorders, and, in adulthood, this level of ego development is associated with immature character disorders, especially of an antisocial or borderline nature.

Self-Protective—Conformity Level

S-149 On the LOEVINGER SENTENCE COMPLETION BLANK, the person's overall performance depicts an individual whose ego development is somewhat below the general conformity level and at a transition stage from a hedonistic, self-protective orientation to one of obedience and conformity. The individual's orientation is external and the emphasis is on pleasing others, but there is still an element of reciprocity in their orientation. This level of ego development is reached by most individuals by the middle school years. In adultood, this level of ego development is almost always associated with an immature character disorder. In a recent study, the majority of antisocial and borderline personalities scored in this range, as well as a third of the histrionic individuals.

Conformity Level

S-150 On the LOEVINGER SENTENCE COMPLETION BLANK, the person's overall performance depicts an individual whose ego development is at the conformity level, which is the level of the majority of the general population. Emphasis is on conformity to external rules, law, order, and authority. The person's outlook is traditional and in line with the values and mores of the polite middle class. Social acceptability and fitting in with one's peers and social group are emphasized. Individual differences are seen only in general terms.

Conformist-Conscientious

S-151 On the LOEVINGER SENTENCE COMPLETION BLANK, the person's overall performance depicts an individual whose ego development is somewhat above the general conformity level. The individual has a heightened consciousness of self and inner feelings. The person is more sensitive to their own feelings and the feelings of others. Contradictions are recognized, rules are seen as having exceptions, and life is seen as complex. This level of ego development is modal for college educated individuals. In mental health settings, persons at this level of ego development are usually seen as free of personality disorders, and character disorders of an immature (dramatic, emotional, or unstable) nature are nonexistent.

Conscientious-Autonomous-Integrated

S-152 On the LOEVINGER SENTENCE COMPLETION BLANK, the person's overall performance depicts an individual whose ego development is above the general conformity level and depicts an individual who is sensitive, capable of insightful evaluation, and views problems as multi-faceted. The person has a strong sense of personal responsibility and is sensitive to the needs of others. About one-fourth to one-third of the adult population score in this range. In mental health settings, persons at these higher levels of ego development are seen as devoid of personality disorder and rarely present on an in-patient basis. When they do need help, their problems tend to center on relationship difficulties, life adjustment problems, or, occasionally, affective disorders.

CHAPTER TWELVE[1]

Interpretative Statements for the MMPI

The Interpretative Statements for the MMPI is essentially a revision of the MMPI Semi-Automated Interpretative Statements which was published in 1980 and was designed to be used on a word processor (Vincent, 1980a,b, 1983a,b; Vincent & Duthie, 1983a). The original system was later fully automated (Vincent et al., 1983). The computerized version of the MMPI Semi-Automated Interpretative Statements was preferred by clinicians when compared to the Lachar (1972) program in a study of private psychiatric patients (Vincent & Castillo, 1984c).

Normally, a longer passage in time ensues between a work and its revision; however, publication of the DSM-III has necessitated updating the MMPI Interpretative Statements, because DSM-III is a radical departure from the diagnostic systems of DSM-I and DSM-II. Because of this, it is extremely difficult, if not impossible in many cases, to merely extrapolate from previous diagnoses to the current ones. The most dramatic example of this is the 6-8 code type, which has in the past been regarded as almost always indicative of psychosis and usually the paranoid schizophrenia. While schizophrenia will still be modal in State Hospital settings (Winters et al., 1985) in private settings, this code type has become almost an indeterminate category (Vincent et al., 1983). The primary reason for this is that schizotypal and borderline personality were previously classified as schizophrenic disorders and are now classified as personality disorders. In a recent study of private psychiatric patients, 43% of the 6-8 code type were classified as having some kind of psychotic disorder in the DSM-III terminology; however, if the borderline personality disorder category were included in the psychotic categories as it would have been in DSM-II terminology, the classification rate would have risen to 72% of the patients evidencing a psychotic disorder.

The new interpretative statements for the MMPI handle the conversion of earlier psychopathological diagnostic systems to the DSM-III whenever possible by use of objective data. The emphasis of this manual is on private hospitalized

[1] This Chapter is taken from the Manual for the Interpretative Statements for the MMPI Computer Version and Interpretative Statements for the MMPI, both copyright 1985. Dr. Ken R. Vincent.

patients and outpatients as opposed to public settings, though, whenever possible, the differences between public and private settings are noted. This will make the revised MMPI Interpretative Statements more viable for the bulk of its users, namely psychiatrists, psychologists, and counselors who predominately serve noninstitutionalized individuals and persons who are in private psychiatric hospitals. Virtually all of the existing MMPI programs, as well as a large amount of research on the MMPI, has had its focus on individuals in public hospital settings, namely State Mental Hospitals and the V.A., and, ironically, private patients have had to make do with extrapolations from this atypical group when it came to objective interpretations of the MMPI. The cornerstone of updating current version are two articles, both of which were done in private practice settings, namely MMPI Code Types of DSM-III Diagnosis (Vincent et al., 1983) and another article titled MMPI Code Types of DSM-III Diagnosis: Some Additional Code Types (Vincent & Costello, 1985). These two sources are the only comprehensive sources of multiple code types in all categories of the psychopathology that had been published to date. There have been some very well done, key, specific articles on particular diagnostic groups; significant articles would include work on schizophrenoform disorder (Walters, 1984); schizophrenics, depressives, and bipolars (Winters et al., 1985); Affective Disorders (Silver, Isaacs, & Mansky, 1981); Borderline Personality Disorder (Gustin et al., 1983; Patrick, 1984); Post-Traumatic Stress Disorder and Psychogenic Pain (Chaney et al., 1984); and Post-Traumatic Stress Syndrome in Veterans (Fairbank, Keave, & Malloy, 1983; Burk & Mayer, 1985; Foy et al., 1984). Additionally, the present work incorporates and reviews over 100 major research articles on the MMPI Validity Scales and Code Types which are listed in the bibliography. In general, the narrative portion of the code types required little modification except for the additional notations of specific studies. Generally, this was related to the change in the diagnostic classification system and such things as the occurrence of Post-Traumatic Stress Disorders on the appropriate code types, as were other categories that are new to the DSM-III Diagnostic System.

For the infrequent code types, conversion to the new system was done via an objective formula, after several alternatives were considered. One of the alternatives was to use the author's skill and insights gleaned as a participant in field trials of DSM-III to make a subjective conversion. Another consideration was to use a system which included more MMPI codes in updated DSM-III form but was done on the MMPI 168 short form. (Vincent et al., 1984). This was a quite tempting alternative, as it was noted in the MMPI 168 Code Book (Vincent et al., 1984) that there was as much variance between public and private populations and between the DSM-III and the earlier classifications systems as there was between the MMPI 168 and the standard form. While there is a good deal of compatibility between the two forms, and, in fact, most studies show that MMPI Code Types are apt to be replicated between a MMPI and a MMPI 168 about as often as they are replicated between the standard form and itself on a test/retest situation, this was discarded because it would still be an extrapolation and there is some significant, though not substantial, variance between the two instruments.

In order to provide an objective classification system for all infrequent code types, the following procedure was adhered to. If the category was identical in the DSM-III to the DSM-II category, it was retained. Examples of this would be Disassociative Disorder as it relates to the 3-8 code type, Paranoid Disorders as related to the 3-6 code type, and various other disorders, such as Passive Aggressive Personality, which are identical in both diagnostic systems. The main system of classification in infrequent code types was through an objective formula developed by the author for use on a new test of psychopathology, namely, the Diagnostic Inventory of Personality and Symptoms (Vincent, in press) and modified for use with the MMPI. This system uses the high point codes of the MMPI, with the exception of 5 and 0, to define symptom clusters that relate to diagnostic categories of DSM-III, and then these categories are ordered in the Differential Diagnostic Section based on a frequency list of base rates of psychodiagnosis worked out by a meta analysis (Vincent & Duthie, in press). The table is listed below:

Frequency Order	MMPI Scale	DSM-III Diagnostic Category
1	D	Affective Disorder: Depression
2	—	Adjustment Disorder
3	Pd	Substance Abuse Disorder
4	Sc	Schizophrenic Disorder
5	Pt	Anxiety Disorder
6	Ma	Affective Disorder: Bipolar
7	Hs & Hy	Somatoform Disorder
8	Hs & Hy	Psychological Factors Affecting Physical Condition
9	Pa	Paranoid Disorder
10	—	Disassociative Disorder

The above base rate frequency was used to arrange the scales in descending order based on their base rate frequency. The following is a list of the MMPI scales and the Disorders which were included in the Differential Diagnostic Section. An elevation on the HS scale would cause the above mentioned diagnostic categories to be included in the analysis in the Differential Diagnostic Section: if HS scale (1) was elevated, Somatoform Disorder, Psychological Factors Affecting Physical Condition and Depression were included for analysis in the Differential Diagnostic Section; if D (2) was elevated, Affective Disorder: Depression was included in the Differential Diagnostic Catagory section for analysis; if Hy (3) was elevated, Somatoform Disorder, Psychological Factors Affecting Physical Condition and Affective Disorder: Depression were included in the Differential Diagnostic Section; if Pd was elevated, Substance Abuse Disorder was included in the Differential Diagnostic Section; if Pa (6) was elevated, Paranoid Disorder and stress Adjustment Disorder were included in the Differential Diagnostic Section; if Pt (7) was elevated, Anxiety Disorder and Affective Disorder: Depression was included in the Differential Diagnostic Section; if Sc (8) was elevated, Schizophrenic Disorder and Adjustment Disorder were included in the Differential Diagnostic Section; if Ma (9) was elevated, then Affective Disorder: Bipolar and Adjustment Disorder was included in the Differential Diagnostic Section. Scales MF (5) and SI (0) were not included in the Axis I analysis. As stated earlier, this system was demonstrated empirically as viable on the Diagnostic Inventory of Personality and Symptoms (Vincent & Duthie, in press) and extrapolated to the MMPI. This system was used to develop a differential diagnostic section for infrequent 2- and 3-point code types. Only the first four diagnostic possibilities are used. In other words, if 19 was the code type in question, Somatoform Disorder, Psychological Factors Affecting Physical Condition and Affective Disorder: Depression, Affective Disorder: Excited and Adjustment Disorder would be the five codes in question for analysis; these would then be reordered for the Differential Diagnostic Section based on the probabilities of their occurrence and would be listed in descending order using the base rate frequency table above. This would result in the Differential Diagnostic Section of the MMPI listing: Diagnostic Possibilities include: Affective Disorder: Depressed, Adjustment Disorder, Affective Disorder: Bipolar, and Somatoform Disorder. Psychological Factors Affecting Physical Condition would be the fifth differential and would not be included, as only the top four are included in the Differential Diagnosis. The Personality Disorder Section was done by the following formula which is also a modification of the system that had been developed for the Diagnostic Inventory of Personality and Symptoms (Vincent, in press). Briefly put, the 11 personality disorders of the DSM-III are broken into three main clusters, namely the odd and eccentric personality disorder category, that includes schizoid and schizotypal paranoid disorders; the dramatic, emotional, and erratic disorder category, that includes histrionic, narcissistic, antisocial, and borderline personality; and the anxious and fearful personality category, including dependent, compulsive, avoidant, and passive-aggressive personality. Scales 1, 2, 3, 5, 7, and 0 were seen as indicative of individuals in the anxious and fearful personality disorder character category. Scales 6 and 8 were seen as representative of individuals in the odd and eccentric personality disorders. Category scales 4 and 9 were seen as typifying individuals in the dramatic, emotional, and erratic personality disorder category. When indeterminate MMPI code types were pure, namely the elevations represented one of these clusters, then that cluster was seen as the most likely differential for the personality disorder section. For example, if the profile type was 137, then the diagnostic possibility section would include dependent personality, avoidant personality, compulsive personality, and passive-aggressive personality.

If the MMPI code type embodied more than one category, the following formula was used to arrive at modal diagnosis. If the code type was composed of scales characterizing all three major personality categories, for example 2, 4, and 8, then the modal diagnosis would be seen as borderline. If the code type embodied two or more categories, and the categories were the odd and eccentric cluster and the dramatic, emotional, or erratic personality cluster—for example, 48 code type -then the modal diagnosis of personality disorder cluster would be seen as also borderline personality disorder. If the combination included the anxious and fearful category and the odd and eccentric category—for example, 78—then the modal personality disorder was seen as avoidant. If the combination included elevations from the anxious and fearful personality disorder category and the dramatic, emotional or erratic personality disorder category, such as 247 code type, then modal personality disorder was seen as passive-aggressive personality disorder.

In order to check this system empirically, the 2- and 3-point code types of the article MMPI Code Types and DSM-III Diagnosis (Vincent et al., 1983) were analyzed using the formula. This enabled the formula's hit rate to be checked against the actuarial data on what was the actual DSM-III Diagnosis for the MMPI Code Type. For the 2- and 3-point code types in that article which represented 169 psychiatric cases, the overall Axis I formula hit rate was 31% that the first diagnosis listed on the differential diagnostic section was the actual diagnosis. A 65% hit rate was obtained that the Axis I differential diagnostic match via the formula would match the actual primary diagnosis. For example, for the 278 code type, the formula listed the following diagnostic categories in order of their probability: Affective Disorder Depressed, Adjustment Disorder, Anxiety Disorder, and Schizophrenia disorder. In actuality, 63% of the persons evidencing the 278 code type had as their primary diagnosis for AXIS I: Affective Disorder: Depressed, 13% were seen as having an Adjustment Disorder, 5% were seen as having an Anxiety Disorder, and 5% were seen as having a Schizophrenic Disorders. This resulted in the primary differential diagnostic code matching the modal diagnosis of the code type 63% of the time, with the differential being correct 86% of the time. Chi square analysis of the formula for all of the 17 code types for the primary diagnosis of AXIS I was significant $X^2(1, N = 169) = 27.38$, $p < .01$ and for the total Differential Diagnostic Section was significant $X^2(1, N = 169) = 4.5$, $p < .05$. For the above-mentioned chi square analysis, the frequency expected was based on the occurrence of diagnosis based on random chance; thus, the elevation of any one code was 12.5%, and the elevation of 4 differential diagnosis was 50%.

Two different analysis for the AXIS II diagnostic statements were used, one for those code types which were pure in the sense that the codes in code type all represented one of the three major clusters for personality disorders. Random chance that this would occur for the odd and eccentric personality disorder cluster would be 27%, as it only contains three personality disorders. The rate of chance prediction for the dramatic, emotional, and erratic personality disorder cluster and the anxious and fearful personality disorder cluster were both 36%, as these each contain four categories. Random chance for any one of the 11 personality disorders to occur would be 9%. The pure personality disorder cluster codes in the MMPI article analyzed, and the mean percent of correct classification of the formula compared to the actual primary diagnosis on Axis I, was 69%, which is roughly two times above chance expectancy. The chi square (corrected for percentage comparison when using a sample smaller than 100 was $X^2(1, N = 88) = 26.4$ $p < .01$. Next, the 10 mixed diagnostic code types where the formula would predict a modal personality disorder were analyzed. Of those 10 cases, the data on three was such that the individual diagnostic categories within the cluster were not easily discerned, and, consequently, only seven of these were used. In these seven cases, the correct classification of the modal personality disorder was 33%, which was roughly four times greater the chance. The chi square analysis (corrected for percent comparison when using a sample smaller than 100) was: $X^2(1, N = 67) = p < .01$. Because this formula works on known code types, the underlying assumption for the infrequent code types in this book is that formula will be the best predictor of differential diagnostic possibilities for infrequent code types. When reading the narratives for the revised interpretative statements for the MMPI, the reader should note that empirically derived statements begin with the phrase: "In a recent study of psychiatric patients. . . ." Other empirically derived information is usually put into the narrative section of the code type, such as notations for post traumatic disorder and direct conversions from DSM I and II to DSM III like passive-aggressive personality, and are phrased with a statement such as "This is the common profile type among individuals suffering from a post traumatic stress disorder." When the formula is used to derive diagnostic possibilities, the Axis I differential diagnostic section always begins with the phrase: "Diagnostic possibilities include . . ." and in Axis II: "Modal personality disorder: . . ." or "Diagnostic Possibilities include: . . . ."

OVERVIEW OF THE INTERPRETATIVE STATEMENTS FOR THE MMPI

The validity scale configuration section includes 14 statements based on validity scale configuration and a statement for when there are thirty omissions. The only Validity Scale Elevation that aborts the program is the one for an elevation on F in excess of a raw score of 26. This results in a narrative statement being printed out that the profile is invalid and a description of the type of individual who usually produces such a profile, namely, individuals who are illiterate, psychotic, or who are suffering from a borderline personality disorder. This section also includes two statements that detail whether the MMPI 168 was given or not. Readers are, however, encouraged to use the MMPI 168 Code Book (Vincent et al., 1984), as it is based on actuarially derived statements based solely on the 168. Nevertheless, two 168 statements are provided—one that states that the MMPI 168 was given, and the other one can be used if the MMPI 168 was administered orally (which is the time when the MMPI 168 is really most appropriately used, namely, when the person in question cannot or will not take the MMPI in the standard form because of illiteracy or intellect, immaturity psychosis, or physical handicap). Next, there are two statements which state that the critical item responses of the person were reviewed. One is for when the answers the person gave fit the intent of the statements, and thereby suggest that the profile in question is apt to accurately fit the person; and one for the opposite situation, in which the reasons the person gave for answering the critical items do not generally fit the intent of the critical items, reflecting possible over-dramatization on the individual's part.

For all multiple code types, namely 5-point, 4-point, 3-point, and 2-point code types, all but one of the codes must be within ten points of one another. All code types are interchangeable; in other words, a 28-code type is an 82-code type, a 346-code type is a 436-code type, and so on. Code types are presented in descending order, from 5-point code types down to 1-point code types. All code types are prefixed with the letter M as the call number, which stands for MMPI, and, with the exception of the adolescent section and one of the supplemental scales, all of the code types relate to codes at or above an elevation of a T score of 70. Adolescent codes relate to scores at or above a T score of 60.

The only low-point code type used is for a score of 40 or under on the Supplemental Scale-Ego Strength. The traditional low-point 5 for females on the MF scale was abandonded because a false normal code type is more accurate and is more complete in its diagnostic and personality section. With few exceptions, all code types relate to both men and woman and, when they relate to one sex only, this is clearly stated in parenthesis next to the code type.

The adolescent code types are meant to be used in addition to, and following code type elevations in excess of, a T score of 70, and, when the adolescent profile does not have an elevation at or in excess of a T score of 70, the adolescent code type narrative is to be used in isolation. For adolescents attaining no elevations at or above a T score of 60 on the clinical scales, the false normal code type is then used. The false normal code type, which gets its name from the fact that there are no critical elevations on the person's code, is based on the assumption that the individual has a problem which has either brought him or her in, or has caused him or her to be brought in, for consultation. This leads us to an important point: THIS PROGRAM IS DESIGNED ONLY FOR USE IN CLINICAL SETTINGS.

Finally, the last portion of the printout provides narratives on the new supplemental scales that NCS has recently added to the MMPI graph, namely the Mac

Andrew scale, Ego Strength scale and the A and R scales. In the author's opinion, a person's time is wasted when he or she is asked to fill out the 566-item MMPI as opposed to the 399-item MMPI for the meager information gained on these supplemental scales. In most cases, the information is redundant. In the case of the Ego-Strength scale, the information on its meaning in the literature is somewhat contradictory. Only the Mac Andrew scale increases the differential diagnostic ability of the MMPI in regard to substance abuse. For all practical purposes, roughly 60% of all alcohol substance abusers can be identified on the basis of elevation of scale 4 (Pd) as one of the 2-point highest codes (Schroeder & Piercy, 1979). The MacAndrew scale ups this to about 78% for alcoholics and 66% for drug abusers, but whether the additional half-hour of torture the person must endure to fill out the 566 version is worth the information on the supplemental scales is up to the user.

VALIDITY SCALES

Rule: If validity statement MVA is used, use no other statements.

MVA If F is a T score of 95 or greater (raw score of 26 or greater) use:

On the MMPI, the person's validity scale configuration is of questionable validity and indicates the person's clinical profile may be invalid, distorted, or exaggerated. Persons exhibiting this type of validity scale configuration fall into several groups: (a) those individuals who read below the 6th grade level and, consequently, are unable to take the test in its standard form; (b) individuals who are manifesting acute psychotic reactions; and (c) individuals who are manifesting an overdramatic cry for help. Numerous studies in psychiatric in-patient settings and mental health centers have found about two-thirds of the persons of this profile type to be evidencing psychosis, while the remainder are seen as behavior disorders. The probability of Behavior Disorder diagnosis increases when the person is under 40 or is a court referral. Persons evidencing this type of validity scale configuration are more prone to engage in acting out, as well as self-destructive or other forms of inappropriate behavior. If persons of this validity scale configuration are literate and nonpsychotic, a diagnosis of Borderline Personality Disorder is quite probable.

In a recent study of private psychiatric patients, half the persons of this profile type were seen as psychotic and primarily evidenced a schizoaffective disorder or bipolar disorder, manic type. The bulk of the remainder were seen as evidencing an adjustment disorder. A third of these individuals were given an additional diagnosis of substance abuse. Half the persons of this profile type had their personality disorder deferred, due to psychosis, with a third of the remainder seen as schizotypal personalities.

MVB If L is a T score of 70 or greater and F is a T score of 70, but less than 95, and K is a T score of 70 or greater, then use:

On the MMPI, the person's validity scale configuration indicates that this profile is is very likely invalid, as it suggests a very deviant response pattern and the person may have, in fact, responded to the test items in an "all false" fashion. Occasionally, this is encountered in individuals who are trying to be defensive while at the same time are under extreme stress, and at the same time admitting to a very significant amount of psychological problems; when this is the case, the patient is apt to be suffering from psychosis. The person's clinical profile, taken as is, indicates the following.

MVC If L is a T score of 70 or greater and F is a T score of 70 or greater, but less than 95, and K is a T score of less than 70, then use:

On the MMPI the person's validity scale configuration indicates that this profile has a deviant response set but may possibly be valid, though it depicts an individual who is defensive, naive, and at the same time admitting to a very significant amount of stress and psychological difficulties. This is most frequently encountered in individuals who are quite defensive about their problems and possibly from a lower socio-economic background. The person's profile taken as is indicates the following.

MVD If L is less than a T score of 70 and F is a T score of 70, but less than 95, and K is a T score of 70 or greater, then use:

On the MMPI, the person's validity scale configuration indicates the profile is of questionable validity and a very deviant response set is suggested, in that the person was both admitting to significant psychological problems, while at the same time attempting to appear well adjusted. This is often encountered in either an individual who has long-standing problems to which they have become adjusted, or in a severely disturbed individual who is trying to be defensive but is not successful. In the latter case, the balance between the person's ability to control themselves and shore up their defenses and their tendency to display clearly deviant psychopathology and is apt to be quite unstable. The person's profile taken as is indicates the following:

MVE If L is a T score of 70 or greater, and F and K are below a T score of 70, use:

On the MMPI, the person's validity scale configuration indicates that the person's clinical scale configuration may be unduly lowered in some way and that the person was quite naively defensive in approaching the questionnaire. This configuration is very infrequent and most often encountered in very rigid, defensive individuals who are naive and apt to be neurotic. These persons are unoriginal in their approach to solving problems, have very little awareness of their behavioral impact on others, and generally lack insight into their own motivations. They are apt to be unduly conventional, insecure, rigid, overly moralistic, and make extreme use of the defense mechanism of repression and denial. This validity scale configuration is more often encountered in neurotics and is more frequent in individuals of lower socio-economic status. These persons are apt to present with somatic concern as a reason for seeking help. The person's clinical profile, taken as is, indicates the following:

MVF If K is a T score of 70 or greater, and L and F are less than a T score of 70, use:

On the MMPI, the person's validity scale configuration indicates this profile is of questionable validity and is apt to have been affected by a response set of an extremely defensive individual and, consequently, the clinical profile may be unduly lowered in some way. These individuals are quite fearful of revealing themselves in any way, and are apt to be extremely resistant to psychotherapeutic intervention. Such persons desperately try to present a facade of adequacy, but are in reality extremely shy, inhibited, and socially anxious, and quite phobic of any implications that their behavior is not the epitome of virtue and normality. Psychological factors affecting physical condition are quite common in these persons. The person's clinical profile, taken as is, indicates the following:

MVG If L and K are less than a T score of 70, and F is a T score of 80 to 94, then use:

On the MMPI, the person's validity scale configuration indicates that the profile is valid and depicts an individual who is apt to be quite negative towards self and currently experiencing a very significant amount of emotional distress. These persons are apt to be aware of their emotional turmoil and desirous of psychotherapeutic assistance. Overdramatization may be operating, and/or the person may be reacting to an acute emotional crisis.

MVH If L and K are less than a T score of 70, and F is at a T score of 70 to 79, then use:

On the MMPI, the person's validity scale configuration indicates the profile is valid and that the person is currently experiencing a significant amount of emotional distress.

MVI If L and K are a T score of 60 to 69, and F is less than a T score of 70, then use:

On the MMPI the person produced a valid profile; however, the person's validity scale configuration depicts a markedly defensive and evasive individual who is lacking in insight and and is apt to be quite resistive to psychotherapeutic intervention. This profile type is most frequently encountered in neurotic individuals who are fearful of revealing themselves in any way.

MVJ If L is less than a T score of 60, and F is less than a T score of 70 and K is a T score of 60 to 69, then use:

On the MMPI, the person produced a valid profile and the person's validity scale configuration depicts an individual who responded to the test items in a defensive fashion and who is apt to be lacking in self insight, and be shy, inhibited, and ill at ease socially. This profile type is most often encountered in neurotic individuals but, when attained in a seriously disturbed person, it may reflect a general lack of awareness on the person's part as to the seriousness of their condition.

MVK If L is a T score of 60 to 69, and F is less than 70 T score and K is less than 60 T, then use:

On the MMPI the person produced a valid profile; however, the person's validity scale configuration indicates a naive, defensive individual who has strong needs to be seen favorably by others. Such individuals are apt to be conventional, conforming, and somewhat rigid; typically, they have a low tolerance for stress and pressure.

MVL If L is less than a T score of 60, and F is less than a T score of 70 and K is less than a T score of 60, then use:

On the MMPI, the person's validity scale configuration indicates that the profile is valid and depicts an individual who was open and honest in approaching the instrument.

MVM If there were over 30 omissions, then use:

While the validity scale configuration indicates the above interpretation, great caution should be used in interpreting the profile, as the person omitted a large number of items and is apt to be a very defensive individual who is fearful of admitting to problems. Analysis of the items omitted may be worthwhile, as they may show trends in avoiding responding. Returning the test booklet to the person for a completion of the items omitted should be considered. The following profile may be unduly lowered in some way. The person's profile, taken as is, indicates the following:

MVN If the 168 short form was used and not read orally, use:

The person was administered the 168 short form.

MVO If the 168 short form was used and administered orally, use:

The 168 short form was administered orally because of problems encountered in having the individual complete the standard form:

MVP If a review of the person's critical items indicate the person's answers fit the intent of the questions, use:

On the MMPI, the person's Critical Item responses were reviewed and the individual's responses given for answering the questions in the deviant direction fit the intent of the questions, and, consequently, the profile is apt to accurately reflect the person's current status.

MVQ If a review of the person's critical item indicates exaggeration, use:

On the MMPI, the person's Critical Item responses were reviewed, and the reasons given by the individual did not generally fit the intent of the questions and suggest the likelihood of overdramatization on the person's part.

MMPI CODE TYPES

Unless otherwise noted, all code types (which are preceded by the letter M) refer to the code type being at or above a T score of 70. Also unless otherwise noted, all code types are interchangeable; that is, 28 is also 82. Unless a code type specifically lists 5 or 0, ignore it; for example, interpret code 154 as code 14, but 250 would become 20 because there is a 20 code type.

5-Point Code Rule: For the following 5-point codes, 4 of the 5 high points must be within 10 points of one another.

M2468F (or M2478F) Persons of this profile type present with a multiplicity of complaints and are emotionally labile and over dramatic. The histories of these people often seem like a text book of psychopathology. Such individuals are apt to be angry, anxious, manipulative, and dysphoric. They are unstable, dependent, and, at the same time, wary and fearful. This profile carries with it a high tendency towards addiction proneness to drugs and alcohol. A history of unstable interpersonal relationships is common; and, if the person is married, marital discord is quite likely. These individuals often present with acute distress. Despite the magnitude and multiplicity of the individuals' complaints, they typically are quite firm in that they do experience them. Diagnostically, the picture is usually one of a Borderline Personality Disorder presenting with an acute psychosis or a severe adjustment disorder or an atypical depression. Substance abuse may be part of the diagnostic picture. Other diagnostic possibilities include: Major Depression and, especially in public hospital inpatient settings, Schizophrenia.

4-Point Code Rule: For the following 4-point code, 3 of the 4 high points must be within 10 points of one another.

M1234 Persons with this profile type show a mixture of long-standing neurotic defenses and character defects which are quite resistant to change. These persons are usually seen as depressed, anxious, and evidencing multiple psychosomatic complaints, especially ulcers and gastro-intestinal difficulties, usually in response to environmental stress or frustration. These persons are likely to have difficulties at work and in their marriages. This profile carries with it a high tendency toward addiction proneness to drugs and alcohol, and these persons quite often are quite hostile and act out when they drink. Diagnostic possibilities include: AXIS I: Affective Disorder: Depression, Somatoform Disorder, Psychological Factors Affecting Physical Condition; AXIS II: Modal Personality Disorder: Passive Aggressive Personality.

3-Point Code Rules: For the following 3-point code, 2 of the 3 high points must be within 10 points of one another.

M123 Persons of this profile type are usually seen as depressed and evidencing multiple somatic complaints. These persons tend to be irritable, overevaluate minor problems, and are apt to be anxious and insecure in social situations and may complain of insomnia or headaches. These individuals are often lacking in aggressiveness and sexual drive. They often react to life stresses via psychosomatic symptomatology. On the positive side, these persons often have life histories characterized by stable work and marital adjustment. The underlying personality of these individuals is usually passive dependence. In older persons and in persons with chronic disease, this is often seen as a declining health profile; and these persons are apt to feel "over the hill," depressed, and preoccupied with somatic concerns. Medical patients evidencing this profile type include: individuals with ulcers, arthritis, and chronic pulmonary disease. This is a mean profile type also of patients suffering from multiple sclerosis.

In a recent study of private psychiatric patients, 92% of the persons of this profile type received somatoform disorders (psychogenic pain or hypochondriasis) or psychological factors affecting physical conditions as their primary, secondary, or tertiary diagnosis. The primary diagnoses, however, were bimodal; namely, affective disorders (major affective disorder: bipolar disorder, depression or major affective disorder: major depression), versus adjustment disorders with depressed mood or mixed emotional features. The modal personality disorder category for persons of this profile type was anxious and fearful personality disorders, namely, dependent, compulsive, or passive/aggressive.

M124 use M 1234 above

M126 use M 1234 above

M127 Persons of this profile type are usually seen as anxious, worrisome individuals who are lacking in assertiveness and have chronic feelings of inadequacy. Depression and psychosomatic complaints are apt to be present. These persons usually lack the wherewithal to stand up to everyday stresses and strains and may, in fact, abdicate such responsibilities to their spouses. This profile carries with it a high tendency toward addiction proneness to drugs and alcohol. These persons have as their primary defense mechanisms repression and somatization, and are typically lacking in insight.

In a recent study of private psychiatric patients, approximately half the persons of this profile type were seen as evidencing affective disorders, either a major depression or dysthymic disorder. One-third of the persons received either a somatoform disorder (somatization disorder or hypochondriasis) or psychological factors affecting physical condition as their primary or secondary diagnosis. The modal diagnostic cluster for personality disorders was anxious and fearful personality disorders; namely, avoidant, dependent, or passive/aggressive.

M128 Persons of this profile type are often seen as overtly psychotic, or acutely pre-psychotic. These patients are apt to present with bizarre somatic complaints and, in addition, complain of fatigue, weakness, depression, and difficulty in concentration. Somatic delusions may be present. Notable psychic distress is usually evidenced in these persons. In addition to feeling alienated from others, these individuals, paradoxically, have strong underlying feelings of dependency. The majority of persons of this profile type are seen as evidencing functional difficulties, but a significant minority are seen as evidencing organic brain syndrome, often secondary to trauma, senility, or alcohol toxicity.

In a recent study of private psychiatric patients, the modal diagnostic cluster for persons of this profile type was major affective disorder. One-third of these patients received either psychological factors affecting physical condition or somatoform disorder (hypochondriasis or somatization disorder) as their primary or secondary profile type. The modal personality cluster for persons of this profile type was anxious and fearful personality disorders; namely, avoidant, dependent, or passive/aggressive.

Mode 129 This profile type is very unusual and infrequent, but depicts an individual who is apt to be tense, agitated, and restless. The person may also be preoccupied with physical complaints, such as gastrointestinal difficulties and headaches. Persons of this profile type are apt to be in acute distress and attempting to ward off impending depression and/or underlying passivity and dependency via hypomanic over-activity.

Diagnostic possibilities include: AXIS I: Affective Disorder: Depressed, Affective Disorder: Bipolar, Somatoform Disorder, Psychological Factors Affecting Physical Condition; AXIS II: Modal Personality Disorder: Passive-Aggressive Personality.

M134 These persons are usually argumentative and generally obnoxious. Despite this, they often have little insight as to the reason why they alienate others. These persons are apt to have functional somatic complaints which may stem from anger which is bottled up inside them. Such anger is also expressed via passive-aggressive maneuvers. These individuals usually have dependency conflicts, and are moody as well as hypochondriacal. This profile carries with it a high tendency toward addiction proneness to drugs and alcohol. Marital problems and disrupted interpersonal relationships are quite likely. In individuals with low back pain, this code type is associated with poor outcome. Diagnostic possibilities include: AXIS I: Affective Disorder: Depressed, Somatoform Disorder, and Psychological Factors Affecting Physical Condition; AXIS II: Modal Personality Disorder: Passive-Aggressive Personality.

M136 This is an infrequent profile type. Persons of this profile type are usually seen as quite over-sensitive. They are apt to have a large amount of repressed hostility and are prone to rationalize their anger away. These individuals are apt to be lacking in insight into their own stimulus value. Functional physical complaints are quite likely. Diagnostic possibilites include: AXIS I: Affective Disorder: Depressed, Somatoform Disorder, Psychological Factors Affecting Physical Condition, Paranoid Disorder; AXIS II: Modal Personality Disorder: Avoidant Personality.

M137 Persons of this profile type are usually seen as evidencing an anxiety-depression syndrome and may experience phobic anxiety-panic attacks. These attacks often are accompanied by such complaints as tachycardia. Epigastric distress is also a frequent complaint. These persons are extremely anxious and apt to be phobic about illness. They typically react to stress via somatic symptomatology. Their underlying personality is usually one of passive dependence, and such persons usually look to their spouses to take the dominant role. These persons are usually unable to accept aggressiveness in themselves or others. Diagnostic possibilities include: AXIS I: Affective Disorder: Depressed, Anxiety Disorder, Somatoform Disorder, Psychological Factors Affecting Physical Condition; AXIS II: Dependent, Passive-Aggressive, Avoidant, and Compulsive.

M138 This is a common profile type in individuals evidencing a Post-Traumatic Stress disorder. These individuals are often depressed, confused, restless, and agitated. They are apt to complain of difficulty in thinking and concentrating, and may complain of memory problems. Somatic complaints are apt to include, headache, pain, dizziness, and possible gastro-intestinal difficulties. Insomnia is likely present. Such individuals are apt to be emotionally vulnerable and fearful, but, at the same time, they are likely to be fearful of dependency. These individuals may have a background of childhood deprivation and have psychotic relatives. These persons respond best to structured environments and may act out in an agitated, overbearing manner when such structure is not present. These individuals are apt to be unconventional in their thinking, may have strong ideas, and may be delusional. A large amount of emotional distress is apt to be present.

Diagnostic possibilities include: AXIS I: Affective Disorder: Depression, Adjustment Disorder, Schizophrenic Disorder, and Post-Traumatic Stress Disorder; AXIS II: Modal personality disorder; Avoidant Personality.

M139 This is a common profile type in persons evidencing a post-traumatic stress disorder. Also a significant number of individuals who produce this profile type are diagnosed as having organic impairment. These persons typically complain of numerous somatic difficulties, including: headaches, hearing and visual problems, tremors, shakiness, and coordination difficulties, all of which are quite vexing to the individual. These persons have a low tolerance for stress and frustration and are irritable and apt to evidence stormy outbursts of temper. Occasionally, such persons are apt to become combative or disruptive. These persons often have poor interpersonal relations with family conflict. Overcompensation for feelings of inferiority or loss of ability are apt to be present. In addition to Post-Traumatic Stress Disorder, diagnostic possibilities include: AXIS I: Affective Disorder: Depressed, Adjustment Disorder, and Somatoform Disorders; AXIS II: Modal Personality Disorder: Passive-Aggressive Personality.

M178 Persons of this profile type are usually hypochondriacal and anxious, are apt to have difficulty concentrating, and may feel confused. They are apt to complain of headaches and insomnia and, typically, are individuals who bottle up their anger and hostility. These persons typically feel inadequate in interpersonal relations, especially with the opposite sex, and generally are wary, distrustful and somewhat fearful of others. Diagnostic possibilities include: AxIS I: Affective Disorder: Depressed, Adjustment Disorder, Schizophrenic Disorder, Anxiety Disorder; AXIS II: Modal Personality Disorder: Avoidant Personality.

M234 Persons of this profile type are usually passive-aggressive characters who are exhibiting reactive depression, usually directly related to problems of their own making. These persons do, however, typically have a large amount of conflict over the release of their anger and tend to deny hostility in themselves and bottle it up, releasing it in passive-aggressive manipulative maneuvers. These individuals are typically immature, egocentric, and lack insight into their own behavior. This profile carries with it a high tendency toward addiction proneness to drugs and alcohol. These persons are typically underachievers, both educationally and vocationally. Additionally, marital problems are quite common. Episodic acting out is a distinct possibility, though, once their distress has abated, these individuals may present a somewhat adequate facade; but, underneath this, they are apt to be passive and feel inadequate. These persons are typically quite sensitive to any demands being made upon them externally by others or institutions. Diagnostic possibilities include: AXIS I: Affective Disorder: Depression, Substance Abuse Disorder, Somatoform Disorder, and Psychological Factors Affecting Physical Condition; AXIS II: Modal Personality Disorder: Passive-Aggressive Personality.

M237 Persons of this profile type are seen as conscientious achievers who are vulnerable to accumulated stress. When stress and anxiety overwhelm them, however, they are apt to present as depressed, dependent, and markedly negative towards self. These persons often have a great deal of trouble handling hostility in themselves and others. Somatic correlates of anxiety are apt to be present. These persons are usually anxious, depressed, and may evidence phobic reactions or panic attacks. These persons are conscientious individuals who are overly hard on themselves, push themselves quite hard, and usually do have a history of achieving. These persons usually have stable work and marital adjustments and are capable of forming emotional ties. Panic attacks—phobic anxiety is common to this profile type. Diagnostic possibilities include: AXIS I: Affective Disorder: Depressed, Anxiety Disorder, Somatoform Disorder, and Psychological Factors Affecting Physical Condition; AXIS II: Dependent Personality, Passive-Aggressive Personality, Avoidant Personality, and Compulsive Personality.

M238 Persons of this profile type are primarily seen as evidencing major depression, though a minority are seen as dysthymic disorders. These persons usually exhibit depressed mood, along with fatigue, exhaustion, and anxiety. These persons typically feel quite negative towards self and are often somewhat inadequate and ineffectual in the business of living. They are apt to be insecure, especially with the opposite sex, and poor sexual performance and marital difficulties are common. They may operate at lower levels of efficiency for a long period of time. These persons have difficulty asserting themselves, typically bottle up their emotions, and make excessive use of the defense mechanisms of repression and denial. These individuals are, consequently, often difficult to motivate psychotherapeutically. Diagnostic possibilities include: AXIS

I: Affective Disorder: Depression, Adjustment Disorder, Schizophrenic Disorder, Somatoform Disorder; AXIS II: Modal Personality Disorder: Avoidant Personality.

M 246 These persons typically present with chronic complaints of depression, anxiety, and nervousness that are apt to be amplified by their tendency to be overdramatic and histrionic. These persons typically are impulsive and quite frequently desirous of sympathy and attention, and are manipulative in their attempts to attain it. Manipulative suicide attempts are a distinct possibility. These individuals typically are egocentric, have significant dependency conflicts, and are apt to be demanding of attention and affection and quite miffed when they do not receive it. Also they are prone to be somewhat skeptical and resentful toward others.

Sexual difficulties and marital problems are quite likely in these persons; and these individuals are quite sensitive to demands being placed upon them by others and are prone to use projection and rationalization as their primary defense mechanisms. This profile type carries with it a high tendency toward addiction proneness to drugs and alcohol. Underachievement and uneven performance is also quite likely. Diagnostic possibilities include: Affective Disorders: Depression, Adjustment Disorder, Substance Abuse Disorder, and Paranoid Disorder; AXIS II: Passive-Aggressive Personality, with the primary differential being Borderline Personality.

M247 Persons of this profile type show a mixture of neurotic symptomatology, primarily in the form of depression and anxiety. They also have long-standing characterological difficulties of a passive-aggressive nature. These individuals often present with marriage and family problems which the patient is apt to feel angry about but unable to deal with or express directly because of simultaneous feelings of guilt. These persons usually feel inadequate and passive and are angry with themselves and others. Despite their difficulties, these individuals are often somewhat evasive and uncomfortable in discussing their problems. This profile carries with it an extremely high tendency toward addiction proneness to drugs and alcohol. This profile has frequently been cited as the mean profile type for alcoholics, and various studies on this code type report drinking problems in frequencies ranging up to 96%. These persons are insecure and typically have insatiable neurotic needs for affection, while at the same time are conflicted over emotional dependency and sexuality.

Psychosomatic symptoms may occasionally also be presented in their symptom cluster. These persons are typically excitable, passively-aggressively manipulative, and may be argumentative. They are typically underachievers, possibly because of a fear of failure. Therapy may be difficult with these patients because they are somewhat fearful of it.

Assertiveness Training may be helpful for patients of this profile type, and, also, this profile type has shown some benefit from Biofeedback Therapy.

In a recent study of private psychiatric patients, the primary diagnostic category for this profile type was bimodal, with half the persons receiving substance abuse as their primary disorder and the remaining half receiving adjustment disorders as their primary disorder. The modal personality diagnosis for persons of this profile type was passive-aggressive personality. In state hospital settings, a significant number of these individuals are seen as having a Major Affective Disorder (unipolar/bipolar).

M248 These persons typically present in acute psychic distress and are apt to be depressed, anxious, nervous, irritable, hostile, suspicious, moody, worrisome, resentful, tense, and oversensitive. These individuals are typically moody and emotionally inappropriate, as well as distrustful of others and fearful of close interpersonal relations. Paradoxically, however, these patients at the same time often have exaggerated needs for attention and affection. These persons typically have erratic, marginal histories of achievement educationally and vocationally. They are apt to be quite sensitive to anything that can be construed as a demand upon them. They occasionally evidence autistic thinking and are withdrawn. They are emotionally labile and apt to suffer from deep-seated feelings of guilt. Nevertheless, these persons do fear a loss of control over their impulses and are apt to be moody, unstable, and unpredictable. Suicide attempts are quite common.

When these patients are married, marital conflict is quite likely. This profile carries with it a high tendency toward addiction proneness to drugs and alcohol, and is a frequent profile type among drug abusers. Impulsive suicide attempts are also quite likely. These persons also have a high incidence of sexual conflicts and sexual difficulties. Projection, rationalization, and acting out are frequent defense mechanisms in patients of this profile type.

In a recent study of state mental hospital patients, a significant number of these individuals were seen as psychotic and about evenly divided between schizophrenia and bipolar disorders. In other settings, diagnostic possibilities include: Affective Disorder: Depressed, Adjustment Disorder, Substance Abuse Disorder, Schizophrenic Disorder; AXIS II: Modal Personality Disorder: Borderline Personality (in fact, one study found this to be the modal borderline personality code type).

M275 (male only) These persons are usually quite self-effacing, submissive, and passive. Typically, they feel most comfortable in subordinate relationships. These individuals are obsessive worriers who are quite depressed and preoccupied over their self-perceived failures and personal deficiencies. These persons typically evidence anxiety, insomnia, and guilt. They are apt to manifest somatic correlates of anxiety and may be concerned about sexual performance. Suicidal ideation and suicidal attempts occur with significant frequency, and these patients have marked difficulty handling negative feelings in themselves. They see themselves as inadequate, insecure, and inferior. These persons are pessimistic, overdutiful, overconscientious worriers. They show a history of difficulty relating to the opposite sex.

In a recent study of private psychiatric patients, the modal diagnosis of patients of this profile type was affective disorders, with the majority of the patients of this profile type receiving major affective disorder, bipolar disorder, mixed, or major affective disorder: major depression as their primary diagnosis. The primary differential would be adjustment disorder with depressed mood. The modal personality cluster for patients of this profile type was anxious and fearful personality disorders; namely, dependent, avoidant, compulsive, or passive-aggressive.

M278 Persons of this profile type typically display pan-neurosis, and the old diagnostic category of pseudoneurotic is an apt descriptor of their overall presentation of self. They usually present with a generalized acute distress syndrome of depression, anxiety, and nervousness, coupled with strong feelings of hopelessness, as well as neurasthenic syndrome of weakness, fatigue, and loss of interest and initiative. These persons are obsessive, introverted individuals who are apt to be withdrawn, indecisive, sensitive, inhibited, and generally fearful worriers who lack self-esteem. Suicidal obsessions and attempts are common in patients of this profile type. These persons are apt to suffer somatic correlates of anxiety and be markedly preoccupied with their own self-perceived feelings of failure. These individuals typically are conscientious, perfectionistic individuals who try hard, set high goals, but feel intensely guilty when they fail to live up to their own standards. They are apt to be fearful of emotional commitment and, consequently, have difficulty establishing close interpersonal relationships with the opposite sex, even though these individuals state they are desirous of such relations. In periods of acute stress, these persons may drink heavily in an attempt to relax. This is a common profile type among post-traumatic stress disorders.

In a recent study of private psychiatric patients, the majority of individuals of this profile type received as a primary diagnosis affective disorders, namely, bipolar disorder, mixed; bipolar disorder, depressed; or major depression. The modal personality disorder cluster for persons of this profile type was anxious and fearful personality disorders, namely, avoidant, compulsive, or passive-aggressive.

M468 Persons of this profile type are typically oversensitive, suspicious, angry, agitated, evasive individuals who are apt to be irritable, demanding, argumentative, and resentful of others. A history of disrupted interpersonal relations and a general wariness in interpersonal relations is quite likely. Additionally, these individuals are typically immature, narcissistic, egocentric, and self-indulgent. These persons usually have symptoms of seething anger, and typically want others to change to solve their own difficulties. Quite often they are quite demanding of sympathy and attention from others. These persons typically have significant sexual conflicts and poor marital adjustment. This profile carries with it a high tendency toward addiction proneness to drugs and alcohol, and is a fairly common profile type among drug abusers. These individuals are hypervigilant, and projection and rationalization are their primary defense mechanisms. Suicide attempts and aggressive acting out are likely. Ideas of reference and delusions may be present.

In state mental hospital settings, these individuals are quite often psychotic and suffering from schizophrenia. In other settings, diagnostic possibilities include: AXIS I: Adjustment Disorder, Substance Abuse Disorder, Schizophrenic Disorder, Paranoid Disorder; AXIS II: Modal Personality Disorder: Borderline Personality.

M469 Persons of this profile type are apt to be angry, aggressive individuals who are easily excitable and display poor judgement and poor emotional control. These individuals are oversensitive, suspicious, and strikingly lacking in insight. They typically project their difficulties on to others and are prone to act out, especially aggressively. These persons typically are alienated interpersonally, lack a viable sense of self, and may at the same time have strong needs for attention and affection, though they are often too fearful of others to be able to establish these to any meaningful degree. Marriage and family problems and disruptive interpersonal relations are quite common to persons of this profile type. This profile type is occasionally evidenced by drug abusers, especially who present in an acute toxic, often psychotic, state. These persons are apt to withdraw when under stress and report difficulty in thinking and concentrating. Delusions and hallucinations may be present, and, occasionally, outright excitement. Diagnostic possibilities include: AXIS I: Adjustment Disorder, Substance Abuse Disorder, Affective Disorder: Bipolar, and Paranoid Disorder; AXIS II: Modal Personality Disorder: Borderline Personality Disorder.

M478 These persons are typically alienated interpersonally and apt to be seen as odd and peculiar, queer and nonconforming. They also are apt to be irritable, hostile, angry, and have disrupted, alienated interpersonal relations. They typically get into trouble because they lack social judgement and typically act out more as a defense than for excitement per se. These persons, however, are more apt to show obsessive concern over their impulses and actions, and evidence anxiety and guilt. They are typically withdrawn and may evidence autistic thinking. They typically are chronically insecure and, though fearful of interpersonal relations, have exaggerated needs for attention and affection. These persons frequently have a significant identity disturbance and a very poor sense of self, and, often, it seems they fail or get into trouble in order to validate their poor self-concept. Sexual conflicts are quite likely and outright sexual deviation is a distinct possibility. These individuals are apt to be manipulative, impulsive, and unpredictable. Their educational and vocational histories are typically characterized by uneven performance and underachievement. This profile type carries with it a high tendency toward addiction proneness to drugs and alcohol and is a common profile type among drug abusers. When married, these persons typically evidence marital discord. Aggressive outbursts and acting out may occur, which are followed by feelings of guilt, remorse, and withdrawal.

In a recent study of private psychiatric patients, 100% of the persons of this profile type received substance abuse as their primary, secondary, or tertiary diagnosis. Substance abuse was one of the two primary diagnoses, with the alternate primary diagnoses being adjustment disorder with either depressed mood or mixed emotional features. The primary personality disorder cluster for patients of this profile type was dramatic, emotional, or erratic personality disorders; namely, histrionic, antisocial, or borderline.

M489 Persons of this profile type tend to be aggressive, acting out individuals with poor impulse control. These persons often present in an agitated, anxious state. These persons are typically aggressive and violent; aggressive acting out is not uncommon in their histories. This profile type carries with it a high tendency toward addiction proneness to drugs and alcohol, and is a fairly common profile type among drug abusers. These individuals are typically manipulative and prone to engage in a wide variety of acting out behavior. They may be somewhat alienated interpersonally, lack a viable sense of self, and have significant identity disturbance. Marriage and family problems, and disrupted interpersonal relations, are quite common in persons of this profile type.

In state hospital settings, this profile type is frequently associated with a psychotic individual who is most frequently manifesting a Bipolar Disorder, Manic type.

In other settings, diagnostic possibilities include: AXIS I: Adjustment Disorder, Substance Abuse Disorder, Schizophrenic Disorder, and

Affective Disorder: Bipolar; AXIS !I: Modal Personality Disorder: Borderline Personality Disorder.

2-Point Code Rules: The only criterion is that the 2 points are at or above a T score of 70 and that a 3-, 4-, or 5-point code type above was not chosen.

M12 Persons of this profile type are usually seen as manifesting significant somatic concerns, along with depression. Somatic difficulties in this profile type can be the result of either functional or organic problems, though, in the case of bona fide physical complaints, amplification of the person's condition is the norm. Physical complaints of these individuals may include headaches, cardiac problems, and gastro-intestinal difficulties, including ulcers and vomiting. These persons are also apt to complain of dizziness, insomnia, weakness, and fatigue. These individuals are generally anxious, tense, and nervous. They are typically lacking in drive and often are hypersensitive to what others think of them. The underlying personality of these persons is apt to be one of passive dependence, and this profile type has a high tendency toward addiction proneness to drugs and alcohol. The individual uses repression and somatization excessively as defense mechanisms and is typically lacking in insight and self-understanding. Medical patients evidencing this profile type include: patients with ulcers, arthritis, and chronic pulmonary conditions.

In a recent study of private psychiatric patients, roughly half the persons of this profile type received somatoform disorders or psychological factors affecting physical condition as their primary or secondary diagnosis. Adjustment disorders were modal, and the differential includes affective disorders and panic disorders. The modal personality diagnosis for persons of this profile type was in the cluster of anxious and fearful personality disorders, namely, dependent, compulsive, and passive-aggressive. This code type in the past has been cited as one associated with substance abuse; however, only 18% of the private sample were substance abusers.

M13 Persons with this profile type are usually seen as neurotic and manifesting physical complaints. A wide variety of physical symptomatology is apt to be presented, including: back pain, headaches, gastro-intestinal difficulties, as well as occasional numbness or tremors. These individuals are occasionally seen as depressed and anxious, but most likely convert their difficulties into functional physical complaints. These persons are usually egocentric, immature, and suggestible, and have long-standing and inordinate needs for sympathy, affection, attention, and reassurance. Few of these patients are incapacitated by their illnesses, at least in regard to doing pleasurable activities. These individuals have a strong need to see and interpret problems in living as sociably acceptable. They typically make excessive use of the defense mechanisms of repression, denial, and somatization. Secondary gain for their illnesses is apt to be operating in the form of either manipulation for the attention of close family members, or avoiding responsibilities. In persons with back pain, this profile type is associated with poor surgery outcome. In a large, well-controlled study, less than 10% of these individuals obtained relief from back pain by purely medical measures alone.

These persons manifest physical problems of all sorts. This is the mean profile type for persons evidencing low back pain, early onset asthma, pseudo-neurologic conditions (including pseudo multiple sclerosis), and female urethral syndrome. In addition to the above-mentioned categories and gastro-intestinal and cardiac complaints, virtually no organ system is immune.

In a recent study of private psychiatric patients, the majority of this profile type received somatoform disorders (somatization, psychogenic pain, and hypochondriasis) or psychological factors affecting physical condition as their primary, secondary, or tertiary diagnoses. Somatoform disorders or psychological factors affecting physical condition were modal, with the differential including affective disorders and adjustment disorders. The modal personality disorder cluster for patients of this profile type was anxious or fearful personality disorders, namely, compulsive, passive-aggressive or dependent.

As there is always the possibility that the person may be evidencing actual physical pathology in conjunction with functional symptomatology, the following is a breakdown of the probabilities of functional physical complaints being evidenced in any individual person, and is based on studies done at the Mayo Clinic on individuals of this profile type. For individuals of this profile type who are the same age and sex as the person tested:

M13(a) (for use with men over 50 years old): the majority were seen as having physical problems. Only one-eighth were seen as having primarily functional problems, and one-fourth presented a mixed picture.

M13(b) (for use with Women over 40): one-third were seen as primarily having functional problems, one-third were seen as having primarily physical problems, and one-third presented a mixed picture.

M13(c) (for use with Men 40–49 years of age): one-half were seen as primarily having physical problems, one-fourth were seen as having primarily functional problems, and one-fourth presented a mixed picture.

M13(d) (for use with men 30–39 years of age): three-fourths were seen as having primarily functional problems, one-sixth were seen as presenting primarily a mixed picture, and only one-twelfth were seen as having primarily physical problems.

M13(e) (for use with women 30–39 years of age): two-thirds were seen as having primarily functional problems, one-tenth presented a mixed picture, and one-fourth were seen as having primarily physical problems.

M13(f) (for use with men less than 30 years of age): one-half were seen as having primarily functional problems, one-fourth presented a mixed picture, and one-fourth were seen as having primarily physical problems.

M13(g) (for use with women less than 30 years of age): 60% were seen as having primarily functional problems, 40% presented a mixed picture, and none were seen as having primarily physical problems.

M14 Persons of this profile type typically report severe hypochondriacal symptoms and especially nonspecific headaches. They are typically indecisive, anxious, and—though superficially extraverted—are apt to lack skills with the opposite sex. These individuals usually have histories of home conflicts, generally lack drive, and are apt to have histories of underachievement and uneven performance. They are typically manipulative and are apt to be grouchy, pessimistic complainers. In general, others see them as difficult to get along with. They have a sour outlook toward life and are, in a word, "bitchy." This profile type carries with it a high tendency toward addiction proneness to drugs and alcohol. They are apt to be quite upset by any external rules, constraints, or obligations placed upon them.

Diagnostic possibilities include, AXIS I: Affective Disorder: Depression, Substance Abuse Disorder, Somatoform Disorder, and Psychological Factors Affecting Physical Condition; AXIS II: Modal Personality Disorder: Passive-Aggressive Personality.

M16 This is a very infrequent profile type. Persons of this profile type tend to be extremely oversensitive, rigid, stubborn, and touchy. They are apt to be somatizers who are vulnerable to accumulated stress. These individuals are quite sensitive to any demands being placed upon them by others. They are often rigid personalities who manifest somatic concern, though occasionally such persons are in the early stages of psychosis and are attempting to hold themselves together by bodily preoccupations. The individuals are emotional worriers who are apt to be distrustful of others.

Diagnostic possibilities include: AXIS I: Affective Disorder: Depression, Somatoform Disorder, Psychological Factors Affecting Physical Condition, and Paranoid Disorder; AXIS II: Modal Personality Disorder: Avoidant Personality.

M17 This is an infrequent profile type. Persons of this profile type are usually seen as chronic neurotic individuals who are tense, anxious, and obsessive. These individuals often manifest somatic complaints which are directly related to their tension and anxiety; however, occasionally they show obsessive overconcern regarding bodily functions. These persons are insecure, inhibited, and lacking in assertiveness, and are apt to have underlying feelings of guilt and inferiority.

Diagnostic possibilities include: AXIS l: Affective Disorder: Depression, Anxiety Disorder, Somatoform Disorder, and Psychological Factors Affecting Physical Condition; AXIS II: Dependent, Passive-Aggressive, Avoidant, and Compulsive.

M18 This is an infrequent profile type. Persons of this profile type have great trouble handling stress and anxiety, and may exhibit somatic delusions. They typically are distrustful of others, are apt to have difficulty in concentration, and may be confused. These persons feel socially inadequate, especially in relation to the opposite sex. They tend to inhibit and bottle up their feelings of anger and hostility.

In a recent study of private psychiatric patients, over half the persons of this profile type were seen as psychotic and primarily evidencing a major affective disorder though schizoaffective disorders was also represented. The major differential was substance abuse disorders, with over 40% of the sample evidencing alcohol or barbiturate abuse - dependence. Underlying personality disorders of this profile type are in the category of anxious and fearful disorders, namely, avoidant and passive-aggressive, with the differential including borderline and schizotypal.

M19 This is an infrequent profile type. Persons of this profile type typically manifest large amounts of distress and turmoil; are tense, anxious, and restless; and may exhibit a variety of complaints, including: gastro-intestinal difficulties, headaches, and exhaustion. This profile is one of overcompensation for basic underlying passivity and dependency needs through overactivity. They may be frustrated because they are unable to achieve up to their expectations. Diagnostically, this profile is an indeterminate one, and, occasionally, these patients are attempting to overcompensate for organic losses or possibly endocrine dysfunction. Generally, this profile is the result of overcompensation and denial of basic passivity or weakness, whether it is the result of functional or organic etiology.

A significant number of individuals with this profile type are seen as having a post-traumatic stress disorder.

Other diagnostic possibilities include: AXIS I: Affective Disorder: Depression, Adjustment Disorder, Affective Disorder: Bipolar, Somatoform Disorder; AXIS II: Modal Personality Disorder: Passive-Aggressive Personality.

M23 Persons of this profile type are almost overwhelmingly seen as depressed. These persons are typically tense, worrisome, and apt to present with sadness and decreased activity. They are apt to feel helpless and manifest multiple somatic complaints. They are typically insecure and have difficulty expressing their feelings, and may be somewhat immature. They often feel socially inadequate, especially with the opposite sex. These persons are typically fearful of failure and overcontrolled, and, consequently, they may avoid additional responsibilities because of a fear of failure. In spite of this, they are usually conscientious workers who take their responsibilities seriously. Poor sexual performance, including frigidity and impotence, is likely. They may have a long history of family unhappiness, but rarely divorce. Ulcers are frequently reported in these patients, and this is a mean profile type for patients with ulcerative colitis.

In a recent study of private psychiatric patients, these individuals were seen primarily as evidencing affective disorders. A very significant minority of this sample (43%) were seen as evidencing either somatoform disorders or psychological factors affecting physical condition, and received this as their primary, secondary, or tertiary diagnosis. The modal personality disorder cluster for patients of this profile type was anxious and fearful personality disorders; namely, avoidant, dependent, or passive-aggressive.

M24 Persons of this profile type are typically seen as immature, impulsive character disorders, most frequently of a passive-aggressive nature—though occasionally they may be seen as antisocial or emotionally unstable personalities who have "been caught" and consequently are exhibiting situational depression in reaction to their external difficulties. These persons typically are insincere in their verbalizations of guilt and remorse, and as soon as their current difficulties are patched over they will return to a pattern of acting out. Often they come from disturbed families. The only long-term remorse these patients are apt to suffer is over their own frustrations and anger over a lack of accomplishments. These patients are quite resistant to demands being placed on them by others. This profile carries with it a very high tendency toward addiction proneness to drugs and alcohol. In a recent study of 500 D.W.I. (D.U.I.) offenders, this was the mean profile type of those having the highest level of drinking. Additionally, these patients typically have marital problems, often as the result of their own sexual acting out. These patients are typically underachievers academically and vocationally. They tend to run from peoples' expectations for them and from their own problems, and are impulsive and self-indulging. Suicide attempts are almost always manipulations on their part to blame or coerce others. In the hospital, these patients usually make a good impression on the staff. Often, under pressure, they will feign a spontaneous recovery. When they do follow through with the therapy, they are at risk for becoming quite dependent on their therapist.

In a recent study of private psychiatric patients, the primary diagnosis for individuals of this profile type was adjustment disorders of depressed mood or mixed emotional features, with a very significant minority (43%) of persons evidencing substance abuse and receiving this as either their primary or secondary diagnosis. The modal personality diagnosis for persons of this profile type was passive-aggressive personality, with the differential being histrionic or antisocial personalities.

M26 Persons of this profile type are typically seen as agitated, depressed, and markedly oversensitive. They are apt to be moody, touchy, demanding, and occasionally have underlying dependency needs which are frustrated. Suicide attempts and thoughts of suicide are a distinct possibility. These persons are angry with others and with themselves, and a vast amount of anger is apt to be present that is channeled into both self-blame and other-blame. These patients tend to be easily offended and may become tired and depressed quickly. They tend to induce rejection by others and have a history of difficulty in interpersonal relations.

In a recent study of private psychiatric patients, half the patients of this profile type are seen as evidencing adjustment disorders with either depressed mood or mixed emotional features. A significant minority, however, were seen as psychotic, evidencing either major depression or paranoid schizophrenia. Underlying personality disorders of most of this profile type tend to cluster in the anxious or fearful category, namely, avoidant, dependent, or compulsive. However, a significant number were seen as histrionic or borderline.

M27 Persons of this profile type are seen as anxious, depressed, tense, high-strung, and obsessive. They typically are chronic worriers and overanticipators of problems who are apt to manifest multiple neurotic manifestations and somatic correlates of anxiety. These individuals typically complain of fatigue, exhaustion, and are apt to suffer from insomnia. They typically are pessimistic, self-punishing worriers. Suicidal thoughts and attempts are fairly common. These persons are often individuals who are easygoing and lack assertiveness. They are capable of forming close emotional ties and usually have stable work and marital adjustment. At the time of seeking psychotherapeutic assistance, the patient may be unable to concentrate or tend to daily duties; however, once their depression and anxiety has abated, these individuals usually return to a positive and achieving stance.

In a recent study of private psychiatric patients, the modal diagnosis of persons of this profile type was affective disorders, with the majority of individuals of this profile type receiving major affective disorder, bipolar disorder, mixed, or major affective disorder: major depression as their primary diagnosis. The primary differential would be adjustment disorder with depressed mood. The modal personality cluster for individuals of this profile type was anxious and fearful personality disorders; namely, avoidant, compulsive, or passive-aggressive or dependent.

M28 Persons of this profile type are seen as withdrawn, anxious, agitated, tense, and jumpy. They are apt to complain of difficulty in concentration, insomnia, confused thinking, and forgetfulness. These individuals also frequently report somatic symptomatology and may, in fact, present themselves as physically ill. However, unlike the hysteric, the presenting problems of these patients are more apt to be atypical and in some cases outright delusional. Also, these persons are withdrawn, unsociable, sensitive, and suspicious. They may have a history of being hurt emotionally and, consequently, fearful of being hurt again. These persons typically have feelings of despair and worthlessness, may suffer from delusions and ideas of reference and, occasionally, auditory hallucinations. These persons feel inadequate in heterosexual relations and are apt to report sexual conflicts. Suicidal ideation and suicide attempts are quite frequent in persons of this profile type, and a significant minority are apt to have a definite plan for suicide. These individuals often fear a loss of self-control. At the time of seeking help, inner turmoil is apt to be evidenced in these persons. The person is also apt to be evidencing emotional lability, irritability, anxiety, and obsessive thinking. Difficulty in thinking and concentration, a stereotyped approach to problem solving, and a general loss of efficiency are likely. Complaints of these persons may include sleep disturbance, memory loss, weakness, easy fatigability, and dizziness.

Though only a minority of persons producing this code type suffer from organic impairment; this is the most common profile type in persons with organic impairment. In cases evidencing organic impairment, this code is usually reflecting depression and possibly agitation in reaction to, and in recognition of, organic loss.

This is also a common profile type among individuals suffering from a Post-Traumatic Stress Disorder. In a recent study on private psychiatric patients, the modal diagnosis of person of this profile type was affective disorder, with 70% of these individuals receiving a diagnosis of major affective disorders; bipolar, depressed or major affective disorder: major depression. The modal diagnostic cluster personality disorder of persons of this profile type was anxious and fearful personality disorders; namely, avoidant, compulsive, or passive-aggressive personality.

M29 This profile type depicts an individual who is apt to present in noticeable psychic distress and is usually seen as being restless, anxious, depressed, and agitated. These persons may evidence hyperactivity. This profile type is rare and paradoxical, and is usually obtained in three distinct categories of patients: (a) in persons who are evidencing an Agitated Depression in the context of a Mixed Affective Disorder—here the person's heightened energy level is seen as an attempt to ward off underlying depression, or manic defenses are no longer successful in blocking such depression, which is increasing; (b) in an agitated, self-absorbed individual who is having an identity crisis and may be narcissistic—such persons may have had to be emotional as children to get attention; (c) in persons suffering from organic impairment, who nevertheless show some awareness of organic losses and consequent depression and who are attempting to overcompensate for such losses and are in dynamic confrontation with them. In such cases, the person is attempting to deny deficits.

M20 Persons of this profile type usually present with mild depression and are introverted. Depression may be of long-standing duration and deeply ingrained into their personality structure. These individuals are usually socially isolated and shy, withdrawn, inhibited, and particularly uneasy in heterosexual relationships. They are apt to worry excessively and may feel physically unattractive or physically inferior. Insomnia, tension, and a general unhappiness is apt to be present. Physically, these persons typically keep a rigid check on their emotions.

In a recent study of private psychiatric patients, the majority of the persons with this profile type were seen as evidencing affective disorders and were evenly divided between major affective disorders, major depression, and dysthymic disorders. The primary differential was adjustment disorders with mixed emotional features. Underlying personality of this code type was avoidant personality. The picture emerges of a depressed, introverted, sensitive individual.

M34 Persons of this profile type are usually seen as chronic impulsive personality disorders who are angry and harbor hostile and aggressive impulses, and are unable to discharge their impulses except in passive-aggressive ways or through episodic angry over-reaction. These persons may go through periods of explosive behavior, which alternates with periods during which the patient is sociable, cooperative, and friendly, but evidences psychosomatic symptomatology. These persons usually have a long history of family unhappiness and chronic marital difficulties. A wide variety of acting out is common to individuals of this profile type. Sexual problems and sexual acting out are common. This profile carries with it a high tendency to addiction proneness to drugs and alcohol. These persons are apt to be demanding of attention and approval from others, and to be quite sensitive to rejection. They are apt to be quite sensitive to any demands made upon them by others. Impulsive suicide attempts usually follow periods of acting out or excessive drinking. Somatic complaints of these persons are apt to include headaches, gastro-intestinal difficulties, and blackout spells.

Occasionally, these persons establish enduring relationships with antisocial individuals and vicariously act out through them. These individuals typically have marked dependency-independency conflicts. This profile type is fertile ground for the occurrence of dissociative phenomena. This is a common profile type for parents of child psychiatry patients, and it would seem that in these cases the parent serves both as a model and a source of reinforcement of the child's unacceptable behavior.

In a recent study of private psychiatric patients, the modal diagnosis of persons of this profile type was adjustment disorder, either with depressed mood or mixed emotional features. The primary personality cluster for patients of this profile type was dramatic, emotional, or erratic personality disorders, namely, histrionic or borderline, with the alternate personality classification being passive-aggressive. This profile type in the past has been associated with a high incidence of substance abuse; however, only 12% of the private sample were substance abusers.

M36 This is an infrequent code type. Persons of this profile type are apt to present as chronically tense and anxious and evidencing somatic complaints such as headaches and gastro-intestinal difficulties. These persons typically have chronic, deep, and often unrecognized anger toward family members. They are apt to express their feelings indirectly and infrequently deny hostile intent in themselves. When they are aware of their anger, they typically present it in a well-rationalized fashion. These individuals are typically rigid, egocentric, and externalize the blame for their difficulties. They are apt to make significant use of denial and to be resistant to psychotherapeutic intervention. Marital unhappiness and disharmony is frequent in patients of this profile type. Disrupted interpersonal relations are likely; often, though the person is often not aware of it, others around them are quite aware of their seething hostility which lies just below the surface.

Diagnostic possibilities include, AXIS I: Affective Disorder: Depressed, Adjustment Disorder, Somatoform Disorder, and Paranoid Disorder; AXIS II: The modal personality disorder is Avoidant Personality.

M37 This code is a very rare profile type and these persons almost always present with neurotic symptomatology. They typically are tense, anxious, depressed, and vulnerable to accumulating stress. They may complain of insomnia and typically have histories of chronic tension. These persons typically lack insight into their behavior and make excessive use of the defense mechanisms of repression and denial. Psychosomatic symptoms are likely. These individuals are anxious and dependent individuals who are overly self-critical.

Diagnostic possibilities include: AXIS I: Affective Disorder: Depressed, Anxiety Disorder, Somatoform Disorder, and Psychological Factors Affecting Physical Condition; AXIS II: Dependent Personality, Passive-Aggressive Personality, Avoidant Personality and Compulsive Personality.

M38 Persons with this profile type are apt to present with a large amount of psychic distress, and are typically anxious, tense, nervous, restless, and depressed. Some of their anxiety is apt to be discharged into somatic complaints, especially gastro-intestinal difficulties, dizziness, pain, headaches, and insomnia. These persons suffer from difficulties in thinking and concentration, are typically schizoid or dependent, and often have strong needs for attention and affection. These individuals typically turn their frustrations inward. These persons are apt to be unconventional in their thinking and occasionally show delusional thinking and loose associations. These persons are prone to obsess, brood, and worry.

They are apt to be somewhat withdrawn upon admission. If physical symptoms are present, secondary gain is apt to be operating. Generally these persons can be expected to be generally fearful, emotionally vulnerable, and chronic worriers. Despite the fact that they are desirous of affection and attention, they are at the same time fearful of emotional dependency.

Diagnostic possibilities include: AXIS I: Affective Disorder: Depression, Adjustment Disorder, Schizophrenic Disorder, Somatoform Disorder. Also, this code type is the most frequent one for the rare disorder group of Disassociative Disorders. AXIS II: Modal Personality Disorder: Avoidant Personality.

M39 This is an uncommon profile type and persons of this profile type are apt to present in the midst of an episodic attack of acute distress. Anxiety and somatic complaints are apt to be present, such as tachycardia and headaches. Occasionally, these persons have underlying depression. Perceptual illusions are occasionally evidenced by individuals of this profile type. These patients typically are hysterical in their approach to others and make excessive use of the defense mechanisms of repression and denial. Often they present with underlying hostility toward a significant other, who has rejected them, and toward whom they are sexually attracted or overly dependent. These persons are often dramatically open, superficial, and highly visible in social situations, and unaware of their impact upon others. They lack insight, and typically have dependency conflicts. Diagnostic possibilities include: AXIS I: Affective Disorder:

Depressed, Anxiety Disorder, Affective Disorder: Bipolar, and Somatoform Disorder; AXIS II: Modal personality disorder, Passive-Aggressive Personality, Histrionic Personality is also quite likely.

M45 Persons of this profile type are apt to be nonconforming, immature, and narcissistic. These patients typically have strong, but unrecognized, dependency needs against which they may be struggling. These persons often have troubles with sexual role identification and are apt to be very sensitive to any demands made upon them by the opposite sex. Despite their nonconformity, these persons rarely act out in a blatant fashion except when under stress or secondary to drug or alcohol abuse. Feelings of guilt and remorse in these individuals are usually caused by external stress, often in relation to interpersonal problems, and generally are transient. This profile carries with it a high tendency toward addiction proneness to drugs and alcohol. Sexual difficulties in these patients may involve overt homosexual problems, but are just as likely to involve latency conflicts or other sexual dysfunctions. These individuals may be anti-establishment and, when educated, are apt to be involved in social causes or social movements. Episodic attacks of aggressiveness may be present in this profile type, as a consequence of repressed anger and a low tolerance for stress and frustration. Diagnostically, the overwhelming majority of persons of this profile type are seen as personality disorders, usually of a passive-aggressive nature, though occasionally these persons are seen as narcissistic. Women of this profile type tend to be more aggressive, whereas the men tend to be more passive and dependent.

M46 Persons of this profile type are typically immature, rebellious, oversensitive, narcissistic, self-indulging individuals who are prone to have disrupted interpersonal relations, especially with the opposite sex. Episodic outbursts of anger are quite likely.

These patients are typically sullen, irritable, argumentative, and generally obnoxious. They are typically quite resentful of authority and sensitive to any demands made upon them by others. These individuals occasionally report somatic complaints—such as asthma, hypertension, headaches, and cardiac complaints. They are apt to present for psychotherapeutic assistance feeling agitated, depressed, and nervous. These persons are insecure and have a long history of disrupted interpersonal relations. Marital problems are quite common in persons of this profile type. In hetrosexual relations, women of this profile type are apt to be quite demanding and dependent, and men of this profile type are apt to be demanding and jealous. This profile type carries with it a high tendency toward addiction proneness to drugs and alcohol. These patients are uncomfortable with and suspicious of others—especially of the opposite sex. They are apt to have a life script of moving against people, and often have disrupted work histories.

In a recent study of private psychiatric patients, persons of this profile type were bimodal in their diagnostic categories, with the primary diagnosis being either affective disorders—major depression, with the alternate diagnostic cluster being substance abuse. Almost one-third of the sample received an additional diagnosis of psychological factors affecting physical condition as their secondary or tertiary diagnosis. Modal cluster for personality disorders was passive-aggressive, with the alternate diagnostic categories being histrionic, borderline, paranoid, or schizotypal.

M47 Persons of this profile type typically show behavioral contradictions, in that they are apt to possess a large amount of insensitivity toward others, while at the same time evidencing guilt over their behavior. Consequently, they often go through cyclic patterns of acting out and then feeling remorseful over their actions. This guilt and self-condemnation, however, is usually insufficient to prevent further episodes of acting out. These persons are typically immature, moody, and insecure. They have a high need for affection, but their erratic behavior serves to alienate others. These individuals are apt to report feelings of inferiority and typically present for psychotherapeutic intervention during their periods of remorse, usually following episodes of acting out. Somatic correlates of anxiety are apt to be present, including headaches and stomach pain. These persons typically have significant dependency conflicts and poor sense of self-worth. This profile carries with it a high tendency toward addiction proneness to drugs and alcohol. Sexual acting out is likely.

In a recent study of private psychiatric patients which somewhat contradicts previous research, which has generally seen these individuals as evidencing reactive adjustment disorders, the majority of our private patient sample with this code type received what would have been previously classified as a psychotic disorder, namely major affective disorder, depressed or bipolar disorder. The latter category, along with a significant minority in the private psychiatric sample who were classified as having a cyclothymic disorder, bears out the alternating and fluctuating pattern previously described in literature for patients of this profile. Also consistent with previous research is the fact that half the patients of this profile type received a personality disorder classification of passive-aggressive personality with the major differential being histrionic, and one-third of the private psychiatric sample were substance abusers.

M48 Persons of this profile type tend to be unpredictable and impulsive, as well as odd and peculiar. These persons usually have severe emotional difficulties. These individuals are apt to suffer from unusual and disturbing thoughts, and frequently act out; however, the acting out in persons of this profile type is often the result of their poor social judgement about how to deal with situations, rather than because they are merely thrill seekers. These persons typically have identity disturbance and suffer from extremely poor sense of self and often seem to set themselves up for rejection by others—thus validating their poor sense of self. These persons have often learned from early childhood to view the world as cold and dangerous, and they typically have, as children, experienced abuse. These persons are basically fearful, unstable, and prone to act out. Suicide attempts are fairly common in persons of this profile type. This profile type carries with it a very high tendency toward addiction proneness to drugs and alcohol, and is a common one among drug abusers.

A high incidence of sexual difficulties and sexual disorders is reported among these individuals. These persons have histories of marginal adjustment and uneven performance. They are socially withdrawn and isolated, but at the same time may have exaggerated needs for attention and affection, which they find difficult to fulfill because of their fears. Episodic, aggressive, violent acting out is a distinct possibility.

In state mental hospital settings, a significant number of persons with this profile type are psychotic and suffering from schizophrenia.

In a recent study of private psychiatric patients, persons of this profile type were bimodal in their primary diagnosis, namely, substance abuse or adjustment disorders with depressed mood; however, 100% of persons of this profile type were substance abusers and received this as either a primary, secondary, or tertiary diagnosis. The sole personality clusters for persons of this profile type were dramatic, emotional, or erratic personality disorders, namely, borderline, antisocial, or histrionic.

M49 Persons of this profile are impulsive, hedonistic, antisocial individuals who are self-indulgent and extremely egocentric. These persons have an extremely poor or no conscience development. A wide variety of acting out is reported in individuals of this profile type. These persons are sensation-seekers who are quite desirous of excitement and thrills. The social histories of these persons almost always include histories of academic underachievement, as well as family, employment, and/or legal difficulties. This profile type is not as devastating in a young person; but, from about the mid-twenties on, it generally represents a chronic, stable, hedonistic adjustment, and the prognosis for change is quite poor. These persons are typically irresponsible, though socially they are apt to make a good first impression. Occasionally, these persons will expend a large amount of their own energy to satisfy their own personal desires and ambitions. When pressed by others, however, they are apt to be hostile and manipulative and quite prone to rationalize.

This profile carries with it a high tendency toward addiction proneness to drugs and alcohol. These persons, upon admission, may show a large amount of distress, but it is because of external difficulties, namely, being caught. Diagnostically, the overwhelming majority of persons of this profile type are seen as character disorders evidencing deficits in impulse control, mainly as antisocial psychopaths or, to a lesser extent, histrionic personalities. A small minority of these persons are diagnosed as psychotic and evidencing primarily a Bipolar Disorder. In fact, one study has shown this to be the mean profile type of patients who are lithium-responders. When the person is presenting in an obvious manic state, the above description should be considered as tentative and an analysis of the patient's underlying character structure should either wait for a remission of their psychosis or be verified from other sources, such as their social history.

In a recent study of private psychiatric patients, persons of this profile received, as a primary diagnosis, substance abuse, and when primary and secondary diagnoses were combined, 75% of the sample were seen as substance abusers. The alternate diagnosis for persons of this profile type was adjustment disorder. Previous research has tended to label these people as antisocial or histrionic; however, virtually all of the private psychiatric sample were seen as evidencing a histrionic personality.

M40 This is a very rare, infrequent profile type and these persons are apt to have substantial anger which is repressed and bottled up inside them. These persons typically have difficulty with assertiveness. They are apt to be passive-aggressive individuals who are sullen and hold grudge feelings, but at the same time have avoidant aspects in their personality structure. These persons typically feel quite uncomfortable with others, and are apt to have a history of dissatisfying interpersonal relationships.

Diagnostic possibilities include: AXIS I: Adjustment Disorder, Substance Abuse; AXIS II: Modal Personality Disorder: Passive-Aggressive Personality.

M67 This is an infrequent profile type. Persons of this profile type are typically seen as anxious, sensitive, and obsessive, and prone to present with complaints of interpersonal difficulties. Somatic correlates of anxiety are occasionally evidenced by patients of this profile type. These persons are apt to be anxious, depressed, tearful, and feel inferior. They are apt to brood and evidence guilt—but at the same time also feel resentful of others. These individuals typically lack social intelligence. They are apt to express their hostility indirectly. This is a very infrequent profile type and, though no consistent diagnostic category is predominant, diagnostic possibilities include: AXIS I: Affective Disorder: Depressed, Adjustment

Disorder, Anxiety Disorder, Paranoid Disorder; AXIS II: Modal Personality Disorder: Avoidant Personality.

M68 Persons of this profile type have chronic feelings of inferiority and insecurity, lack confidence and self-esteem, and suffer from guilt over their perceived failures. These individuals have marked difficulty establishing emotional ties with others and are prone to live in a world of fantasy. They are typically suspicious and distrustful of others and prefer seclusion. They may be seen as moody and irritable. Depression, emotional inappropriateness, and fears and phobias may be present. These persons are typically unpredictable. They are usually single, and typically have severe inner conflicts about sexuality.

Delusions of persecution and/or grandeur and/or hallucinations are apt to be present. Feelings of unreality and loose associations are the norm. These persons typically handle stress via withdrawal from reality and, in fact, have marked difficulty differentiating between the two. They are apt to complain of difficulties in concentration, tension, and memory. These persons typically lack adequate judgement. Their thinking is usually seen as autistic, fragmented, tangential, or circumstantial. They may episodically act out aggressively, especially following periods of drinking. Diagnostically, previous research has always identified this code type as associated with psychotic disorders, primarily paranoid schizophrenia, or, to a lesser extent, bipolar disorders, and this is still largely true in state mental hospitals. However, DSM-III is a major change in the classification system, and in a recent study of private psychiatric patients, the primary category for persons of this profile type was adjustment disorder with mixed emotional features or depressed mood, with the major differential being schizoaffective disorders. The major personality cluster was bimodal and either being borderline personality or deferred because of being obscured by the AXIS I diagnosis. Paranoid and avoidant personalities were also represented. It should be noted that, if the above cluster of diagnoses were reclassified in line with DSM-II terminology, 72% of the private psychiatric patients would be classified as psychotic, namely, those classified as having a schizoaffective disorder, major affective disorder, and those individuals now classified in the personality disorder category of borderline personality disorder.

M69 Persons of this profile type typically present with extreme anxiety or nervousness, and may actually tremble. They typically withdraw into fantasy when threatened and may vascillate between overcontrol and manic excitement. They are apt to overreact in minor matters as if they were crises, and they typically have strong underlying dependency needs; however, they are also apt to be suspicious and wary of others despite this. These persons seem unable to express their emotions in a modulated, adaptive fashion. They are apt to complain of difficulties in thinking and concentration, and be irritable, perplexed, overideational, and obsessional. These persons may evidence delusions and hallucinations, ideas of reference, and incoherent speech.

In state mental hospital settings, the majority of these patients are apt to be psychotic and are almost always seen as Bipolar Disorders, though a few are seen as having schizophrenia. In other settings diagnostic possibilities include: AXIS I: Adjustment Disorder, Affective Disorder: Bipolar, Paranoid Disorder; AXIS II: Modal personality disorder: Borderline Personality.

M60 This is an extremely rare profile type and little is known about it, except these persons are apt to report feelings of physical inferiority and be shy, withdrawn, oversensitive, and socially uncomfortable. These persons are apt to be avoidant individuals who are conforming, constricted, and have difficulty relating to others—especially of the opposite sex.

Diagnostic possibilities include: AXIS I: Adjustment Disorder, Paranoid Disorder; AXIS II: Modal Personality Disorder: Avoidant Personality.

M78 Persons of this profile type typically are obsessive, worrisome, oversensitive individuals who are apt to present with complaints of anxiety, nervousness, tension, and depression. They almost always show marked psychic distress on admission, and are apt to complain of difficulty in thinking and concentration. Occasionally, they are quite confused and in a state of panic. These persons are overideational in approach to solving problems, and are generally worrisome, insecure, and have chronic feelings of inadequacy and inferiority. They are apt to be indecisive and passive in their relationships with others, and typically have difficulty establishing close interpersonal ties with the opposite sex. A rich fantasy life, and much daydreaming, are characteristic of patients of this profile type. Sexual conflict and poor sexual performance are quite likely. These persons are apt to be withdrawn, depressed, and suffer from somatic correlates of anxiety. They are usually conscientious, but somewhat stereotyped in their approach to solving problems. Occasionally, these persons drink excessively in an attempt to relax. Delusions and hallucinations are sometimes present. These persons may suffer from depersonalization. In state hospital settings, the majority of these persons are seen as psychotic, and these are divided between major depressions and schizophrenia. In a recent study of private psychiatric patients, these persons were not seen as a homogenous group, and had a primary diagnoses of adjustment disorders; tied for second place were three categories: psychotic disorders not elsewhere classified (schizophreniform or schizoaffective disorders), affective disorders, and substance abuse. Though the latter was a small factor in primary classification, substance abuse was included as a primary, secondary, or tertiary diagnosis in 64% of this sample. This is greater than normally has been reported in the general literature, with the exception of work that has been done with female college students. The modal personality cluster for patients of this profile type was dramatic, emotional, erratic personality disorders, namely, borderline or histrionic. This differs from previous findings; however, here again, this was not a homogenous sample, and the differential would include schizoid, schizotypal, avoidant, and passive-aggressive.

M79 This is a very infrequent profile type, and persons of this profile type are apt to be seen as anxious and agitated and generally worrisome. Sexual difficulties are quite common in persons of this profile type. These individuals may be somewhat suspicious, as well as tense and nervous. They may complain of depression. These persons tend to be somewhat immature and go through periods of impulsive and inconsiderate behavior, which are apt to be followed by feelings of guilt and obsessive self-condemnation. Disrupted interpersonal relations are likely. These persons may also complain of somatic symptoms such as backaches, muscle spasms, and insomnia. They are apt to have disrupted thinking and poor judgement.

Diagnostic possibilities include: AXIS I: Affective Disorder: Depressed, Adjustment Disorder, Anxiety Disorder, Affective Disorder: Bipolar; AXIS II: Modal personality disorder: Passive-Aggressive Personality.

M89 Persons of this profile type usually present in an acute state of hyperactivity and restless agitation. They are apt to be seen as indecisive, perplexed, intense, hostile, and irritable. These persons are emotionally labile, unrealistic, and often have delusions of grandeur. They typically lack insight into their own behavior, and do not see themselves as having problems or needing hospitalization. These persons are typically fearful of, and avoid, close interpersonal relations, and are distrustful of others. At the same time, they are desirous of attention and apt to be quite upset when not receiving it. These individuals typically have difficulty in heterosexual relationships, and have significant sexual conflicts and poor sexual adjustment. These persons are quite distractible and, in the extreme, may be disoriented, perplexed, and suffering from delusions and hallucinations. These individuals are likely to disorganize under stress and, though they have a strong need to achieve high goals, often their performance is only fair. These persons are apt to suffer from feelings of inadequacy and inferiority and, consequently, have educational and vocational difficulties. Their social relations are also disrupted.

In state mental hospital settings, the majority of these patients are seen as psychotic and most often are diagnosed as Bipolar Disorders, but a few are seen as having schizophrenia. In a recent study of private psychiatric patients, this was an indeterminant code type, though a third of all patients of this profile type were seen as substance abusers, and this is a significant difference compared to previous research; but it should be noted that drug abuse was not as prominant in America when a good deal of the earlier work was done on the MMPI. A third of the patients of this profile type were seen as adjustment disorders with either mixed emotional features or depressed mood. A fifth were seen as psychotic and evidencing schizoaffective disorders and major depression. The primary personality disorder diagnostic category of this profile type was borderline, with the differential including schizotypal, histrionic, and avoidant. This code type has also been affected by changes in the nomenclature. In the private psychiatric patient study, the majority of the patients of this profile type (56%) would have been seen as psychotic if they were reclassified DSM-II terminology, the primary factor being that the borderline and schizotypal personality disorders of the present classification system would be counted as psychotic (borderline schizophrenia) in the earlier classification systems.

M80 This is a very infrequent profile type, and persons of this profile type tend to be quite withdrawn socially and avoid interpersonal relationships. These individuals are apt to be anxious, feel alienated from others, and be depressed. They may be somewhat perplexed and confused and suffer from insomnia. These people have difficulty establishing interpersonal relations, and they are typically seen as oversensitive individuals who spend much time in personal fantasy and daydreaming.

Diagnostic possibilities include: AXIS l: Adjustment Disorder, Schizophrenic Disorder; AXIS II: Modal Personality Disorder: Avoidant Personality.

M90 This is an extremely rare profile type and little is known about this code, except that these individuals tend to be shy and withdrawn and may be in confrontation with depression, which they are seeking to alleviate by restless overactivity.

Diagnostic possibilities include: AXIS I: Adjustment Disorder, Affective Disorder: Bipolar; AXIS II Modal Personality Disorder: Avoidant Personality.

1-Point Codes: The only criteria is that the high point is above a T score of 70 and that none of the above 2-, 3-, 4-, or 5-point code types were chosen:

M1 Persons of this profile type typically evidence overconcern with somatic complaints and tend to be passive individuals. A wide variety of somatic complaints is apt to be vocalized by these patients, including chronic fatigue, pain, and weakness, as well as diarrhea, loss of appetite, and insomia. These persons are generally listless and anxious, lack self confidence, and tend to turn hostile feelings inward on self. They may be very defensive and unable to deal with negative emotions. This code type is not always associated with pure functional complaints, and this is especially true in older individuals, though their verbalizations almost always suggest a strong psychological component. Passive, whiney personality features are apt to be evidenced, even when chronic disease is present. When chronic disease is documented, one can expect an exaggeration of complaints and symptomatology. These individuals occasionally shop from physician to physician. Their problems are usually of longstanding duration and not a reaction to immediate stress. This profile is related to poor outcome from back pain surgery.

Diagnostic possibilities include: AXIS I: Affective Disorder: Depressed, Somatoform Disorder, and Psychological Factors Affecting Physical Condition; AXIS II: Dependent Personality, Passive-Aggressive Personality, Avoidant Personality, and Compulsive Personality.

M2 Persons of this profile type are seen as evidencing depression, even when such patients deny depression. These individuals typically feel depressed, pessimistic, and negative towards self, and are often individuals who tend to turn their anger inward on themselves, though occasionally in younger persons such anger may be episodically expressed in brief outbursts. Somatic symptoms, loss of appetite, insomnia, and anxiety often accompany the clinical picture. These persons are apt to verbalize feelings of failure, lack self confidence, and may be somewhat shy, timid, and retiring. They are typically apt to be relatively conventional in their outlook and unaggressive. These individuals may be overcontrolled, indecisive, and typically avoid confrontations with others. Frequent nervousness and a general lack of assertiveness is the norm.

In a recent study of private psychiatric patients, persons of this profile type are divided primarily into two groups: Those seen as evidencing a major affective disorder, and those seen as evidencing adjustment disorder with either depressed mood or mixed emotional features. The underlying personality primarily was seen as falling into the cluster of anxious and fearful personality disorder, namely, avoidant, dependent, compulsive, or passive-aggressive.

M3 Persons of this profile type are constricted, overconventional individuals who have a strong need to be liked and have a large amount of difficulty handling hostility and stress. These individuals are apt to react to stress and responsibility via somatization, and a wide variety of symptomatology is presented in patients of this profile type. Anxiety attacks and physical concomitants of anxiety are apt to be prominent, and among the symptoms frequently reported by these persons are such things as headaches, chest pains, weakness, and tachycardia. These persons usually make an initially good first impression, as they are often talkative, enthusiastic, and desire to be liked; however, underneath this facade, these persons are often immature and narcissistic and grossly lacking in insight. These patients are quite desirous of attention, support, and affection from others.

They are suggestible. These individuals are more apt to see physicians with their somatic complaints than to seek psychotherapeutic treatment on their own; however, when they do, it is often regarding achievement difficulties, conflicts with authority figures, or lack of acceptance by their social group. A history of family unhappiness and/or marital difficulties is likely. These persons have great difficulty handling situations where assertive behavior is required.

Diagnostic possibilities include: AXIS I: Affective Disorder: Depression, Somatoform Disorder and Psychological Factors Affecting Physical Condition; AXIS II: Dependent Personality, Passive-Aggressive Personality, Avoidant Personality, and Compulsive Personality.

M4 Persons of this profile type tend to be rebellious, immature, irresponsible, egocentric, emotionally unstable individuals who are almost always seen as character disorders, associated with deficits of impulse control. They are primarily seen as emotionally unstable, hysterical, passive-aggressive, or (to a lesser extent) antisocial or narcissistic. A wide variety of acting out behavior is presented in patients of this profile type, including lying, cheating, stealing, and sexual acting out. These persons tend to be rebellious toward authority, are impulsive, and apt to have a history of poor educational and/or vocational adjustment. These people tend to made good impressions, but after longer acquaintance their unreliability and egocentricity becomes apparent. They may be seen as exhibitionistic and ostentatious. These persons are self-indulgent. Individuals of this profile type have a high tendency toward addiction proneness to drugs and alcohol. When pressed, they may react with hostility and/or aggressive temper outbursts. These persons are generally free from anxiety and depression, with the exception of situational external reactions to having been caught. These persons, however, may be somewhat self-dissatisifed and empty inside. They are easily bored and, in addition to acting out, may use rationalization and intellectualization as defense mechanisms. Marital adjustment and difficulties are quite common in patients of this profile type. These persons are occasionally sexual deviates. This is a frequent profile for mothers of problem children. These individuals tend to blame others for their difficulties and often seek out psychotherapeutic treatment to smooth over relations and problems with others—such as a marital crisis of their own making, or to avoid legal difficulties. This profile type is less deviant in younger individuals, such as adolescents and young adults; however, beyond the mid-twenties this is a rather enduring and stable personality pattern that is apt to be quite resistant to any significant change.

In a recent study of private psychiatric patients, persons of this profile type were seen as having a modal diagnosis of adjustment disorder with depressed mood or mixed emotional features, with the differential being either substance abuse or affective disorders. The underlying personalities were divided evenly between the cluster of dramatic, emotional, or erratic personalities, namely, histrionic or borderline, and the cluster of anxious and fearful personality disorders, namely, passive-aggressive.

M5 M (use with males) Men of this profile type are typically seen as passive individuals who are apt to be sociable and sensitive to others, and capable of expressing their feelings. They may be somewhat dependent and submissive in interpersonal relationships and unassertive. Men of this profile type typically avoid confrontations. They may have an element of compulsivity in their personality stance. This profile type occasionally reflects an individual who is conflicted over their sexual identity and occasionally may be overtly homosexual. In general, these men do not identify with the stereotype of the masculine role. These men typically have a wide range of interests, and are apt to be concerned with social issues and be idealistic.

M5 F (use with Females) Women of this profile type typically do not identify with the culturally prescribed feminine role, and, consequently, tend to be more aggressive. They are apt to become anxious when they are expected to behave in the traditionally feminine manner. These women typically have masculine interests, are assertive, but may be a bit coarse. They typically are sexually inhibited but self-confident. These women may have some difficulty relating to the opposite sex in a boy–girl fashion, and may have sexual conflicts.

M6 Persons of this profile type are almost always paranoid individuals who are overly sensitive, suspicious, and prone to brood. These persons are hypervigilant, quite apt to have a life script of moving against people, and use projection and rationalization as their primary defense mechanisms. These individuals are typically angry with others and may plot revenge on them. These persons are difficult to engage psychotherapeutically. They are apt to have a large amount of hostility and resentment toward family members. Delusions of persecution and/or grandeur, and ideas of reference, are quite likely. These individuals typically feel pressed, both interpersonally and vocationally. These persons are brittle, have a history of disrupted interpersonal relations, and are prone to jump to conclusions based on inadequate data.

Diagnostic possibilities include: AXIS I: Adjustment Disorder, Paranoid Disorder, and, especially in state mental hospitals, Paranoid Schizophrenia; AXIS II: Schizoid, Schizotypal, Paranoid.

M7 Persons of this profile type are apt to present with a virtual smorgasbord of anxiety-related disorders, including: tension, worry, obsessions, phobias, irrational fears, morbid self-doubt, guilt, and worrisome introspection. These persons are typically obsessive individuals who feel inadequate, insecure, and chronically lacking in self confidence. They typically are overly self-critical and prone to engage in marked sub-vocal self-flagellation. These individuals are rigid, perfectionistic, suffer from unwarranted guilt, and are shy, sensitive worriers who over react to problems. These persons are typically well socialized, sentimental, sensitive individuals who are dependable and overly conforming. They are intellectualizers who may also rationalize. Somatic correlates of anxiety are apt to be present, such as tachycardia, headaches, gastro-intestinal and genito-urinary complaints, as well as complaints of fatigue, exhaustion, and insomnia. These persons typically are organized, neat, and orderly.

Diagnostic possibilities include: AXIS I: Affective Disorder: Depressed, Anxiety Disorder; AXIS II: Dependent Personality, Passive-Aggressive Personality, Avoidant Personality, and Compulsive Personality.

M8 Persons of this profile type always feel alienated and withdrawn from others and misunderstood by them. They tend to handle life's stresses by withdrawing into need-fulfilling fantasies. These persons feel unaccepted by others and, though they may be dependent, may lack the wherewithal to establish close interpersonal relations. These individuals are occasionally in acute distress and overly psychotic, and may exhibit disoriented, disorganized, confused behavior, accompanied by delusions and hallucinations.

These persons show poor judgement, especially in social situations, are withdrawn, and generally do not have much in the way of an understanding of what it is to be or become a socialized human being. Nevertheless, these persons may be painfully aware of their lack of social confidence. Original, unusual, or eccentric qualities are apt to be present in their thinking. Sexual conflicts, sexual preoccupation, or sex role confusion are likely. These individuals have difficulty expressing their feelings, and are apt to be plagued by self-doubts. Uneven educational and occupational performance are likely.

In a recent study of private psychiatric patients, persons of this profile type were not seen as a homogenous group. The most homogenous finding was that 69% of the patients of this profile type received as a primary or secondary diagnosis substance abuse; adjustment disorder was the second major group, followed by psychotic disorders not elsewhere classified, namely, brief reactive or schizoaffective disorders. Eight percent were seen as evidencing organic affective syndrome. The modal personality disorder cluster of persons of this profile type was dramatic, emotional erratic personality disorders, namely, borderline or histrionic. It appears that, in private psychiatric patients, code 8 is most typical of drug abusers. In other settings, diagnostic possibilities are apt to include: AXIS I: Adjustment Disorder, Schizophrenic Disorder; AXIS II: Schizoid, Schizotypal, and Paranoid Personality.

M9 Persons of this profile type are typically hyperactive, restless, and talkative, and may be agitated. They typically show an insufficient capacity for delay, and are apt to get easily angered when obstacles are placed in their path. They are apt to be impulsive and irritable. These persons are often enterprising and industrious, have a wide range of interests, and may be involved in many activities; however, they are also apt to spin their wheels and manifest intense, but short-lived, enthusiasm for various undertakings. They typically do not see limitations in themselves, and are extremely optimistic. These persons are usually quite sociable and likeable. They may become bored easily, dislike routine, and have a low frustration tolerance. These persons may be excitable and occasionally blantantly manic and agitated, and suffer from delusions of grandeur. Behaviorally, they are apt to be quite hyperactive, may pace, and be distractible and unpredictable. These individuals occasionally evidence a flight of ideas.

In a recent study of private psychiatric patients, substance abuse was also a hallmark of this code type, as 57% of the patients received either primary, secondary, or tertiary diagnosis of substance abuse. The modal diagnosis was affective disorders, followed by a primary differential of substance abuse. The modal personality cluster of persons of this profile type was dramatic emotional, erratic personality disorders, with 72% of persons of this profile type seen as evidencing a histrionic personality. This is discrepant from the classic differential on this high point of hypomanic personality, and may be due to the fact that this data was from a private psychiatric sample, or it may be due to the fact that DSM-III does not include hypomanic personality as a category, but rather places cyclothymic disorders as a primary diagnostic problem under other specific affective disorders.

M0 Persons of this profile type tend to be withdrawn, aloof, and anxious in interpersonal relationships. These individuals are typically quite aware of their social discomfort and are apt to have feelings of personal inferiority. These persons are particularly uncomfortable around members of the opposite sex. They tend to be self-effacing, hard to get to know, and generally lacking in self-confidence. These individuals are usually very sensitive to what others are thinking and doing. They are typically serious, reliable, dependent individuals who tend to be slow in personal tempo. They are typically cautious, conservative, submissive, overcontrolled, and overly accepting of authority. These persons are somewhat rigid and have difficulty making decisions. They usually have good work adjustment and take pleasure from personal achievement. These persons tend to be anxious worriers and to suffer from guilt feelings and depression. They most often present psychotherapeutically with complaints of marital maladjustment. Diagnostically, the majority of patients of this profile type are seen as avoidant personalities.

If no clinical scale (1–0) was a T score of 70 or greater, and the person was 18 years old or older or was under 18 years old and no clinical scale (1–0) was a T score of 60 or greater, use MFN. If the person was under 18 years old and has an elevation of a T score of 60 or greater on the clinical scale (1–0), then don't use MFN but proceed to the Adolescent code section.

MFN (''False Normal'') The person's profile is devoid of significant clinical scale elevations. In outpatient settings, about half the time, such a performance is indicative of individuals who are presenting with either an adjustment disorder and/or marital problems, and who are quite often devoid of a personality disorder.

In psychiatric inpatients, the other extreme of the diagnostic spectrum is apt to be present, in that approximately half of the persons producing this ''false normal'' profile are psychotic and evidencing, most probably, a Major Affective Disorder (Major Depression or Bipolar Disorder) or, to a lesser extent, Schizophrenia.

The remainder of individuals who produce this ''false normal'' profile, in both inpatient and outpatient settings, tend to be in what pre-DSM-III terminology would be classified as chronic mixed neurotics. Such individuals are apt to present with somatoform disorders and psychological factors affecting physical conditions, as well as anxiety disorders or dysthymic disorders. The underlying personality of these persons is apt to be in a category of anxious and fearful personality disorder, namely, Avoidant, Dependent, Compulsive, Passive-Aggressive, though a small minority are seen as evidencing histrionic personalities.

Persons of this profile type are usually defensive about psychological problems and are apt to be naive, rigid, and lacking in insight. Such individuals tend to make heavy use of the defense mechanisms of repression and denial, and are unduly conventional and insecure. Such individuals are quite apt to be resistant to psychotherapeutic intervention because of a fear of revealing themselves. They are usually quite upset and distressed when they cannot present a facade of adequacy, formality, and moral virtue.

ADOLESCENT CODE SECTION

This section assumes that the adolescent norms (without K correction) have been used.

Adolescent 2-point codes: Use the following 2-point code with persons under 18 who attain a T score of 60 or greater on both 2-point codes (which are interchangeable—12 is also 21) and they are the highest 2-point codes (in the case of ties, use the codes in order from left to right). The adolescent codes can be added to the above adult code types when the elevations are at or above a T score of 70, or used alone if none of the codes are at or above a T score of 70.

MJ 12 Adolescents of this profile type are usually shy, oversensitive, and have few friends. They are apt to be despondent and worrisome, have difficulty at school, and occasionally present school phobia.

MJ 13 Adolescents of this profile type are often referred because of attention-seeking behavior and/or somatization. These adolescents are typically insecure, often have school difficulties, and may be seen as somewhat depressed.

MJ 14 Adolescents of this profile type are apt to be defiant, disobedient, and provocative, and are apt to act out in a wide variety of ways. They typically have problems both at home and at school. These adolescents occasionally make impulsive suicide attempts. They may be hyperactive.

MJ 15 Adolescents of this profile type are seen as impulsive and hyperactive, but at the same time are also apt to be somewhat compulsive. They typically have hypochondriacal tendencies and are anxious.

MJ 16 Adolescents of this profile type are typically emotionally insecure and have strong needs for attention. About half the patients of this profile type are emotionally overcontrolled. Family conflict is likely, with aggressive outbursts of family members often in evidence.

MJ 17 Adolescents of this profile type typically are anxious, lacking in self confidence, and apt to complain of headaches and insomnia. They are likely to be socially insecure. This is an infrequent profile type for adolescents.

MJ 18 Adolescents of this profile type are typically anxious, despondent, introverted, self conscious, and socially insecure. They are indecisive and may complain of headaches and insomnia. They are often worried about being teased at school and are also worried about their school performance. These adolescents may have sexual conflicts, use drugs, and engage in suicide attempts.

MJ 19 This is a very infrequent profile type among adolescents. Boys of this profile type are apt to be aggressive and prone to rationalize, while girls of this profile type are apt to be extraverted. Tension, distress, and restlessness may be evidenced by both sexes.

MJ 10 Adolescents of this profile type are apt to be seen as passive, shy, and socially insecure, especially with the opposite sex. They typically lack self confidence, and they may complain of headaches and insomnia. This is an infrequent profile among adolescents.

MJ 23 Adolescents of this profile type are typically lonely individuals who are lacking in self confidence, may feel inferior, and be prone to worry a great deal. They typically have poor relationships with their peers, and few friends. They are often seen as lacking in skills with the opposite sex, have difficulties with self-assertion, and may suffer from insomnia. A wide variety of somatic complains and/or anxiety hysteria are apt to be evidenced.

MJ 24 Adolescents of this profile type are often seen as anxious and have difficulty in concentration. Home conflict is also apt to be in evidence. These patients are apt to act out as a defense, have conflicts over emotional dependency, and occasionally engage in impulsive suicide attempts. Drug abuse and runaway behavior is common among these adolescents.

MJ 25 Adolescents of this profile type are typically seen as lacking in self confidence and are socially insecure and introverted. They typically have poor relationships with their siblings, are apt to evidence sexual conflicts and be worrisome, somewhat obsessional, and quite negative towards self.

MJ 26 Adolescents of this profile type are typically anxious and depressed, are apt to have home conflicts, and are prone to worry a great deal and to suffer from insomnia. They are typically somewhat introverted and lacking in skills with the opposite sex.

MJ 27 Adolescents of this profile type are typically anxious, despondent, worrisome individuals who are self conscious and socially insecure. They typically feel confused and are apt to complain of headaches, insomnia, and exhaustion. They are often introverted and are apt to be passive and unassertive.

MJ 28 Adolescents of this profile type are frequently seen as being emotionally inappropriate. They are apt to be anxious, depressed, distractible, and lacking in self confidence, and to have significant home conflict. They are typically introverted, lack skills with the opposite sex, and have conflicts over sexuality and emotional dependency. Suicide attempts are a distinct possibility. While not the majority, occasionally these adolescents evidence organic deficits. They are apt to have school difficulties. Occasionally, they are seen as psychotic.

MJ 29 This is a very infrequent code among adolescents and is apt to reflect an acute "identity crisis." Narcissistic, ruminative self-absorption is likely. These adolescents are tense, anxious, socially insecure, and restless.

MJ 20 Adolescents of this profile type are typically introverted, self-conscious, socially insecure, lacking in skills with the opposite sex, and may feel physically inferior. They are usually tense, unhappy, and prone to worry. These adolescents typically dislike school and have few friends.

MJ 34 Adolescents of this profile type are typically hostile and aggressive youths who have home conflicts as well as school problems. They are apt to be despondent and insecure, and they occasionally manifest suicidal thoughts. They are quite prone to use drugs, and may have histories of school truancy and runaway behavior.

MJ 35 Adolescents of this profile type are apt to be seen as inhibited, withdrawn, and depressed. They are also apt to be socially insecure, anxious, inhibited worriers who have strong needs for attention. Often, these adolescents have weight problems. They are apt to especially lack skills with the opposite sex.

MJ 36 Adolescents of this profile type typically have home conflict and are apt to engage in impulsive suicide attempts. They may abuse drugs. Typically they deny their difficulties, and are apt to be oversensitive, resentful, and prone to rationalize.

MJ 37 Adolescents of this profile type are anxious, shy individuals who are typically lacking in self confidence and are prone to suffer from headaches and insomnia. This is an infrequent code type for adolescents.

MJ 38 Adolescents of this profile type typically are unhappy worriers who are anxious and apt to complain of headaches, insomnia, and exhaustion. This is an infrequent profile type for adolescents.

MJ 39 Adolescents of this profile type are apt to have family conflicts. Boys of this profile type are apt to be aggressive and prone to rationalize, and girls of this profile type are to to be socially extraverted and marriage-oriented. This is an infrequent profile type for adolescents.

MJ 30 Adolescents of this profile type tend to be shy, insecure, and self conscious. They are especially apt to be ill-at-ease with the opposite sex. They may have family conflicts. This is an infrequent profile type among adolescents.

MJ 45 Adolescents of this profile type are apt to be rebellious, impulsive, and evidence home conflict. They are prone to rationalize and to act out. They are apt to be argumentative and are quite prone to use drugs. They are also apt to have a history of juvenile delinquency and be quite emotionally over-reactive.

MJ 46 Adolescents of this profile type are typically rebellious youth who are apt to be quite resentful of authority. They dislike school and, typically, externalize blame for their difficulties. They are hedonistic, provocative, and apt to have very intense conflicts with their parents. These adolescents are apt to be drug abusers.

MJ 47 Adolescents of this profile type typically act out as a defense, and are apt to be impulsive and irresponsible, but at the same time are basically insecure and may feel quite deprived of affection and attention. Conflicts over emotional dependency and sexuality are likely. They are typically superficially extraverted. They may complain of anxiety and to suffer from insomnia. A history of drug abuse is likely.

MJ 48 Adolescents of this profile type are typically anxious and immature, and are apt to be somewhat narcissistic. They are apt to engage in runaway behavior, to be unsocialized and aggressive, and are quite likely to abuse drugs. They typically have intense family conflicts. They also are quite likely to have problems at school. They typically manifest poor social judgement. They are quite resentful of authority, are apt to be wary of others, oversensitive, and generally miserable.

MJ 49 Adolescents of this profile type typically are defiant, hedonistic, rebellious, impulsive, and prone to engage in a wide variety of acting out behavior. They are superficially good-natured and socially extraverted. They are quite apt to use drugs and typically have histories of school truancy and runaway behavior. Sexual acting out and legal difficulties are also quite likely.

MJ 40 Adolescents of this profile type are typically shy, sensitive, and distrustful of others. They typically are self conscious and are apt to be especially ill-at-ease with the opposite sex. They act out and typically resent authority. They are prone to be skeptical of others, and often manifest paranoid tendencies. They are over-anxious and prone to overreact. They are apt to be disinterested in school and to have only a few friends.

MJ 56 Adolescents of this profile type are typically distractible, anxious, and fearful of emotional involvement. They are also seen as irritable, resentful, and oversensitive. School difficulties and histories of legal problems are likely, as is a tendency for a significant number of these adolescents to evidence violent acting out and drug abuse.

MJ 57 This is a very infrequent profile type among adolescents, and these adolescents are apt to have family conflict, to desire reassurance, and to be anxious and worrisome.

MJ 58 Adolescents of this profile type typically have a high incidence of family conflict and are anxious, worrisome, and insecure. This is a very infrequent profile type among adolescents.

MJ 59 Adolescents of this profile type are typically anxious and prone to use rationalization as their primary defense mechanism. They are typically conflicted over emotional dependency and self assertion. These patients are typically rebellious toward their parents, but do get along well with their peers. Adolescents of this profile type are apt to abuse drugs.

MJ 50 Adolescents of this profile type are typically seen as anxious, awkward, and socially insecure individuals who are shy and have difficulty relating to others, especially the opposite sex. They typically have sexual conflicts and are desirous of attention and affection. They tend to be obsessive, perfectionistic individuals.

MJ 67 This is a very infrequent profile type among adolescents. These youth are typically lacking in self confidence, are socially insecure, and are prone to be anxious worriers. They are apt to be to be oversensitive, may complain of difficulties in concentration, and feel confused.

MJ 68 Adolescents of this profile type are typically introverted, self conscious, socially insecure, and indecisive. They are apt to be withdrawn, feel confused, feel physically inferior, and to be distractible. They occasionally evidence bizarre behavior and violent temper outbursts. They typically have sexual conflicts, are extremely oversensitive, and occasionally are seen as psychotic. They are also quite likely to attempt suicide. Brain damage and learning difficulties are present in a significant minority of these adolescents.

MJ 69 This is a very infrequent profile type among adolescents. These adolescents are apt to be oversensitive, nonresponsive, and to have difficulty with criticism. They may evidence aggressive outbursts occasionally, and they typically over-react to danger. They are apt to be self-conscious, socially insecure, and may feel physically inferior.

MJ 60 Adolescents of this profile are usually shy, insecure, self conscious, and oversensitive. They are especially apt to be ill-at-ease with the opposite sex, and may feel physically inferior. This is an infrequent profile type among adolescents.

MJ 78 Adolescents of this profile type typically are lacking in self confidence, and are prone to evidence anxiety, headaches, and insomnia. They are typically lacking in self confidence, are socially insecure, and are often quite fearful of school failure. They typically have dependency conflicts, are negativistic towards self, and are apt to complain of nightmares. Occasionally these adolescents are seen as psychotic. Suicide attempts are not uncommon in these adolescents.

MJ 79 Adolescents of this profile type are typically anxious, confused, and worrisome. They often have school difficulties and are worried about school failure. They typically have dependency conflicts, and are oversensitive and fearful of loss of control.

MJ 70 Adolescents of this profile type are apt to be shy, oversensitive individuals who are despondent and socially insecure, especially with the opposite sex, and are generally overcontrolled. They are insecure worriers who have dependency conflicts and are apt to be lacking in assertiveness.

MJ 89 Adolescents of this profile type are typically anxious, indecisive, and prone to overreact emotionally. They are apt to be shy, inhibited, and fearful of making mistakes. They occasionally act out, have authority conflicts, and are apt to be somewhat self-defeating. They are also prone to be overdramatic and generally emotionally undercontrolled. Occasionally these adolescents are seen as psychotic, though this may be secondary to drug ingestion. This is a fairly common profile type for adolescents on drugs. It is also quite common for adolescents of this profile type to be in the midst of an acute identity crisis.

MJ 80 This is a very infrequent profile type among adolescents. These youth are apt to be indecisive, shy, and unhappy. They are also prone to be socially insecure, especially with the opposite sex, and are generally described as being self conscious and worrisome.

MJ 90 Adolescents of this profile type tend to be shy, withdrawn and self conscious. This is a very infrequent profile type among adolescents.

Adolescent 1-Point Codes: Use with persons under 18 who have attained a T score of 60 or greater on the following codes, and the code is the only one elevated. Use these statements alone or, if the code is also at a T score of 70 or greater, add it to the above statement for codes at or above a T score of 70.

MJ 1 Adolescents of this profile type tend to be anxious and withdrawn. They are apt to be dependent and verbalize somatic complaints.

MJ 2 Adolescents of this profile type tend to be despondent, insecure, and self conscious. They are apt to be tense, worried, and suffer from insomnia.

MJ 3 Adolescents of this profile type tend to have high levels of denial and somatization. When hospitalized, they tend to require longer periods of treatment.

MJ 4 Adolescents of this profile type are apt to be rebellious, have poor school adjustment and poor school conduct, and are prone to engage in a wide variety of acting out behavior. They are apt to be aggressive, if not belligerent, toward authority. They are apt to abuse drugs and are typically rebellious and impulsive. Conduct Disorders are modal.

MJ 5 Adolescents of this profile type tend to be ill at ease with the opposite sex. Boys tend to be passive, introverted, and self conscious, while girls tend to be more outgoing and distractable.

MJ 6 This is an extremely infrequent code type among adolescents. Sensitivity, avoidance, and anxiety are likely.

MJ 7 Adolescents of this profile type tend to be anxious and withdrawn. Indecisiveness, insecurity, and worry are likely.

MJ 8 Adolescents of this profile type are typically introverted, withdrawn individuals who are prone to engage in a large amount of fantasy and daydreaming. They are apt to have sexual conflicts, and may abuse drugs. They also have a high incidence of school difficulties and dropping out of school.

MJ 9 Adolescents of this profile type tend to be socially extraverted, outgoing, and aggressive. They may occasionally be underachievers and have a moderate potential for acting out and drug abuse.

MJ 0 Adolescents of this profile type tend to be anxious and withdrawn. A lack of skill with the opposite sex, and social insecurity, are the norm.

SPECIAL SCALE SECTION

Use the following in addition to the above sections:

MA T score of 70 or greater or the A scale (raw score of 32 or greater for females; raw score of 28 or greater for males).

The person has a significant elevation on the Anxiety (A) supplemental scale. Such individuals are apt to be consciously anxious, especially in social situations. A lack of self assurance and trust in oneself is likely. The person is apt to be pessimistic about the future, but because of emotional discomfort is motivated for treatment.

MR T score of 70 or greater on the R scale (raw score of 27 or greater for females; raw score of 25 or greater for males).

The person has a significant elevation on the Repression (R) Supplemental Scale. Such individuals are apt to make heavy use of the defense mechanisms of repression and denial. These individuals often lack in sight into their own behavior, and often are resistant to discussing problems in therapy.

MES T2 score of 70 or greater on the Es Scale (raw score of 53 or more for females; raw score of 57 or more for males).

The person has a significant elevation on the Ego Strength (Es) supplemental scale. While the research on this scale is somewhat contradictory, the person is apt to possess more psychological resources than the average individual seeking therapeutic assistance. Such individuals are apt to be able to profit from psychotherapy, providing they are self referred. These individuals are capable of forming mature relationships with others.

MEL T score of 40 or less or the Es scale (raw score of 33 or less for females; raw score of 38 or less for males).

The person has a significant low score on th Ego Strength (Es) supplemental scale. While the research on this scale is somewhat contradictory, the person is apt to be lacking in psychological resources and less able to profit from traditional psychotherapeutic modalities. The person is apt to be negative toward self and lacking in the ability to stand up to significant stress and problems. A treatment approach that is concrete, behaviorally oriented, and pragmatic may be helpful.

MAC T score of 70 or greater on the MacAndrew scale (MAC) (raw score of 27 or more for females; raw score of 29 or more for males).

The person has a significant elevation on the MacAndrew (MAC) supplemental scale, indicating a high potential for substance abuse. Roughly, 80% of persons with an elevation on this scale are alcohol abusers or alcohol dependent, and about two thirds of all drug abusers also have elevation on this scale. A history of drug abuse is more likely if scale 8 and/or 9 are among the highest three codes of the person's code type.

CHAPTER THIRTEEN

Interpretative Statements for the Diagnostic Inventory of Personality and Symptoms (DIPS)[1]

The Diagnostic Inventory of Personality and Symptoms (DIPS) is a brief test of psychopathology built from those items which were most predictive of abnormality from the Psychological Inventory of Personality and Symptoms. The purpose was to devise a test of psychopathology that was comprehensive but, like the Millon Multiaxal Clinical Inventory (Millon, 1977), was brief in the number of items and quickly administered. Brevity is especially useful when the test must be read to patients. The Diagnostic Inventory of Personality and Symptoms has approximately half as many items as the Psychological Inventory of Personality and Symptoms (171 compared to 345), and consequently should be able to be taken in about half the time, about 15 minutes.

METHODOLOGY

The subjects for developing the Diagnostic Inventory of Personality and Symptoms were the same normal population sample as the Psychological Inventory of Personality and Symptoms (N = 140) and the comparison samples of abnormality were the 50 private patient sample used on the PIPS as well as a 40 V.A. patient sample which were also used in at least one study of the PIPS. Several scales on the DIPS are identical to that of the PIPS in that the entire number of items was retained. The validity scale was retained intact as was the Alcohol Abuse Scale (AA), the Drug Abuse Scale (DA), and the Stress-Adjustment Disorder Scale (SA). SA was left intact because, while some of the items in the scale are of low frequency of endorsement, such as death of a spouse, they are of paramount importance in assessing stressful life events in patients' lives. All clinical scales

[1] This Chapter is based on the Diagnostic Inventory of Personality and Symptoms (DIPS), the Revised Manual for the Diagnostic Inventory of Personality and Symptoms (DIPS) and the Interpretative Program for the Diagnostic Inventory of Personality and Symptoms (DIPS) all copyright 1985 by Dr. Ken R. Vincent.

with the exception of Affective Depressed (AD) and Anxiety Disorders (AX) were reduced to the 12 most predictive items which best discriminated the general sample from the two clinical samples. In this process, both clinical samples were used and the normal patient sample was compared to both clinical samples, with the lowest differential between both comparisons of the normal versus each clinical sample being used in the decision process. The Alcohol Abuse and Drug Abuse scales were left intact, as they initially had only 12 items. The Anxiety Disorder (AX) and Affective Depressed (AD) scales were reduced to 20 rather than 12 items because of their prevalence as psychiatric disease entities (Dohranwend et al., 1980).

The Axis II disorders were collapsed into the three major categories of DSM-III but were given briefer names. The first cluster from DSM-III is the odd or eccentric category, which includes paranoid, schizoid, and schizotypal personality. This corresponds to the Withdrawn Character (WC) scale of the DIPS. The second DSM-III cluster is called dramatic, emotional, and erratic personality disorders and includes histrionic, narcissistic, antisocial, and borderline personality disorders. This corresponds to the Immature Character scale (IC) of the DIPS. The third DSM-III cluster is the anxious or fearful personality disorder cluster, and includes avoidant, dependent, compulsive, and passive-aggressive disorders and corresponds to the Neurotic Character scale (NC) of the DIPS.

The Withdrawn Character (WC) scale, Immature Character (IC), and the Neurotic Character (NC) scale were developed from the overlap from both within and between their respective clusters of the PIPS which differentiated at 20% or greater between the general sample and either the public or private sample. An additional requirement was added, with the Immature Character scale, that all overlapping items also must have been on the Antisocial scale. Collapsing the 11 personality disorder scales into three clusters was done partially for brevity, but there is a theoretical reason for restructuring the test. This not only makes it easier to deal with but, considering the present state of our knowledge, personality disorders are less well defined then Axis I disorders.

When only one of the Axis II disorder scales on the DIPS is elevated, namely, Withdrawn Character, Immature Character, or Neurotic Character, diagnosis can be made within that cluster of character disorders. When two of the personality disorder scales are elevated above 70, differential prediction is based on what might be called "personality bridges" within the DSM-III personality disorder section. When Withdrawn Character and Immature Character are elevated, the diagnostic likelihood is that the individual will be a Borderline Personality Disorder. This draws support from the literature, which shows that borderline individuals are apt to be a combination of the emotional lability of a hysteric coupled with the fear of people of the schizoid individual. In MMPI literature, this would be the 48 profile. Other variants of the borderline syndrome occur when all three of the personality disorder character scales (Withdrawn, Immature, and Neurotic) are elevated. Research on the response sets of borderline personality disorders and on identifiable patterns of the MMPI such as 248 and 487 (Vincent et al., 1984) supports this condition. When the Withdrawn Character is elevated above 70 and the Neurotic Character is also elevated, another "personality bridge" is likely. Avoidant Personality which combines the sensitivity of mild paranoids and people avoidance similar to schizoid individuals with the anxiety of the classic neurotic characters such as the compulsive illustrates this "bridge." An example of this from MMPI literature would be the 7-8 pattern. When the Immature Character and the Neurotic Character are both elevated, the likelihood is the individual is Passive-Aggressive. The Passive-Aggressive personality disorder combines episodic acting out, if only through subterfuge, with anxiety and worry. Classic patterns on the MMPI which are synonomous with the passive-aggressive personalities are the 2-4, the 4-7, and the 2-4-7 (Vincent et al., 1984).

SUBSTANTIVE DATA FOR THE VALIDITY SCALE

Because it shares the identical items on the validity scale, the following research on the PIPS validity scale is completely applicable to the DIPS (Vincent, in press).

In order to access the utility of the validity scale, a comparison of the overall frequency of responses of individuals was made in both the private patient sample and the V.A. sample. The purpose was to assess the validity of the validity scale. In order to do this, it was assumed that individuals who responded randomly would have a higher rate of response than those who did not respond randomly or carelessly. In this sample, 57 private patients were used, 43 from Houston International Hospital and 14 from Memorial Hospital in Houston, Texas, and 60 Veteran's Administration Hospital patients were used. Those who marked zero or 1 item (which were all but two of the sample) endorsed the item, number 258. This may be confusing to some, because it is stated negatively, namely: "I have never seen a mailman." The two patients who marked yes to items other than 258 had a mean frequency of response of 216 items; those at the V.A. who marked yes to item number 258 as their one critical item on the validity scale had a mean response rate of 210 items. Both of these were quite close to the overall average response rate of the V.A. patients, which was 179 responses per record. Of those marking "yes" to three or four items on the Validity Scale, the mean response rate for the V.A. patients was 257 items per record. Comparing those who endorsed zero or one item marked "yes" on the validity scale with those who endorsed "no" items on the validity scale, no significant difference was found, X^2 (1, N=60) = 3.9, $P< .05$. The difference between those marking "yes" to zero or one item and those marking "yes" to three or four items on the validity scale was quite significant in the V.A. sample, X^2 (1,N=60) = 13.95, $P< .01$. The same general response was found in the private sample. Mean number of responses marking one item "yes" on the validity scale, all of which were on the confusing item number 258, was 156, with the mean average number of "yes" responses for the private patient sample being 153. There was no significant difference between the two, X^2 (1, N=57) = .003, $P > .05$. The difference between this and individuals marking "yes" to three or four items on the validity scale was 320 items. This was quite significant, X^2 (1, N=57) = 58.8, $P < .01$. It remains to be seen whether individuals who endorse two items or more are suspect or just invalid. None of the two samples endorsed two items on the validity scale. At the present time, it may be best to count individuals endorsing two items on the validity scale as invalid, or at least to interpret the profile with great caution.

CRITERION RELATED VALIDITY

Figures 1 and 2 show that the DIPS scales are viable and differentiate normality from abnormality. The Figures 1 and 2 profiles of the DIPS compare the means of normal subjects (a T-score of 50 on the profile sheet) with the mean profiles for private patients (Figure 1) and Veteran's Administration patients (Figure 2). The private sample consisted of 50 individuals, 36 from Houston International Hospital and 14 from Memorial Hospital, and had a mean age of 37.3 years. The V.A. patient sample consisted of 40 individuals from the Veteran's Administration Hospital, with a mean age of 43.9 years.

The average number of responses from the normal sample from the DIPS was 25, the average number of responses from the private patient sample was 64, and the average number of responses from the V.A. population sample was 74. Comparing the private sample with the normal sample resulted in a highly significant difference between the two means, X^2 (1, N=50) = 16.9, $P < .001$. However, comparing the two abnormal samples (private and V.A.) resulted in nonsignificant findings between them, X^2 (1, N=50/40) = 0.72, $P > .05$).

The mean profiles for the two abnormal samples (private and V.A.) of the DIPS were elevated to approximately one standard deviation higher than the same samples on the PIPS. This is most likely due to the fact that the more predictive items are used in the DIPS as opposed to the PIPS.

CONTENT VALIDITY

The content validity of the DIPS is based on the fact that it is derived from the Psychological Inventory of Personality and Symptoms, which was made from the descriptions and criterion sections for the various syndromes of the DSM-III (American Psychiatric Association, 1980).

Figure 1. DIPS (Diagnostic Inventory of Personality and Symptoms)

PROFILE SHEET

Name or ID# PRIVATE PATIENT SAMPLE Marital Status ______

Age 37.3 Sex M29/F21 Date ______ Examiner ______

Validity Score [0.3] Fake Good Score [64]

			Raw Score	50		60		70		80		90	
1.	(AA)	Alcohol Abuse	3	1	2			4	5	6		7	(AA)
2.	(DA)	Drug Abuse	3	2		4	.	6	.	8	.	10	(DA)
3.	(SP)	Schizophrenic Psychosis	3	1		2				4		5	(SP)
4.	(PP)	Paranoid Psychosis	3	1		2				4		5	(PP)
5.	(AD)	Affective Depressed	9	3	. .	. .	.	8	.	. .	.	13	(AD)
6.	(AE)	Affective Excited	3	1	2			4	5	6		7	(AE)
7.	(AX)	Anxiety Disorders	9	3	. .	6	. .	.	. .	12	. .	15	(AX)
8.	(SO)	Somatoform Disorders	4	2		3				5		6	(SO)
9.	(DD)	Dissociative Disorders	3	1		2				4		5	(DD)
10.	(SA)	Stress-Adjustment Disorders	3	1		2				4		5	(SA)
11.	(PC)	Psychological Factors Affecting Physical Condition	3	1		2				4		5	(PC)

			Raw Score	50		60		70		80		90	
12.	(WC)	Withdrawn Character	5	2	.	.			.	.	.	8	(WC)
13.	(IC)	Immature Character	5	2	.	4		6	.	8	.	10	(IC)
14.	(NC)	Neurotic Character	8	4	. .	7		10	. .	13	. .	16	(NC)

SCORING SHEET

AA [ ] DA [ ] SP [ ] PP [ ]

AD [ ] AE [ ] AX [ ] SO [ ]

DD [ ] SA [ ] PC [ ] VS [ ]

WC [ ] IC [ ] NC [ ]

300a

Figure 2. DIPS (Diagnostic Inventory of Personality and Symptoms)

PROFILE SHEET

Name or ID# VA PATIENT SAMPLE Marital Status ______

Age 43.9 Sex M37/F3 Date ______ Examiner ______

Validity Score [0.6] Fake Good Score [74]

	Raw Score	50		60		70		80		90	
1. (AA) Alcohol Abuse	3	1	2			4	5		6	7	(AA)
2. (DA) Drug Abuse	3	2		4	.	6	.	8	.	10	(DA)
3. (SP) Schizophrenic Psychosis	4	1		2		3				5	(SP)
4. (PP) Paranoid Psychosis	4	1		2		3				5	(PP)
5. (AD) Affective Depressed	10	3	. . . . .			8	. . . .			13	(AD)
6. (AE) Affective Excited	4	1	2		3		5		6	7	(AE)
7. (AX) Anxiety Disorders	9	3	. .	6	. .	. .		12	. .	15	(AX)
8. (SO) Somatoform Disorders	5	2		3		4				6	(SO)
9. (DD) Dissociative Disorders	4	1		2		3				5	(DD)
10. (SA) Stress-Adjustment Disorders	4	1		2		3				5	(SA)
11. (PC) Psychological Factors Affecting Physical Condition	3	1		2				4		5	(PC)

	Raw Score	50		60		70		80		90	
12. (WC) Withdrawn Character	5	2	.	.	.		.	.	.	8	(WC)
13. (IC) Immature Character	7	2	.	4	.	6		8	.	10	(IC)
14. (NC) Neurotic Character	9	4	. .	7	.	10	. .	13	. .	16	(NC)

SCORING SHEET

AA [ ] DA [ ] SP [ ] PP [ ]

AD [ ] AE [ ] AX [ ] SO [ ]

DD [ ] SA [ ] PC [ ] VS [ ]

WC [ ] IC [ ] NC [ ]

PACIFIC PSYCHOLOGICAL

300b

Table 1. DIPS Intercorrelation Matrix

	AA	DA	SP	PP	AD	AE	AX	SO	DD	SA	PC	WC	IC	NC
AA	1	.58	.26	.16	.12	.41	.26	.22	.38	.32	.23	.31	.71	.16
DA		1	.29	.29	.02	.51	.19	.27	.39	.18	.21	.32	.78	.06
SP			1	.78	.32	.50	.41	.35	.78	.40	.39	.72	.21	.33
PP				1	.46	.47	.52	.43	.72	.38	.33	.73	.26	.44
AD					1	.31	.80	.41	.52	.37	.44	.44	.14	.90
AE						1	.44	.19	.52	.29	.37	.55	.48	.33
AX							1	.48	.60	.33	.51	.48	.21	.77
SO								1	.40	.31	.48	.43	.12	.24
DD									1	.41	.49	.71	.45	.53
SA										1	.50	.31	.36	.41
PC											1	.51	.20	.47
WC												1	.26	.46
IC													1	.23
NC														1

CONSTRUCT VALIDITY

A factor analytic study was conducted on the DIPS using the hospitalized psychiatric patients from private hospitals. Principal components factor analysis with the varimax rotation yielded three well-defined factors accounting for 70% of the total variance. These factors could be conceptualized as Neurotic, Psychotic, and Characterological. Factor one accounted for 46% of the common variance, and showed its highest positive loadings on the scales of: Affective Depressed (AD), Anxiety Disorder (AX), and Neurotic Character (NC). Factor two, which accounted for 15% of the common variance, showed its highest positive loadings to be on the scales of: Alcohol Abuse (AA), Drug Abuse (DA), and Immature Character (IC). Factor three, which accounted for 9% of the common variance, showed its highest positive loadings to be on the scales of: Schizophrenic Psychosis (SP), Paranoid Psychosis (PP), Dissociative Disorders (DD), and Withdrawn Character (WC) (Vincent & Duthie, in press).

Table 1 presents the Intercorrelation Matrix used in the Factor Study.

Further Validation with Specific Scale—The Alcohol Abuse Scale

Vincent and Williams (1985) investigated the clinical validity of the Alcohol Abuse Scale of the DIPS, using the PIPS (the instrument from which the DIPS was developed) on two separate populations. These two populations were from a private psychiatric hospital setting (patients from Houston International Hospital and Memorial Hospital in Houston, Texas), and from a public hospital setting (Patients from the Veteran's Administration Hospital (V.A.) in Houston, Texas). Using a cut-off T-score of 70 on the Alcohol Abuse Scale, 82% of the private patient sample was correctly identified and 84% of the public hospital patient sample was correctly identified (Vincent and Williams, in press). Setting the cut-

Table 2. DIPS Test/Retest Reliability Correlations and Standard Error of Measurement (In T Score Points)

Scale	Reliability	SE_M
AA	.90	3.2
DA	.91	3.0
SP	.64	6.0
PP	.70	5.5
AD	.88	3.5
AE	.58	6.5
AX	.76	4.9
SO	.80	4.5
DD	.50	7.1
SA	.80	4.5
PC	.82	4.2
WC	.74	5.1
IC	.88	3.5
NC	.86	3.7

off point at 65 and at 75 did not result in improving the hit rate and did result in slightly lower ratings (Vincent & Williams, 1985). This 82% correct classification for the private sample, and 84% correct classification for the public sample, for the Alcohol Abuse Scale compares favorably with previous studies done on the MacAndrews Scale of the MMPI (Butcher & Owen, 1978). Butcher and Owen (1978) cite 10 studies on the overall accuracy of the MacAndrews Scale, with correct classification of alcoholics vs. nonalcoholics ranging from 62% to 82%, with a mean overall accuracy rate of 78%.

Reliability

Table 2 presents Test/Retest Correlations for the clinical scales of the DIPS. The interval between test and retest was 1 week. These were based on a sample of 40 adult students in a small private university, and are extracted from the PIPS data from an article on the reliability of that instrument (McMurrey & Vincent, 1985). The overall reliability of the DIPS was .78. Also provided in Table 2 is the standard error of measurement for the DIPS clinical scales.

RATIONALE FOR INTERPRETATION AND COMPUTER PROGRAM DOCUMENTATION

The DIPS interpretation relies on previous research relating to response sets, exaggerated profiles, and false normal profiles in the interpretation of said scores. Most of the work previously done relating to response and psychopathology has been with the MMPI and, to a lesser extent, instruments such as the SCL-90 and MCMI (Vincent et al., 1983; Millon, 1977).

When a patient omits over 20 statements, the profile is considered highly suspect. The printout has a statement about possible reasons for omissions, based on previous work on other psychological instruments. The report states that the patient is apt to be quite guarded and possibly paranoid or obsessive to the point of inability to make a decision, or, possibly, is uncooperative and passive-aggressive. Because of the nature of the construction of the DIPS, the profile is still printed, as some problem areas may still be brought to light; however, a note of caution as to possible distortion is added.

The Validity scale of the DIPS is built solely to assess whether the individual can and/or has read the instrument. Answering 0 or 1 item on the validity scale is a valid profile. A score of 2 to 4 on the validity scale is interpreted as invalid. Here the program only prints out a paragraph stating that the profile is invalid, and the possible reasons for this. These reasons are based on previous research on this type of response set, which is usually characteristic of an Immature Personality Disorder, most likely a Borderline or severe Histrionic Personality who is in the midst of acute reactive emotional distress, or the individual is apt to be psychotic. The program notes that, in public settings, the individual is more apt to be psychotic, while, in private settings, the diagnosis of Immature Character, Situational Stress, and possible Substance Abuse is more likely.

The false normal profile which gets its name from the fact that the individual has come or has been presented to a mental health facility for help, but nevertheless produces a normal profile, is based on previous psychological research on this response style. The subsequent narrative notes that, in psychiatric inpatient settings, half of these patients are seen as psychotic, whereas, in out-patient settings, usually half are presenting with adjustment and/or marital problems and are usually devoid of a personality disorder. The other half of the individuals producing the false-normal profile of both inpatient and outpatient settings tend to be individuals who would previously have been classified as chronic mixed neurotics who are often suffering from, among other things, somatization.

The DIPS includes a "fake good" scale which serves to flag people who present as too-good-to-be-true, as they scored one standard deviation below the normal mean (five or less). This is interpreted as an individual who is extremely defensive and unable to admit to problems and symptoms. If the DIPS is used in screening normals, this can serve to flag individuals who may be under-reporting problems. The fake good scale has a test/retest reliability score of .92.

The AXIS I descriptive statements of the DIPS Computer Version has a brief descriptive statement for each scale above the T score of 70. All scales, with the exception of alcohol and drug abuse, which are assumed to be very pathological at a T score of 70 (this is based on Vincent & Williams, 1985), have an additional stronger statement when the respective scale is a T score of 90 or greater. T scores in excess of 90 are not reported. A further differential beyond four standard deviations beyond a normal mean is, for all practical purposes, meaningless. Elevations among scales in excess of 90 should be ranked for developing code types in the order of frequency of base rate psychiatric data. (See below, in the AXIS I Differential Diagnostic Section, for a further explanation.) The second portion of the narrative for AXIS I disorders in excess of a T score of 70 introduces a system that has not yet been possible without computer interpretation, and makes the DIPS interpretation unique. Briefly, each individual item is considered, and statements relating to that item, or clusters of items relating to the same thing, all have a narrative statment printed out for them. For example, if a person answers "yes" to item number 5, "I can't think," and/or item 40, "I have trouble thinking," the narrative statement "Difficulty in concentration is reported" is printed. As there is always a chance that carelessness or lack of concentration, or simply a clerical error, has occurred, and that the person may have answered an individual question in error, caution is needed in giving undue weight to any one sentence in the narrative. Because the DIPS AXIS I Disorder Narrative prints out a report on those items answered by the patient in those scales above a T score of 70, which are unique to him or her, each DIPS report will be unique to the individual being tested and also will vary as a function of his or her reported pathology rather than merely as a function of what is known about a disorder in general or a code type. A T score of 70 is used as the cut off. Hospitalized psychiatric patients, as a group, tend to score about two standard deviations above the normal mean (T score 70) (Vincent, 1985d).

RATIONALE FOR AXIS I: DIFFERENTIAL DIAGNOSTIC SECTION

The second innovative and unique feature of the DIPS Computer Interpretation is one that can be used by clinicians without the computer version. It is the method of determining differential diagnosis. This portion was based on analysis of the tests of a sample of 60 psychiatric inpatients from private hospital settings, who were also the sample for the factor analytic study. This was done to establish the rules and test their validity. It should be noted that the DIPS is a new test, and thus has not been cross-validated. Therefore, it is more apt to be tentative with regard to individuals who are in public hospital settings.

RULE: If six of the AXIS I scales are in excess of T score 90, the following diagnostic statement is used, which is based on what has been previously known about so-called "floating profiles."

The person's clinical profile is quite elevated. Individuals producing this profile type most often fit into one of two categories.

Persons with this profile are often seen as borderline personality disorders who are evidencing either an extreme adjustment disorder or a brief reactive psychosis. Substance abuse is frequently part of the clinical picture.

The alternative picture is one of an individual presenting with an acute psychotic episode, which is most frequently Schizophrenia; however, Bipolar Disorders also evidence this profile type. In outpatient and private settings, the individual is more likely to be a borderline personality in acute distress. In public inpatient settings, acute psychosis is more likely.

RULE: For the remainder, always list, in the AXIS I Differential Diagnostic Section, the scales in descending order, based on the following base rate frequency list, and use the corresponding DSM-III Diagnostic category, which is for the Axis I Differential Diagnostic Section.

Frequency Order	DIPS Scale	DSM-III Diagnostic Category
1	AD	Affective Disorder: Depression
2	SA	Adjustment Disorder
3	AA	Substance Abuse Disorder: Alcohol
4	SP	Schizophrenic Disorder
5	DA	Substance Abuse Disorder: Drugs
6	AX	Anxiety Disorder
7	AE	Affective Disorder: Bipolar
8	SO	Somatoform Disorder
9	PC	Psychological Factors Affecting Physical Condition
10	PP	Paranoid Disorder
11	DD	Dissociative Disorder

NOTE: On adolescents, the frequency order is reversed for 1 and 2, so that 1 is Adjustment Disorder and 2 is Affective Disorder: Depression.

If five or less scales of Axis I are at a T score of 90 or less, use the highest four scales 70 T or greater in the Axis I Differential Diagnostic Section based on their frequency order listed above. Ask if the person is an outpatient or private hospital inpatient or state mental or VA hospital inpatient. If they are *not* a state mental or VA hospital inpatient, or if this information is unknown, then add the following rule: if SP, PP, AE and/or DD are among the highest scales, always include SA as if it were one of the highest (at a T score of 90); and, for *everyone tested,* if SO or AX are among the highest, include AD as if it were one of the highest (at a T score of 90).

For *example,* if a person who was an outpatient or private hospital inpatient had a profile that included: AA at 76 T, SP at 90 T, SO at 90 T, this would result in the following hierarchy for the Axis I: Differential Diagnostic Section.

1. Affective Disorder: Depressed
2. Adjustment Disorder

3. Substance Abuse Disorder: Alcohol
4. Schizophrenic Disorder
5. Somatoform Disorder

Note: The fifth category would not be printed out; only the first four are listed.

The rationale for the diagnostic classification system is that, if the diagnostician knew nothing about the person who had taken the DIPS except that he or she was seeking therapeutic help, probabilities derived from the base rate would be the most likely differential diagnosis. The person's reporting of his or her symptoms (in this case via the DIPS) changes the picture. While the construction of code types is one way to deal with the simultaneous elevation of several scales (symptom clusters), the DIPS formula of assigning probable diagnostic priority of elevated scores via base rates is another.

The base rate frequency list is a meta-analysis that was built by averaging the four DSM-III studies listed in Tables 1 and 2 of Appendix F of the DSM-III, the data listed in the MMCI Manual (Millon, 1977), the data on MMPI Code Types (Vincent et al., 1983), and a survey of the Mid-Columbia Mental Health Center's 1984 cases. Using the averaging method, in which the highest and lowest cases were thrown out and the remainder averaged, the result is the frequency order listed above. The validity of this data was checked against the sample used in the above mentioned factor study of the DIPS, and the result was a 44% hit rate for the first diagnosis listed in the differential diagnostic section and a 95% hit rate for one of the four differential diagnoses. This would correspond to a correlation coefficient of .66 with the discharge diagnosis, and is roughly equivalent to the kappa coefficients of interrater agreement on AXIS I diagnosis from the DSM-III which range from .52 to .72 (see Appendix F, DSM-III).

INTERPRETATION RATIONALE FOR THE AXIS II DISORDERS SECTION

In this section, narratives are provided for elevations of the three AXIS II scales for one elevation and all combinations of elevations.

When there is no elevation on any of the three scales in AXIS II, and Stress Adjustment is the only scale elevation in AXIS I, the person is considered to be devoid of a personality disorder or features of a personality disorder. When there are no elevations in the AXIS II section, but there are AXIS I elevations above the T score of 70 on scales other than the Stress Adjustment scale, notations are made to possible personality features that may coexist with those elevations. For example, passive-aggressive features are apt to be present when the AA scale is elevated. Features common to the Immature Character cluster are apt to be present if the AA or the DA scale is elevated. The traits associated with the

Withdrawn Character cluster may be present if the SP, PP, and/or DD scale is elevated. Aspects associated with the Neurotic Character are noted if the AD or AX scale is elevated. Histrionic Personality Features may be present if there is an elevation on the AE scale. Dependent Personality Features are suggested if there is an elevation on the SO or PC scale. The rationale for all of these is the author's synthesis of what is known from the literature on psychopathology.

INTERPRETATION RATIONALE ON THE AXIS II STATEMENTS FOR ADOLESCENTS

The DIPS interpretation for adolescents converts the personality disorder section into the corresponding disorders as per the conversion table for childhood or adolescence in the personality disorder section and the section on disorders usually first evidenced during infancy, childhood, or adolescence of the DSM-III.

RATIONALE FOR THE PSYCHOTHERAPY RECOMMENDATION SECTION

This section is based on the author's synthesis of general approaches to treatment that are viable with corresponding types of presenting problems. These are obviously not meant to be substitutes for the therapist's judgement.

FURTHER NOTES AND GUIDELINES FOR DIPS INTERPRETATION

The DIPS is sold only to qualified professionals. DIPS users should have a doctorate or master's degree in behavior science or its substantial equivalent that includes, at minimum, a course on test and measurement and a course in abnormal psychology-psychopathology.

The DIPS is a new test, and research is still in progress regarding its application to various groups. Research has been done in both public and private settings, and cross-validation has been carried out regarding the DIPS's ability to differentiate normals from abnormals and alcoholics from other psychiatric patients in both public and private settings. At this point in time, the DIPS interpretive manual verification has been done solely on private patients. Consequently, users in public settings need to bear this in mind when reviewing the priorities assigned in the differential diagnostic section. All differential diagnostic possibilities should be considered. In general, the skills which the clinician has developed from interpreting other tests, such as the MMPI and MMCI, should transfer easily to analyzing the total profile. Users will note that the DIPS does not have separate norms for males and females. This is intentional. The rational for unisex norms is that the DIPS is a criterion-referenced test based on the descriptions and criterion of the DSM-III. To adjust reporting rates of these disorders would be adding an element of distortion to them. Men and women have different frequencies for various disorders as noted in the DSM-III. Some of the most widely known of these differential frequencies are the fact that women tend to have a higher rate of depression and that men tend to have a higher rate of alcoholism. Separate norms would add distortion to the test and lower the hit rate for individuals presenting with these disorders or other disorders more common to his or her sex. In a recent study on male and female alcoholics, no significant differences were found on the DIPS AA scale hit rate for men and women (Vincent & Williams, 1985b).

When using the DIPS with adolescents, it should be noted that the AXIS II personality disorder clusters and the base rate frequency order have been modified for adolescents. Though a normative study has not been conducted on adolescents, a recent study of 45 high school students found the mean scores to be the same for adolescents as for adults on all but four scales, and on each of those scales the difference was only one raw score point (Duthie, personal communication, 1985). The DA score for adolescents was one raw score point less than for the adults and for SP, AE and AX the adolescent scores were one raw score point higher (Duthie, personal communication, 1985). Additional norming needs to be done.

A final caution should be noted in that the research on the DIPS has been done largely via the paper and pencil version, and the comparability of the Computer Version has not been assessed; however, research is under way in this area. One should note that there is little reason to suspect that the two forms should not be comparable based on the myriad of research presented by Hedlund et al. (1981). In this monumental review of articles related to computers in mental health, the research to date shows that, unless complex graphics are used (which are hard to transpose to the computer medium), the difference between the two forms of presentation is nil. Study after study of yes/no, true/false, and multiple choice tests have shown no significant difference between the two media.

Administration and Scoring of the Diagnostic Inventory of Personality and Symptoms (DIPS)

The DIPS is a straightforward instrument with instructions printed on the form. The instructions state: "Please blacken the appropriate box for each statement as it best applies to you." Additional instructions, when asked for, should be along the lines of telling the patient to go with their initial feelings and mark the answer which is mostly true. The Test Administrator may state, "This test is written in everyday language, although there are some medical diagnostic statements which you may not know, such as 'angina pectoris'.'' A good rule is that ''if you don't know what it is, you don't have it,'' or ''you only have it if your doctor told you that you have it.'' It is also permissible to rephrase the question and explain it, provided the decision of whether to mark it ''yes'' or ''no'' is not made for the person.

On scoring, only questions marked ''yes'' are scored. Score all blanks ''no,'' and there can be up to 20 omissions before the profile is considered invalid. Score all items marked both yes and no as ''yes.''

To score the profile, place the scoring stick (key) flush against the test questionnaire so that the test questions are next to the corresponding items on the scoring stick (key). Go down the items, making tally marks in the scoring boxes which are at the bottom of the profile sheet of the DIPS. Make hash marks for each of the special scale categories, and then sum them into arabic numerals and post the scores in the raw score blanks of the profile sheet. It is good to double check all of this work.

Next, the profile graph is to be plotted. When a person makes a score below the mean T score, it is to be plotted on the mean T-score category. For instance, if a subject earns a 1 point on drug abuse and the mean is 2 points, plot the graph on the mean of 2 anyway. Also, if the subject earns a score greater than the normal number of points beyond the T-score of 90, plot this at the T-score of 90 range rather than off the paper. For example, if the subject earns 12 points on the drug abuse scale, the highest factor listed is 10. Ten is where the graph should be plotted, rather than off the page. Draw lines connecting the points on the graph. It should be noted that two standard deviations above the mean or a T-score of 70 is considered significant. The graph is not carried out further than 4 standard deviations, because meaning is lost as the graph approaches infinity. Conversely, research on such instruments as the MMPI have shown that, in assessing psychopathology, scores that are below the mean are of little value. Consequently, the scores below the mean were not made part of the profile graph, as the DIPS is designed as a test of psychopathology and not as a general personality test.

DIAGNOSTIC INVENTORY OF PERSONALITY AND SYMPTOMS (DIPS): *ITEM COMPOSITION OF THE SCALES*

Validity Scale (VS) N = 4

DIPS No.	PIPS Item No.	Test Item
36.	74.	I am a potato.
72.	143.	I have a pet gorilla.
108.	208.	I go to the North Pole a lot.
140.	258.	I have never seen a mailman.

Alcohol Abuse (AA) N = 12

Scale Overlap	DIPS No.	PIPS Item No.	Test Item
	11.	27.	I lost my job because of drinking.
	25.	71.	I have ten drinks of alcohol a day.
	39.	112.	I have been drunk on the job.
IC	52.	117.	I have had a DWI.
	67.	119.	I have six hangovers a year.
	82.	178.	My drinking causes family problems.
	96.	199.	I have had the D.T.s
	111.	218.	I am a binge drinker.
IC	125.	270.	I like to get drunk.
	141.	284.	I have had blackouts.
IC	157.	297.	I like to drink a lot.
	165.	332.	I have been in jail for being drunk.

Drug Abuse (DA) N = 12

Scale Overlap	DIPS No.	PIPS Item No.	Test Item
	18.	23.	I have been high on the job.
	31.	53.	I have been arrested for drugs.
	45.	62.	I like to get high.
IC	59.	89.	I have sold drugs.
	75.	111.	My drug use has caused family problems.
IC	78.	118.	I have been in trouble for drugs.
	89.	174.	I feel bad for taking drugs.
	103.	183.	Some drug use is O.K.
	118.	221.	If you're healthy you can use drugs.
IC	132.	242.	I take drugs for fun.
	148.	268.	I need drugs.
	161.	281.	My drug use has cost me friends.

Schizophrenic Psychosis (SP) N = 12

Scale Overlap	DIPS No.	PIPS Item No.	Test Item
WC	16.	57.	I have a "sixth" sense.
	29.	114.	I hear voices.
WC	43.	220.	I do not feel close to others.
	57.	241.	I am really dead.
WC	64.	272.	Others can feel my feelings.
DD	73.	283.	My identity has changed.
PP	101.	298.	I am being controlled.
	116.	300.	My thinking is not the same.
DD	105.	305.	I have another identity.
	130.	306.	I am aware of outside forces and powers.
	146.	320.	My thinking controls others.

Paranoid Psychosis (PP) N = 12

Scale Overlap	DIPS No.	PIPS Item No.	Test Item
	13.	5.	I am being followed.
WC,NC	23.	16.	I feel isolated.
	27.	50.	I am being watched.
	41.	150.	I am being observed.
WC	54.	184.	I cannot trust many people.
	69.	196.	I am being harassed.
	84.	230.	I feel my house is bugged.
WC	93.	316.	I am being talked about.
	98.	254.	I feel paranoid.
SP	101.	298.	I am being controlled.
	113.	318.	Others blame me for their problems.
	127.	334.	I have been drugged.

Affective Depressed (AD) N = 20

Scale Overlap	DIPS No.	PIPS Item No.	Test Item
AX	2.	21.	I can't sleep.
	5.	42.	I can't think.
AX	8.	82.	At times I feel as if I am going to die.
	12.	102.	I cannot stay asleep.
	26.	127.	I feel worthless.
AX	40.	146.	I have trouble thinking.
	50.	160.	I avoid decisions.
	53.	163.	I cannot remember things.
	68.	190.	I am discouraged.
NC	83.	193.	I feel unwanted.
NC	94.	202.	I feel nothing works out.
	97.	223.	I have no energy.
NC	112.	228.	I feel guilty.
	126.	252.	I have tried suicide.
NC	137.	286.	I feel sad.
NC	142.	301.	I am irritable.
	158.	308.	I feel depressed.
	169.	322.	I feel hopeless.
NC	155.	326.	I am indecisive.
	166.	328.	I have lost interest in sex.

Affected Excited (AE) N = 12

Scale Overlap	DIPS No.	PIPS Item No.	Test Item
	17.	13.	I have cosmic thought.
	30.	69.	I feel my speech is speeded up.
	44.	81.	I am hyper.
	58.	142.	I call friends in the middle of the night.
	74.	167.	I can do six things at once.
	88.	172.	I am hyperactive.
	102.	261.	I feel my thoughts racing.
	117.	264.	I am manic.
	131.	267.	I do not need sleep.
	147.	287.	I can go days without sleep.
	160.	288.	I have more energy.
	167.	327.	I am on top of the world.

Anxiety Disorders (AX) N = 20

Scale Overlap	DIPS No.	PIPS Item No.	Test Item
AD	2.	21.	I can't sleep.
	3.	14.	I have anxiety attacks.
NC	6.	20.	I am a worrier.
AD	8.	82.	At times I feel as if I am going to die.
	9.	70.	I have to re-check things often.
NC	14.	31.	I feel blocked completing tasks.
PC	28.	107.	I have had tachycardia.
NC	37.	115.	I fear being alone.
AD	40.	146.	I have trouble thinking.
SO	42.	125.	I have had chest pains.
	55.	129.	I have panic attacks.
NC	65.	175.	I am nervous.
	70.	158.	I shake.
	85.	168.	I cannot get to sleep.
	99.	188.	I feel unsteady.
NC	109.	215.	I am anxious.
	114.	260.	I tremble.
DD	120.	311.	I feel unreal.
	128.	266.	I am tense.
	144.	331.	My feet and hands tingle.

Somatoform Disorders (SO) N = 12

Scale Overlap	DIPS No.	PIPS Item No.	Test Item
	15.	58.	I have had double vision.
AX	42.	125.	I have had chest pains.
PC	46.	88.	I have had vomiting spells.
	56.	136.	I have had shortness of breath.
	71.	139.	I have had joint pain.
	86.	157.	I have had memory loss.
PC	90.	224.	I have had a lot of nausea.
	100.	187.	I have had muscle weakness.
	115.	240.	I have had loss of vision.
	129.	250.	I have had trouble walking.
	145.	285.	I have dizziness.
	159.	321.	I have had blurred vision.

Dissociative Disorders (DD) N = 12

Scale Overlap	DIPS No.	PIPS Item No.	Test Item
	20.	46.	I feel in a trance.
	33.	103.	I feel apart from the world.
	47.	203.	I feel that time has slowed.
	61.	239.	I feel I am watching myself.
	77.	247.	I feel like more than one person.
SP	73.	283.	My identity has changed.
SP	87.	296.	I feel mechanical.
	91.	302.	I feel things are slowed.
SP	105.	305.	I have another identity.
AX	120.	311.	I feel unreal.
	134.	345.	I have more than one personality.
	138.	251.	I have an identity problem.

Stress-Adjustment Disorders (SA) N = 20

DIPS No.	PIPS Item No.	Test Item
1.	35.	In the past year my wife/husband died.
4.	289.	This year I quit school.
7.	76.	My spouse and I separated this past year.
10.	96.	I retired this past year.
24.	99.	This year our house was destroyed.
38.	131.	This year I have had a major illness.
51.	137.	One of my parents died this year.
66.	153.	This past year I went on disability.
81.	165.	This year I was in the hospital.
95.	181.	I have had a family crisis this year.
110.	185.	I was divorced this year.
124.	209.	I was pregnant this year.
135.	226.	My child died this year.
139.	231.	We had a new baby this year.
153.	248.	I have been laid off this year.
156.	273.	This year I had a miscarriage.
154.	282.	I got married this year.
168.	72.	In the past year I have been in jail.
170.	319.	This year I was fired at work.
171.	330.	I have a chronic illness.

Psychological Factors Affecting Physical Condition (PC) N = 12

Scale Overlap	DIPS No.	PIPS Item No.	Test Item
	19.	15.	I have had arrhythmia.
	32.	124.	I have had a duodenal ulcer.
AX	28.	107.	I have had tachycardia.
SO	46.	88.	I have had vomiting spells.
	60.	128.	I have had migraine headaches.
	76.	182.	I have had essential hypertension.
SO	90.	224.	I have had a lot of nausea.
	104.	227.	I have had colitis.
	119.	229.	I have had a gastric ulcer.
	133.	245.	I have tension headaches.
	149.	335.	I have had asthma.
	162.	338.	I have arthritis.

Withdrawn Character (WC) N = 14

Scale Overlap	DIPS No.	PIPS Item No.	Test Item
SP	16.	57.	I have a "sixth" sense.
	22.	11.	I feel others can feel my life force.
PP,NC	23.	16.	I feel isolated.
	35.	154.	It is wise not to trust people.
SP	43.	220.	I do not feel close to others.
	49.	33.	I have telepathy.
PP	51.	184.	I cannot trust many people.
SP	64.	272.	Others can feel my feelings.
	79.	276.	I am vacant.
			I am being talked about.
	107.	337.	I have few friends.
	122.	339.	I feel bland.
	151.	344.	I am lifeless.
	154.	159.	Fantasy and reality are close.

Immature Character (IC) N = 18

Scale Overlap	DIPS No.	PIPS Item No.	Test Item
	21.	6.	I move around a lot.
	34.	17.	I get in fights.
	48.	44.	I have had affairs.
AA	52.	117.	I have had a D.W.I.
DA	59.	89.	I have sold drugs.
	62.	51.	I have had two divorces.
	63.	66.	I have been arrested.
DA	78.	118.	I have been in trouble for drugs.
	92.	133.	I have been arrested two times.
	106.	148.	I have been on probation.
	121.	164.	I have had three marriages.
AA	125.	270.	I like to get drunk.
DA	132.	242.	I take drugs for fun.
	136.	176.	I have been in jail.
	153.	179.	I have been fired two times.
	150.	277.	I change jobs a lot.
AA	157.	297.	I like to drink a lot.
	163.	207.	I act out my anger.

Neurotic Character (NC) N = 16

Scale Overlap	DIPS No.	PIPS Item No.	Test Item
AX	6.	20.	I am a worrier.
AX	14.	31.	I feel blocked completing tasks.
PP,WC	23.	16.	I feel isolated.
AX	37.	115.	I fear being alone.
AD	50.	160.	I avoid decisions.
AX	65.	175.	I am nervous.
	80.	189.	I fear making mistakes.
AD	83.	193.	I feel unwanted.
AD	94.	202.	I feel nothing works out.
AX	109.	215.	I am anxious.
AD	112.	228.	I feel guilty.
	123.	275.	I feel powerless.
AD	137.	286.	I feel sad.
AD	142.	301.	I am irritable.
	152.	317.	I lack self-confidence.
AD	155.	326.	I am indecisive.

DIPS STATEMENTS FOR THE VALIDITY SCALE AND FALSE NORMAL

1. Rule: Over Twenty (20) Omissions

Use the following statement:

> The validity of the person's profile on the Psychological Inventory of Personality and Symptoms (PIPS) is questionable, as the individual left unanswered 20 of the test items. This, consequently, may unduly lower the person's clinical profile. Assuming the individual is literate, the possible reasons for this large number of omissions are: (a) The person is extremely defensive, guarded, and possibly paranoid; (b) the person may be obsessive, worried, and ambivalent to the degree that it precludes making a decision; (c) the person may be uncooperative in a passive-aggressive manner. The clinician may wish to discuss the test with the individual and then have the individual retake the test. The clinical profile, as is, is presented because, even though the patient omitted a large number of items, the construction of the Diagnostic Inventory of Personality and Symptoms (PIPS) is such that significant problem areas of the person may still be brought to light despite the number of omissions; however, as stated earlier, the profile should be considered suspect and interpreted with great caution.

2. Rule: The PIPS Validity Scale in the Valid Range (A Score of 0 to 1 on the Validity Scale)

Use the following statement:

> On The Psychological Inventory of Personality and Symptoms (PIPS), the person produced a valid profile.

3. Rule: Valid Profile (Score 2–4 on the Validity Scale)

Use the following statement and *no* other statement:

> The person's validity scale indicates that the Personality Inventory and Personality Symptoms (PIPS) is invalid. Assuming the person is not retarded or demented and can read at the sixth grade level, the person is apt to fall into one of two distinct groups: (a) Individuals exhibiting dramatic emotional or erratic character disorders, primarily borderline or histrionic personality disorder, who tend to react to the world and test in an over dramatic way; (b) Individuals who are psychotic and evidencing either functional or drug-induced psychosis. All in all, persons producing invalid profiles are apt to be a highly volatile or unstable group. In public institutional settings, these individuals are quite often psychotic; in private settings, they are more apt to have a diagnosis of dramatic, emotional, or erratic personality disorder and substance abuse.

NOTE: All of the following assume a valid profile, or profile omissions. The invalid profile is due to 2–4 answered "yes," and is the only one where the clinical narrative is not printed.

4. Rule: False Normal (No Clinical Scales in Axis I or Axis II Disorders)

Use the following statement:

> The person's clinical profile on the Psychological Inventory of Personality and Symptoms (PIPS) for both Axis I and Axis II disorders is within normal limits.

In outpatient settings about half the time, such a performance is quite often indicative of individuals who are presenting with either an adjustment disorder and/or marital problems, and who are quite often devoid of a personality disorder.

In psychiatric inpatients, the other extreme of the diagnostic spectrum is apt to be present in that approximately half of the persons producing this "false normal" profile are psychotic and evidencing, most probably, a Major Affective Disorder (Major Depression or Bipolar Disorder) or, to a lesser extent, Schizophrenia.

The remainder of individuals who produce this false normal profile, in both inpatient and outpatient settings, tend to be in what pre-DSM-III terminology would be classified as chronic mixed neurotics. Such individuals are apt to present with somatoform disorders and psychological factors affecting physical conditions, as well as anxiety disorders or dysthymic disorders. The underlying personality of these persons is apt to be in the category of anxious and fearful personality disorder, namely, Avoidant, Dependent, Compulsive, Passive, Aggressive, though a small minority are seen as evidencing histrionic personalities.

Persons of this profile type are usually defensive about psychological problems and are apt to be naive, rigid, and lacking in insight. Such individuals tend to make heavy use of the defense mechanisms of repression and denial, and are unduly conventional and insecure. Such individuals are quite apt to be resistant to psychotherapeutic intervention because of a fear of revealing themselves. They are usually quite upset and distressed when they cannot present a facade of adequacy, formality, and moral virtue.

5. Rule: If the Fake Good Scale is 5 or Less

Use:

> The persons score on the "Fake Good Scale" indicates that the individual is quite defensive and naive. Scores in this range are obtained by less than 15% of the

general population. Such persons are apt to be fearful of revealing themselves in any way, and feel they must present themselves as angelic characters who are free of symptoms and problems.

DIPS STATEMENTS FOR AXIS I PRINT HEADING: AXIS I DISORDERS

Scale 1 AA Rules

If the AA scale has a T score of 70 or greater (raw score of 4 or more), use the following statement:

> The overwhelming majority of persons who score in this range on the AA scale are alcohol abusers or alcohol dependent.

And (with the AA T score greater than 70), if the person answered *yes* to the DIPS question number listed below, use the corresponding statement

157 The person reports a strong desire to drink.
125 Liking to "get drunk" is admitted.
25 Regular consumption in excess of ten drinks a day is reported.
111 The individual reports a binge drinking pattern.
67 Problem drinking results in the person having six or more hangovers a year.
141 A history of blackouts is reported.
96 Serious addiction problems indicated as the individual reports having had the D.T.s.
39 Alcohol abuse is affecting the person's job performance, as the patient admits to being drunk on the job.
11 The person reports a job loss due to drinking.
82 Family problems due to drinking are indicated.
52 Legal problems in the form of D.W.I. are reported.
165 The individual reports having been jailed for being drunk.

Scale 2 DA Rules

If the DA scale has a T score of 70 or greater (raw score of 6 or greater), use the following statement:

> A history of significant subsance abuse is likely,

And (with SP T score greater than 70), if the patient answered *yes* to the DIPS question number listed below, use the corresponding statement.

45	The person reports a liking to get "high."
132	Drug use is seen as "fun."
103 and/or 118	The person holds the belief that drug use can be done in moderation.
89	Guilt over substance abuse is verbalized.
78	The person admits that drug use has caused problems.
148	Physical or psychological addiction is suggested.
59	A history of selling drugs is reported.
18	The individual reports being "high" on the job.
161	Drug use is seen as having a negative effect on the person's social life.
75	Family problems due to substance abuse are reported.
31	Substance abuse has resulted in a drug-related arrest.

Scale 3 SP Rules

If the SP scale has a T score of 90 or greater (raw score of 5 or more), use the following statement:

> Marked emotional withdrawal and feelings of alienation are indicated; impaired reality testing is likely. A thought disorder may be present, and a very significant number of individuals of this profile type are psychotic.

If the SP scale has a T score of 70 or greater (raw score of 3 or 4), use the following statement:

> Emotional alienation and withdrawal, as well as disrupted and confused thinking, are suggested. Reality distortion is a possibility.

And (with SP T score of 70 or greater), if the patient answered *yes* to the DIPS question number listed below, use the corresponding statement:

116	The person reports difficulty thinking.
43	Withdrawal and emotional isolation are indicated.
87	Feelings of personal estrangement are indicated.
73 & 105	An identity disturbance is likely.
16, 64 & 130	Magical thinking is suggested.

146	Delusions of thought broadcasting may be present.
29	The person reports hearing voices.
57	Nihilistic delusions are suggested.
101	The person alludes to experiencing delusions of control.

Scale 4 PP Rules

If the PP scale has a T score of 90 or greater (raw score of 5 or more), use the following statement:

> Marked feelings of suspiciousness, wariness, resentment, and anger are present. The person is apt to be hypervigilant and hostile. Paranoia of psychotic proportions is likely.

If the PP scale has a T score of 70 or greater but less than 90 (raw score of 3 or 4), use the following statement:

> Feelings of suspiciousness and guardedness are apt to be present. Over-sensitivity and anger are likely. Paranoid feelings are a possibility.

And (with PP T score 70 or greater), if the patient answered *yes* to the DIPS question number listed below, use the corresponding statement:

23	Feelings of social isolation are apt to be present.
54	The person is apt to be distrustful of others.
93	The individual reports feeling talked about.
98	Feelings of oversensitivity are indicated.
69 and/or 113	Harassment and blame from others is verbalized.
13	The person reports being followed.
27, 41 and/or 84	A feeling of being monitored is reported.
127	The person reports they have been drugged by others.
101	(Note: use only if this statement was not used in the SP section above) The person alludes to experiencing delusions of control.

Scale 5 AD Rules

If the AD scale has a T score of 90 or greater (raw score of 13 or more), use the following statement:

> Marked feelings of dysphoria are reported. A loss of interest or pleasure is indicated. Very significant depression is likely.

If the AD Scale has a T score of 70 but less than 90 (Raw score of 8–12), use the following statement:

> Feelings of dysphoria and loss of interest or pleasure is reported. A significant amount of depression is likely.

And (with the AD scale T score of 70 or greater), if the person answered *yes* to the DIPS question number listed below, use the corresponding statement:

2	Sleep disturbance is indicated.
12	The person reports difficulty staying asleep.
5 and/or 40	Difficulty in concentration is reported.
53	The person reports difficulty with memory.
50 and/or 155	The individual feels indecisive.
68, 137 and/or 158	Despondence is reported.
26 and/or 83	A lack of self worth is verbalized.
112	The person feels guilty.
142	Feelings of irritability are present.
94 and/or 169	The person verbalizes a feeling of hopelessness.
97	Fatigue is reported.
166	A loss of sex drive is indicated.
8	The person reports feelings of acute panic.
126	A suicide attempt is reported.

Scale 6 AE Rules

If the AE Scale is a T score of 90 or greater (raw score of 7 or greater), use the following statement.

> An elevated, expansive mood is likely. The person may be easily irritated. Restlessness, distractibility, agitation, and/or hyperactivity is likely. Manic features may be present.

If the AE scale is greater than a T score of 70 but less than 90 (raw score of 4-6), use:

> The person is apt to be restless, energetic, and distractable. Irritability, agitation, and/or hyperactivity may be present.

And (with the AE T score of 70 or greater), if the person answered *yes* to the DIPS question number listed below, use the corresponding statement:

44, 78, 88, 117, and/or 160	Hyperactivity and/or overactivity is reported.
131 and/or 147	A decreased need for sleep is acknowledged.
167	A feeling of euphoria is indicated.
30	The person reports a pressure of speech.
102	The individual reports experiencing their thoughts racing.
58	Uninhibited people-seeking behavior is suggested.
17	The person reports having cosmic insight.

Scale 7 AX Rules

If the AX scale is a T score of 90 or greater (raw score of 15 or greater), use the following statement:

> Marked feelings of anxiety are present. The person is experiencing tension and apprehension. Compulsions, phobias, panic, and/or depression is likely.

If the AX scale is greater than a T score of 70 but less than 90 (raw score of 9-14), use:

> Feelings of anxiety are present. The person is apt to be tense and apprehensive. Anxiety disorders and/or depression are most likely present in the clinical picture.

And (with the AX T score of 70 or greater), if the person answered *yes* to the question number listed below on the DIPS, use the corresponding statement:

65, 109 and/or 128	Generalized anxiety is reported.
6	The person reports being a worrier.
70, 99 and/or 114	Motor tension is present.
14	The person feels blocked.
28, 42 and/or 144	Physical manifestations of anxiety are present.
120	The individual indicates feeling unreal.
40	(Note: use only if 40 not used above in the AD section) Difficulty in concentration is reported.
2	(Note: Use only if 2 not used above in AD section) Sleep disturbance is indicated.
85	The person reports difficulty going to sleep.
8	(Note: use only if 8 not used above in the AD section) The person reports feelings of acute panic.

3 and/or 55	Episodes of acute anxiety are reported; a Panic Disorder may be present.
9	Minor compulsive behavior is reported.
37	The person is fearful of being alone; agoraphobia may be present.

Scale 8 SO Rules

If the SO scale is a T score of 90 or greater (raw score of 6 or more), use the following statement:

> The person is reporting an unusually large number of symptoms that collectively indicate a psychosomatic component is present in any reported or actual illness. A somatoform disorder or depression with marked somatic complaints is likely.

If SO scale is greater than a T score of 70 but less than 90 (raw score of 4 or 5), use the following statement:

> A significant number of somatic symptoms are verbalized. This may suggest a psychosomatic component is present in any reported or actual illness.

And (with the SO T score of 70 or greater), if the person answered *yes* to the DIPS question number listed below, use the corresponding statement:

> The person reports the following symptoms:

And then use:

15 double vision,
42 chest pain,
46 vomiting spells,
56 shortness of breath,
71 joint pain,
86 memory loss,
90 nausea,
100 muscle weakness,
115 loss of vision,
129 trouble walking,
145 dizziness,
159 blurred vision,
(Note: add *and* to the next to last symptoms, and end with a period.

Scale 9 DD Rules

If DD scale is a T score of 90 or greater (raw score of 5 or more), use the following statement:

> The person is reporting experiencing a very significant amount of dissociative phenomena. Feelings of unreality are present. Depersonalization may be present. There is a likelihood that the individual has problems with identity may be present.

If DD scale is greater than a T score of 70, but less than 90 (raw score of 3 or 4), use the following statement:

> Feelings of unreality may be present. Problems with identity are a possibility.

And (with the DD T score of 70 or greater), if the person answered *yes* to the DIPS question number listed below, use the corresponding statement:

33, 61 and/or 87	(Note: use only if 87 not used above in the section) Feelings of personal estrangement are indicated.
73, 105 and/or 138	(Note: use only if 73 and/or 105 not used above in SP section) An identity disturbance is likely.
120	(Note: use only if 120 not used in the AX section above) The individual indicates feeling unreal.
47 and/or 91	A sense of time distortion may be present.
77 and/or 134	The individual indicates feeling like more than one person.
20	A feeling of being in a trance is reported.

Scale 10 SA Rules

If the SA scale is a T score of 90 or greater (raw score of 5 or more), use the following statement:

> The person is reporting experiencing a severe amount of environmental stress in the past year, the most significant of which are:

If the SA scale is greater than a T score of 70, but less than 90 (raw score of 3 or 4), use the following statement:

> The person is reporting experiencing a significant amount of environmental stress in the past year, the most significant of which are:

And (with the SA T score of 70 or greater), if the peson answered *yes* to the DIPS question number listed below, use the corresponding statement:

1. death of a spouse,
4. dropping out of school,
7. marital separation,
10. retirement from work,
24. destruction of the person's home,
38. major illness of the person's child,
51. death of a parent,
66. becoming disabled,
81. being in the hospital,
95. having a family crisis,
110. being divorced,
124. getting pregnant,
135. death of a child,
139. birth of a baby,
153. being laid off from work,
156. having a marital crisis,
164. getting married,
168. being in jail,
170. being fired from work,
171. having a chronic illness,
(Note: add *and* to the last statement, and end with a period.)

Scale 11 PC Rules

If the PC scale is a T score of 90 or greater (raw score of 5 or more), use the following statement:

> The person is reporting a very large number of physical conditions in which psychological factors often (but not always) contribute to the onset or exacerbation of the physical problem. The person is apt to develop psychophysiological symptoms and/or illness under periods of emotional stress. The individual reports the following conditions:

If the PC scale is greater than a T score of 70 but less than 90 (raw score of 3 or 4), use the following statement:

> The person is reporting a large number of physical conditions in which psychological factors often (but not always) contribute to the onset or exacerbation of the physical problem. The person is at risk for developing psychophysiological symp-

> toms under periods of emotional stress. The individual reports having had the following conditions:

And, (with the PC T score of 70 or greater), if the person answered *yes* to the DIPS question number listed below, use the corresponding statement:

19. arrhythmia,
32. duodenal ulcer,
28. tachycardia,
46. (Note: use only if 46 is not used above in the SO section).
    vomiting spells,
60. migraine headaches,
76. essential hypertension,
90. (Note: use only if 90 not used above in the SO section).
    nausea,
104. colitis,
119. gastric ulcer,
133. headaches,
149. asthma,
162. arthritis,
    (Note: add *and* to the last statement and end with a period.)

AXIS I DIFFERENTIAL DIAGNOSTIC SECTION

If 6 of Axis I scales are at a T score of 90, use:

> The person's clinical profile is quite elevated. Individuals producing this profile type most often fit into one of two categories.

Persons making this profile are often seen as borderline personality disorders who are evidencing either an extreme adjustment disorder or a brief reactive psychosis. Substance abuse is also often part of the clinical picture.

The alternative picture is one of an individual presenting with an acute psychotic episode which is most frequently Schizophrenia; however, Biopolar Disorders also evidence this profile type.

In outpatient and private settings, the individual is more likely to be a borderline personality in acute distress. In public inpatient settings, acute psychosis is more likely.

RULE: For the following in the Axis I Differential Diagnostic Section, always list the scales in descending order based on the following base rate frequency list, and use the corresponding DSM-III Diagnostic Category, which is for the Axis I Differential Diagnostic Section.

Frequency Order	DIPS Scale	DSM-III Diagnostic Category
1	AD	Affective Disorder: Depression
2	SA	Adjustment Disorder
3	AA	Substance Abuse Disorder: Alcohol
4	SP	Schizophrenic Disorder
5	DA	Substance Abuse Disorder: Drugs
6	AX	Anxiety Disorder
7	AE	Affective Disorder: Bipolar
8	SO	Somatoform Disorder
9	PC	Psychological Factors Affecting Physical Condition
10	PP	Paranoid Disorder
11	DD	Dissociative Disorder

Note: For adolescents, the frequency is reversed for one and two, so that 1 is Adjustment Disorder and 2 is Affective Disorder: Depressed.

If 5 or less scales of Axis I are at a T score of 90 or less, use the highest 4 scales in the Axis I Differential Diagnostic Section based on their frequency order listed above. Ask if the person is an outpatient or private hospital inpatient, or if he or she is a state mental or VA hospital inpatient. If they are *not* a state mental or VA hospital inpatient, or if this information is unknown, then add the following rule: if SP, PP, AE, and/or DD are among the highest scales, always include SA as if it were one of the highest (at a T score of 90), and, for everyone tested, if SO or AX are among the highest, include AD as if it were one of the highest (at a T score of 90).

NOTE: Always begin this section by using the heading and narrative:

AXIS I Differential Diagnostic Section

Based on analysis of the individual's profile, the following is a list of the most likely diagnostic categories for the person, in order of their probability:

For example, if a person who was an outpatient or private hospital inpatient had a profile that included: AA at 76 T, SP at 90 T, SO at 90 T: this would result in the following hierarchy for the Axis I: Differential Diagnostic Section.

1. Affective Disorder: Depressed
2. Adjustment Disorder
3. Substance Abuse Disorder: Alcohol

4. Schizophrenic Disorder
5. Somatoform Disorder

Note: The fifth category would not be printed out; always, only the four highest are listed.

Print Heading: AXIS II DISORDERS

If the person is 18 or over, and the WC scale is a T score of 70 or greater and IC and NC are less than 70 T, use:

> The individual's personality disorder cluster has a significant evaluation on the withdrawn character scale. This scale corresponds to the ''odd'' or eccentric cluster of the DSM-III.
>
> Such individuals are apt to be withdrawn, suspicious, and isolated. An unusual presentation of self may be present, and individuals of this profile type often verbalize significant discomfort in interpersonal relationships. This may be due to fear, distrust, or apathy. Persons scoring high on this personality disorder cluster are often seen as having a paranoid, schizoid, or schizotypal personality. Occasionally, persons with avoidant personalities score high on this scale.

If the person is 18 or over, and the IC scale is a T score of 70 or greater and WC and NC are less than 70 T, use:

> The individual's personality disorder cluster has a significant elevation on the immature character scale. This scale corresponds to the dramatic, emotional, or erratic cluster of the DSM-III. Such individuals are apt to be impulsive, hedonistic, emotionally labile, and exploitative. A wide variety of irresponsible, self-centered behavior is apt to be evidenced by individuals of this profile type, that may range from egocentric self indulgence and neglect of adult responsibilities to substance abuse and legal difficulties. Persons of this profile type often have difficulty sustaining long-term interpersonal relationships, and marital difficulties are common. Persons scoring high on this personality disorder cluster are often seen as having a histrionic, narcissistic, antisocial, or borderline personality. Occasionally, persons with passive-aggressive personalities score high on this scale.

If the person is 18 or over, and the NC scale is a T score of 70 or greater and WC and IC are less than 70, use:

> The individual's personality disorder cluster has a significant elevation on the neurotic character scale. This corresponds to the anxious or fearful cluster of the DSM-III. Such individuals are apt to be overconscientious, sensitive, passive, and rigid. Persons of this profile type are often negative towards self and chronically anxious. They usually have a stable family life and are capable of forming lasting

emotional relationships. Persons scoring high on this personality disorder cluster are often seen as having an avoidant, dependent, compulsive, or passive aggressive personality.

If the person is 18 or over, and the WC and IC scores are both a T score of 70 or over and the NC scale is under 70 T, use:

The individual's personality disorder cluster has significant elevations on both the withdrawn character scale and the immature character scale. This corresponds to elevations on the "odd" or eccentric cluster (paranoid, schizoid, and schizotypal) and the dramatic, emotional, or erratic cluster (histrionic, narcissistic, antisocial, and borderline) of the DSM-III. The simultaneous elevation of these clusters indicate a combination of wariness and fear of people with emotional liability and potential for irresponsible behavior that is most apt to be seen as in individuals having a borderline personality disorder.

If the person is 18 or over, and the WC, IC, and NC scales are all a T score of 70 or greater, use:

The individual's personality disorder cluster has significant elevations on all three of the character disorder scales, namely, withdrawn character, immature character, and neurotic character. These correspond to elevations in all three of the personality disorder clusters of DSM-III: "odd" or eccentric; dramatic, emotional, or erratic; and anxious or fearful. Whether this is due to a response set of acquiescence or to the fact that the disorder encompasses such a broad spectrum of behaviors and symptoms, a diagnosis of borderline personality disorder is likely.

If the person is 18 or over, and the WC and NC scales are both a T score of 70 or greater, and the IC scale is under 70 T, use:

The individual's personality disorder cluster has significant elevations on both the withdrawn character scale the the neurotic character scale. This corresponds to elevations on the "odd" or eccentric cluster (paranoid, schizoid, and schizotypal) and the anxious or fearful cluster (avoidant, dependent, compulsive, and passive-aggressive) of the DSM-III. The simultaneous elevations of these clusters indicate a combination of oversensitivity and social withdrawal with anxiety and passivity that is most apt to be seen in individuals with an avoidant personality.

If the person is 18 or over, and the IC and NC scales are both a T score of 70 or greater and the WC scale is less than 70 T, use:

The individual's personality disorder cluster has significant elevations on both the immature character scale and the neurotic character scale. This corresponds to elevations on the dramatic, emotional, or erratic cluster (histrionic, narcissistic, antisocial, and borderline) and the anxious or fearful cluster (avoidant, dependent, compulsive, and passive-aggressive) of the DSM-III. The simultaneous elevation of these clusters indicates a combination of impulsivity and irresponsibility with anxiety and passivity that is most apt to be seen in individuals with a passive-aggressive personality.

If the person is 18 or over, and the WC, IC, and NC scales are all below a T score of 70 and there is/are elevation at a T score of 70 or above other than SA in Axis I, use:

The individual's scores on the personality disorder cluster are within normal limits. The full symptom cluster of a personality disorder is not apt to be present. Analysis of the person's overall profile indicates the following personality features may be present:

If the following scales on Axis I are at or above a T score of 70, use in the order of the base rate frequency (which is the order they are listed in below). If AA, Use:

Passive-Aggressive personality features are likely.

If AA or DA, use:

Features common to the Immature Character are apt to be present.

If SP, PP, and/or DD, use:

Traits associated with the Withdrawn Character may be present.

If AD and/or AX, use:

Aspects associated with the Neurotic Character are apt to be present.

If AE, use:

Histrionic Personality features may be present.

If SO or PC, use:

Dependent Personality features are indicated.

If the person is 18 or over, and the WC, IC, and NC scales are below a T score of 70 and SA is the only scale above a T score of 70 in Axis I, use:

The individual's score on the personality disorder cluster is within normal limits. A normal personality is likely.

AXIS II STATEMENTS FOR ADOLESCENTS

Print Heading: DISORDERS OF ADOLESCENCE

If the person is 12 to 17, and the WC scale is a T score of 70 or greater and IC and NC are less than 70 T, use:

> The individual's personality disorder cluster has a significant evaluation on the withdrawn character scale. Such adolescents are apt to be withdrawn, suspicious, and isolated. An unusual presentation of self may be present and individuals of this profile type often verbalize significant discomfort in interpersonal relationships. This may be due to fear, distrust, or apathy. Adolescents scoring high on this scale are often seen as having a Schizoid Disorder of Adolescence. Occasionally, adolescents with an Avoidant Disorder of Adolescence score high on this scale.

If the person is 12 to 17, and the IC scale is a T score of 70 or greater and WC and NC are less than 70 T, use:

> The individual's personality disorder cluster has a significant evaluation on the immature character scale. Such adolescents are apt to be impulsive, hedonistic, emotionally labile, and exploitative. A wide variety of irresponsible, self-centered behavior is apt to be evidenced by individuals of this profile type that may range from egocentric self-indulgence and neglect of responsibilities to substance abuse and legal difficulties. Adolescents of this profile type often have difficulty sustaining long-term interpersonal relationships. Adolescents scoring high on this personality disorder cluster are often seen as having Conduct Disorders. Occasionally, adolescents with an Oppositional Disorder or Identity Disorder score high on this scale.

If the person is 12 to 17, and the NC scale is a T score of 70 or greater and WC and IC are less than 70, use:

> The adolescent's personality disorder cluster has a significant elevation to the neurotic character scale. Such adolescents are apt to be overconscientious, sensitive, passive, and rigid. Persons of this profile type are often negative towards self and chronically anxious. They usually have a stable family life and are capable of forming lasting emotional relationships. Adolescents scoring high on this personality disorder cluster are often seen as having an Overanxious Disorder, Separation Anxiety Disorder, or Avoidant Disorder of Adolescence.

If the person is 12 to 17, and the WC and IC scores are both a T score of 70 or over and the NC scale is under 70 T, use:

> The adolescent's personality disorder cluster has significant elevations on both the withdrawn character scale and the immature character scale. The simultaneous elevation of these clusters indicates a combination of wariness and fear of people

> with emotional lability and potential for irresponsible behavior that is most apt to be seen in adolescent's having an Identity Disorder.

If the person is 12 to 17, and the WC, IC, and NC scales are all a T score of 70 or greater, use:

> The adolescent's personality disorder cluster has significant elevations on all three of the character disorder scales, namely, withdrawn character, immature character, and neurotic character. Whether this is due to a response set of acquiescence or to the fact that the disorder encompasses such a broad spectrum of behaviors and symptoms, a diagnosis of Identity Disorder is likely.

If the person is 12 to 17, and the WC and NC scales are both a T score of 70 or greater, and the IC scale is under 70 T, use:

> The adolescent's personality disorder cluster has significant elevations on both the withdrawn character scale and the neurotic character scale. The simultaneous elevations of these clusters indicates a combination of oversensitivity and social withdrawal with anxiety and passivity that is most apt to be seen in adolescents with an Avoidant Disorder of Adolescence.

If the person is 12 to 17, and the IC and NC scales are both a T score of 70 or greater, and the WC scale is less than 70 T, use:

> The adolescent's personality disorder cluster has significant elevations on both the immature character scale and the Neurotic character scale. The simultaneous elevation of these clusters indicate a combination of impulsivity and irresponsibility with anxiety and passivity that is most apt to be seen in adolescents with an Oppositional Disorder.

If the person is 12 to 17, and WC, IC, and NC Scales are all below a T score of 70, use:

> The adolescent's personality disorder cluster is within normal limits.

Next, ask, Do you want psychotherapy recommendations on your report?

If No and 18 or above, print the report.

If Yes, then print the heading *Psychotherapy Recommendations*.

The following are *suggestions* about treatment planning based on the individual's test scores, and are not substitutes for the skilled therapist's judgement. They are merely possibilities put forth to stimulate the therapist's thinking in planning the individual's therapy.

If AA is at a T score of 70 or greater, and items 96 and/or 111 answered *no*, print:

The person needs to be in a program that emphasizes either abstinence or controlled drinking.

If AA is at a T score of 70 or greater, and item 96 and/or 111 answered *yes*, print:

It is essential that the person participate in a program that emphasizes abstinence from drinking.

If DA is at a T score of 70 or greater, use:

Psychotherapeutically, in addition to abstinence, the person will probably profit best from a treatment approach that emphasizes taking greater responsibility for their own actions, and which reinforces the benefits of long-range, as opposed to short-range, hedonism.

If IC is greater than a T score of 70, and WC and NC are less than a T score of 70 and the DA statement not used, print:

Psychotherapeutically, the person will probably profit best from a treatment approach that is pragmatic and no-nonsense and which places the burden of responsibility for the individual's actions squarely upon the person's own needs and shoulders.

If IC and WC are *both* greater than a T score of 70, or if IC, WC, and NC are all greater than a T score of 70, use:

The person will probably benefit most from treatment that focuses on concrete, here-and-now issues and modulating the individual's emotions. Insight Therapy is apt to be contraindicated, as it is apt to cause the person to decompensate.

If WC or WC and NC are *both* greater than a T score of 70, and IC is less than a T score of 70; or if WC, IC, and NC are all below a T score of 70, and SP, PP, and/or DD is a T score of 70 or more, use:

Psychotherapeutically, the person will probably profit best from a treatment approach that emphasizes developing an increased repertoire of behavioral-emotional skills and general interpersonal sensitivity.

If NC is greater than a T score of 70, and WC and IC are less than a T score of 70; or if WC, IC, *and* NC are all below a T score of 70, and AD and/or AX is a T score of 70 or more, use:

The person will probably profit from a treatment approach that emphasizes action and doing and which de-emphasizes further ruminative introspection.

If IC and NC are *both* greater than a T score of 70, and WC is less than a T score of 70; or if AE is above a T score of 70, and all other scales in Axis I and II except SA are below a T score of 70, use:

Psychotherapeutically, the person will probably profit best from a treatment approach that emphasizes modulating the individual's emotions, thinking things through, and developing a more assertive and balanced stance toward life.

If the WC and IC are all below 70, and SO and/or PC is a T score of 70 or greater, use:

Assertiveness training may be helpful. Additionally, the person needs to be coaxed back into becoming active again in the business of living, and sick-role behavior is to be discouraged.

If SA is the only scale above a T score of 70, use:

Short term, goal-focused psychotherapy appears indicated.

If 95 and/or 156 answered *yes* and the person is married, use:

Marital therapy should be considered for incorporation into the person's overall treatment plan.

CHAPTER FOURTEEN

Interpretative Statements for the Personality Inventory for Children

The Personality Inventory for Children (PIC) is a unique test in the field of child personality assessment in that the parent takes the test. Various studies have shown that the Personality Inventory for Children is more than just merely a parent-rating check list, and should be interpreted as pertaining directly to the child (Wirt & Lachar, 1981). Like an adaptive behavior measure in which the parent is interviewed, the Personality Inventory for Children uses the parent as the informant, but, unlike an adaptive behavior measure, the Personality Inventory for Children is an objective test taken by the parent. The test is now available in short form and a brief screening form. Statements are included for all forms of the Personality Inventory for Children. Because it is objective, it is a real breakthrough in child assessment. The Personality Inventory for Children was developed at the University of Minnesota and in many ways parallels the MMPI, but, unlike the MMPI, it usually does not result in an elevated configural profile for interpretation, and, in fact, in one study only 12% of the profiles had clinical scales in excess of a T score of 69 (DeHorn, Lachar, & Gdowski, 1979). When more than one code type is enumerated, the interpretative statements can be assembled together to form a coherent report.

P. 1. (Introductory Statement—Informant)
On the **PERSONALITY INVENTORY FOR CHILDREN** the informant was:

P. 2. L<60, F<100, DEF<70
The validity scales indicate that the profile is valid.

P. 3. L 60–69
The Lie Scale indicates that the informant may have been naively defensive in their approach to the questionaire. This is not apt to be a problem if the informant is the parent and initiated the referral.

P. 4. L 70
The Lie Scale indicates that the informant may have been quite defensive in their approach to the questionaire and, consequently, the child's clinical profile may be unduly lowered in some way. The

informant is apt to be naive and needs to see the child as free of even "normal" problems. With an elevation on this Scale, the child is not apt to have a conduct disorder, and the informant's denial is not apt to be a problem when the informant is the parent and initiated the referral.

P. 5. F 100–119
The F Scale is quite elevated and indicates that the informant's response set was one of exaggeration and probable distortion of the child's current state. Assuming the informant is literate, this is apt to be either a "cry for help" or tendency for the informant to be overdramatic.

P. 6. F 120
The F Scale indicates that the profile is likely invalid due to a random response set. The literacy, emotional states, and/or lack of motivation of the informant should be evaluated.

P. 7. DEF 70
The Defensiveness Scale indicates that the informant is apt to have been quite defensive in their approach to the questionaire. The informant, in all probability, has under-reported the child's problems, and, consequently, the clinical profile may be unduly lowered in some way. The informant may be resistive to psychotherapeutic intervention.

P. 8. ADJ 60–69
The Adjustment Scale indicates that the child may have some significant emotional/behavioral problem requiring psychotherapeutic intervention.

P. 9. ADJ 70
The Adjustment Scale indicates that the child has significant emotional/behavioral problems requiring psychotherapeutic intervention.

P. 10. ACH 60–69
The Achievement Scale indicates that the child may have learning problems. A psychoeducational evaluation is indicated.

P. 11. ACH 70
The Achievement Scale indicates that the child has learning problems, and a thorough psychological evaluation is indicated.

P. 12. IS 70
The Intellectual Screening Scale indicates that the child may have significant deficits in the area of intellectual ability, and individually administered intelligence testing is indicated to further assess the child's cognitive functioning.

P. 13. DVL 60–69

The Development Scale is mildly elevated and indicates that the child may have deficits in cognitive functions, language skills, and social skills. Scool problems may result.

P. 14. DVL 70

The Development Scale is significantly elevated and indicates that the child is apt to have problems in the areas of cognitive ability, language skills, and social skills.

Neurological impairment is a significant occurrence, and a neurological evaluation by a physician and neuropsychological screening is recommended.

Children with evaluations on this scale tend to be concrete, clumsy, withdrawn, and isolated. Their development is behind that of their same-age peers. Because of their intellectual speech, motor, and social handicaps, school problems are common.

P. 15. SOM 70

The Somatic Concern Scale is significantly elevated and indicates that the child is apt to have health problems with a functional component. Fatigue, somatic concern, and pain are frequent complaints. Boys of this profile type may also have separation anxiety and frequent headaches.

P. 16. D 70

The Depression Scale is significantly elevated and indicates the presence of significant depression in the child's symptom cluster. Such children are apt to be despondent, pessimistic, shy, and self critical. Males of this profile type are apt to evidence sleep disturbance, social withdrawal, suicidal ideation, and somatic complaints. Females of this profile type are apt to be seen as chronic worriers.

P. 17. FAM 60–69

The Family Relations Scale is mildly elevated and suggests the presence of family unhappiness, marital discord, and/or separation/divorce. The child is apt to experience inconsistent discipline and limit setting by the parents. Parent maladjustment and a need for parent counseling is likely.

P. 18. FAM 70

The Family Relations Scale is significantly elevated and indicates the presence of significant problems in the home. Parental maladjustment and a need for parent counseling is likely. The possibility exists that a parent has a substance abuse problem and should be further examined. This profile type is associated with major family unhappiness and marital discord and/or separation/divorce. It is also quite likely that the impulsive and hostile behavior which children of this profile type often exhibit is the result of modeling the parents' behavior. These children are also apt to experience inconsistent limit-setting and discipline by parents.

P. 19. DLQ 80–89
The Delinquency Scale is significantly elevated, and children of this profile type are apt to be described as impulsive, hostile, and antisocial. These children display poor social judgment and evidence irresponsible behavior. A wide variety of conduct problems and poor self control are apt to be manifest by the child.

P. 20. DLQ 90
The Delinquency Scale is markedly elevated, and children of this profile type are apt to be described as impulsive, hostile, and antisocial. These children display poor social judgment and evidence a wide variety of acting out behaviors, including truancy, stealing, running away, lying, and aggression. These children dislike school and are seen by the school as problem children. They are quite often known by the legal authorities. These children are hostile, aggressive, and irresponsible. They need close supervision, consistent discipline, and firm limits. The modal diagnosis for children of this profile type is conduct disorder.

P. 21. WDL 70
The Withdrawal Scale is significantly elevated, and children of this profile type are apt to be isolated, shy, and anxious. They typically have few friends and prefer solitary activities.

P. 22. ANX 70
The Anxiety Scale is significantly elevated, and children of this profile type are anxious, fearful, and worried. They are apt to have frequent nightmares. These children may exhibit social withdrawal and occasionally evidence suicidal ideation and/or suicidal behavior. Occasionally, their worries reflect parental concerns. These children are overideational and frequently worry about the past and future. They are desirous of constant reassurance. An overanxious disorder is likely.

P. 23. PSY 80–99
The Psychosis Scale is significantly elevated and depicts a child who is apt to be isolated, restless, and easily upset. The child is apt to be a concrete thinker who is lacking in social skills and is socially withdrawn. Sleep problems are common to children of this profile type. Often, these children are described as being dazed or confused.

P. 24. PSY 100

The Psychosis Scale is markedly elevated and depicts a child who is isolated, agitated, and apt to be emotionally labile. These children are concrete thinkers who are withdrawn and quite deficient in social skills. The child should be carefully evaluated for the presence of overt psychosis.

Boys of this profile are more apt to display psychotic behavior, whereas girls more often display more impulsive, hostile behavior. Suicidal ideation and suicidal behavior are a possibility, and, occasionally, these children have intellectual and/or neurological deficits. Poor social skills and judgment and inappropriate affect are the norm.

P. 25. HPR 60–69

The Hyperactivity Scale is significantly elevated, and depicts a child who is apt to be impulsive, distractable, irresponsible, and inattentive. The child is apt to be agitated, restless, and hostile, and to have conflicts with all individuals around him or her. Such children are often described as bossy, disobedient, and argumentative. An Attention Deficit Disorder with Hyperactivity is likely.

P. 26. HPR 70

The Hyperactivity Scale is very significantly elevated, and children of this profile type are usually seen as having an Attention Deficit Disorder with Hyperactivity. Such children are often described as inattentive, impulsive, and hyperactive. The child is apt to be agitated, restless, and hostile. Such children are bossy, disobedient, and argumentative. Their behavior is apt to alienate, not only teachers and other adults, but also their peers, as such children are typically bossy, impulsive, and irresponsible. They are apt to tease and fight with their peers. A medical evaluation for chemotherapy is indicated.

P. 27. SSK 70

The Social Skills Scale is significantly elevated and depicts a child who is lacking in social skills and self esteem, and who is apt to be socially withdrawn. Such children often display a lack of self-confidence. They are typically shy and have few friends.

P. 28. FACTOR SCALE I 70

The Undisciplined/Self Control Factor Scale is significantly elevated and depicts a child who is apt to be manifesting a behavioral disturbance or conduct disorder. Such children are prone to act out aggressively and display a wide variety of antisocial behavior. They tend to be restless, distractable, hostile, emotionally labile, and impulsive. A history of runaway behavior and delinquency is common in older children. These children have histories of poor school performance, both academically and behaviorly. Lying, cheating, stealing, and fighting are common. These children lack social judgment and self control.

P. 29. FACTOR SCALE I 70

The Social Incompetence Factor Scale is significantly elevated, and depicts a child who is socially withdrawn and lacking in social skills. They are social isolates who are often described as anxious, depressed, and fearful. Such children may present with somatic symptoms and sleep difficulties. They tend to be overly self-critical. These children are ill at ease with others and prefer to be alone or with their family.

P. 30. FACTOR SCALE III 70

The Internalization/Somatic Symptoms Factor Scale is significantly elevated, and depicts a child who is apt to be seen as depressed and anxious. Additionally, they are apt to manifest somatic complaints such as pain and headaches. These children frequently have sleep problems. Children of this profile type are seen as perfectionistic, fearful, and inhibited. Often they are described as sad, but may be seen as emotionally labile.

P. 31. FACTOR SCALE IV 70

The Cognitive Development Factor Scale is significantly elevated, and depicts a child who is apt to evidence deficits in intellectual and/or adaptive behavior. Poor school progress is likely, and the child may be seen as withdrawn and/or impulsive. Occasionally, these children have neurological deficits. A thorough psychoeducational and medical evaluation is indicated.

P. 32. STATEMENTS 3 THROUGH 32 *NOT* USED

This appears to be an essentially normal performance. The child's problems are apt to be within normal limits.

CHAPTER FIFTEEN

Interpretative Statements for Vineland Scales

The Vineland Social Maturity Scale is the granddaddy of all adaptive behavior measures, and the most widely used. It has recently undergone a substantial revision, and the new Vineland Adaptive Behavior Scales are in three editions: the basic Survey Form, an Expanded Form, and the Classroom Edition. Interestingly, the Expanded Form is an extrapolation from the shorter version, rather than the survey form being an abbreviation of the long form. The Classroom Edition is meant to be filled out by the classroom teacher.

Interpretative statements are provided in this section for all three Vineland Adaptive Behavior Scales as well as for the original Vineland Social Maturity Scale. It should be noted, and cannot be emphasized enough, that it is not only not good practice to *not* give an adaptive behavior measure when assessing whether an individual is retarded, but that giving one is now mandated by law. The Vineland Adaptive Behavior Scales can be used with nonretarded individuals to assess their overall maturity, and it has been the author's experience that parents more readily accept adaptive behavior measures with regard to the child's affective functioning. This is probably because the parent not only participates in the process, but also, when parents are informed of what is age appropriate, the information can be presented to them in a concrete fashion and concrete recommendations made for remediation. Thus, the adaptive behavior measure can serve as a springboard for parent counseling to begin.

INTERPRETATIVE STATEMENTS FOR THE VINELAND SOCIAL MATURITY SCALE

B1 (Informant Statement) On the VINELAND SOCIAL MATURTY SCALE the informant was:

B2 (Social Statement) The person's overall Social Age (SA) is:

B3 (Social Quotient Statement) This converts to a Social Quotient (SQ) of:

B4 (Use if the person's social quotient is 83 or less)
The person's social maturity is significantly below that of their age

group. The individual is lacking in social skills and is deficient in adaptive behavior when compared to those at the same age.

B5 (Use if the person's social quotient is 68 or less)
The person's social maturity is markedly below that of their age group. The individual's social skills and adaptive behavior are at the level of retarded individuals.

B6 (Use if the person's social quotient is between 84 and 116)
The person's social maturity is average for the individual's age group. The person possesses an adequate number of age-appropriate social skills and adaptive behavior when compared to others the same age.

B7 (Use if the person's social quotient is 117 or more)
The person's social maturity is above average for the individual's age group. The person is more mature than most individuals the same age.

B8 (Use if the person's social quotient is 16 points below their IQ and below 84)
The person's social maturity is not only below that of their age group but also is significantly below what would be expected for an individual of their intellectual ability.

B9 (Use if the person's social quotient is 16 points below their IQ and below 68)
The person's social maturity is markedly below, not only their age group, and at a level of retarded individuals, but also is significantly below what would be expected for an individual of their intellectual ability.

B10 (Use if the person's IQ is below the retarded cut-off, e.g., 68–70, and the person's social quotient is above 68)
The person's social quotient is above their IQ and above the range usually attained by retarded individuals. It is likely that the person is not retarded and that their IQ is depressed due to other factors, such as cultural bias, English as a second language, or other health impairment.

INTERPRETATIVE STATEMENTS FOR THE VINELAND ADAPTIVE BEHAVIOR SCALES

B11 (Informant Statement - Survey Form)
On the VINELAND ADAPTIVE BEHAVIOR SCALE - Survey Form the informant was:

B12 (Informant Statement - Expanded Form)
On the VINELAND ADAPTIVE BEHAVIOR SCALE - Expanded Form the informant was:

B13 (Informant Statement - Classroom Edition)
On the VINELAND ADAPTIVE BEHAVIOR SCALE - Classroom Edition the informant was:

B14 (Adaptive Behavior Composite Score Statement)
The person's adaptive behavior composite score was: (insert the score and the words): above average for 116+, average for 85–115, below average for 70–84, and quite low for 69 or less).

B15 (Use if the person's adaptive behavior composite score is 84 or less)
The person's overall social maturity is significantly below that of their age group. The individual is lacking in social skills and is deficient in adaptive behavior when compared to those of the same age.

B16 (Use if the person's adaptive behavior composite score is 69 or less)
The person's overall social maturity is markedly below that of their age group. The individual's social skills and adaptive behavior are at the level of retarded individuals.

B17 (Use if the person's adaptive behavior composite score is between 85 and 115)
The person's overall social maturity is average for the individual's age group. The person possesses an adequate amount of age-appropriate social skills and adaptive behavior when compared to others the same age.

B18 (Use if the person's adaptive behavior composite score is 116 or more)
The person's overall social maturity is above average for the individual's age group. The person is more mature than most individuals the same age.

B19 (Use if the person's adaptive behavior composite score is 15 points below their IQ and below 85)
The person's overall social maturity is not only below that of their age group but also is significantly below what would be expected for an individual of their intellectual ability.

B20 (Use if the person's adaptive behavior composite score is 15 points below their IQ and below 70)
The person's overall social maturity is markedly below, not only that of their age group, and at a level of retarded individuals, but also is significantly below what would be expected for an individual of their intellectual ability.

B21 (Use if the person's IQ is below the retarded cut-off, e.g. 68–70, and the person's adaptive behavior composite score is above 69)
The individual's social quotient is above their IQ and above the range usually attained by retarded individuals. It is likely that the person is not retarded and that their IQ is depressed due to other factors, such as cultural bias, English as a second language, or other handicap.

B22 The person's Adaptive Behavior Composite Score is equal to a social age equivalent of: (report 18+ as 18 years or older).

B23 (Use for Communication Domain)
The individual's performance in the Communication Domain of adaptive behavior is: (insert the score and the words: above average for 116+, average for 85–115, below average for 70–84, or quite low for 69 or less).

B24 The person's Communication Domain Scale is average performance (Social Age equivalent) for: (report 18+ as 18 years or older)

B25 (Use for Daily Living Skills Domain)
The individual's performance in the Daily Living Skills Domain of adaptive behavior is: (insert the score and the words: above average for 116+, average for 85–115, below average for 70–84, or quite low for 69 or less).

B26 The person's Daily Living Skills Domain Scale is average performance (Social Age equivalent) for: (report 18+ as 18 years or older).

B27 (Use for Socialization Domain)
The individual's performance in the Socialization Domain of adaptive behavior is: (insert the score and the words: above average for 116+, average for 85–115, below average for 70–84, or quite low for 69 or less).

B28 The person's Socialization Domain Scale is average performance (Social Age equivalent) for: (report 18+ as 18 years or older).

B29 (Use for Motor Skills Domain if child is under 6)
(insert the score and the words: above average for 116+, average for 85–115, below average for 70–84, or quite low for 69 or less).

B30 The person's Motor Skills Domain Scale is average performance (Social Age equivalent) for:

B31 (Use for Maladaptive Behavior Domain)
The person's performance on the Maladaptive Behavior Domain is:

B32 (50% or less use)
Nonsignificant

B33 (51–84% use)
Of Intermediate significance, and additional psychological evaluation of the child's emotional functioning is suggested.

B34 (85%+ use)
Significant, and additional psychological evaluation of the child's emotional functioning is indicated.

CHAPTER SIXTEEN

Interpretative Statement for the Assessment of Stressful Life Events

This section includes the now famous Social Readjustment Rating Scale, which has been the primary research instrument for assessing the relationship between stressful life events and physical, emotional, and psychosomatic disorders since its development in 1967. Indeed, Holmes and Rahe (1967) have been probably more responsible than anyone else for clarifying the relationship between emotional factors and health. In the author's experience, it has not only helped individuals to understand the relationship between stressful life events and psychosomatic problems, but also is a good instrument to use to help individuals understand that emotional factors, such as depression and anxiety, are directly related to the turmoil engendered by stressful life events. Also, the research of Holmes and Rahe (1967) has led to the greater acceptance of the fact that emotional factors do play a role in health by physicians at large, because research with the Social Readjustment Rating Scales clarifies the relationship between stress and illness.

The Social Readjustment Rating Scale and the other instruments in this section can serve as a handy interview aid, and, occasionally, information that is not picked up in the standard interview may be reviewed and clarified by going through the items on the Social Readjustment Rating Scale or the other stress adjustment instruments for stressful life events in this section. When the instrument is given by the examiner, the Social Readjustment Rating Scale form is used. When the assessment of stressful life events is taken directly by the patient, the Survey of Recent Experience should be used. For adolescents, R. Dean Coddington (1981) has devised the Life Event Scale for Adolescents, and the Life Event Scale for Children. The adolescent can take the Life Event Scale for Adolescents, and it has items that are more pertinent to an adolescent's life, such as failing a grade in school. Interestingly, Coddington omitted dropping out of school from his scale, but, in the author's use of the scale, this is its only limitation.

The Life Events for Children, which was also developed by Coddington (1981), is an assessment instrument of stressful life events for children. This scale is given to the parent, as opposed to the child.

SOCIAL READJUSTMENT RATING SCALE

E-1 Less than 150 Life Change Units
On the SOCIAL READJUSTMENT RATING SCALE, the person's overall performance is indicative of an individual who has not incurred a significant amount of environmental stress in the last year.

E-2 150 to 199 Life Change Units
On the SOCIAL READJUSTMENT RATING SCALE, the person's overall performance is indicative of an individual who has incurred a mild number of environmental stresses in the last year, the most significant of which are:

E-3 200 to 299 Life Change Units
On the SOCIAL READJUSTMENT RATING SCALE, the person's overall performance is indicative of an individual who has incurred a moderate number of stresses in the past year, the most significant of which are:

E-4 300 to 399 Life Change Units
On the SOCIAL READJUSTMENT RATING SCALE, the person's overall performance is indicative of an individual who has incurred a severe number of environmental stresses in the past year, the most significant of which are:

E-5 400+ Life Change Units
On the SOCIAL READJUSTMENT RATING SCALE, the person's overall performance is indicative of an individual who has incurred an extreme number of environmental stresses in the past year, the most significant of which are:

SCHEDULE OF RECENT EXPERIENCE

E-6 Less than 150 Life Change Units
On the SCHEDULE OF RECENT EXPERIENCE, the person's overall performance is indicative of an individual who has not incurred a significant amount of environmental stress in the last year.

E-7 150 to 199 Life Change Units
On the SCHEDULE OF RECENT EXPERIENCE, the person's overall performance is indicative of an individual who has incurred a mild number of environmental stresses in the last year, the most significant of which are:

E-8 200 to 299 Life Change Units
On the SCHEDULE OF RECENT EXPERIENCE, the person's over-

all performance is indicative of an individual who has incurred a moderate number of stresses in the past year, the most significant of which are:

E-9 300 to 399 Life Change Units
On the SCHEDULE OF RECENT EXPERIENCE, the person's overall performance is indicative of an individual who has incurred a severe number of environmental stresses in the past year, the most significant of which are:

E-10 400+ Life Change Units
On the SCHEDULE OF RECENT EXPERIENCE, the person's overall performance is indicative of an individual who has incurred an extreme number of environmental stresses in the past year, the most significant of which are:

E-11 Death of a spouse

E-12 Divorce

E-13 Marital separation from mate

E-14 Detention in jail or other institution

E-15 Death of a close family member

E-16 Major personal injury or illness

E-17 Marriage

E-18 Being fired from work

E-19 Marital reconciliation with mate

E-20 Retirement from work

E-21 Major change in the health or behavior of a family member

E-22 Pregnancy

E-23 Sexual difficulties

E-24 Gaining a new family member (e.g., through birth, adoption, oldster moving in, etc.)

E-25 Major business readjustment (e.g., merger, reorganization, bankruptcy, etc.)

E-26 Major change in financial state (e.g., a lot worse off or a lot better off than usual)

E-27 Death of a close friend

E-28 Changing to a different line of work

E-29 Major change in the number of arguments with spouse (e.g., either a lot more or a lot less than usual regarding child-rearing, personal habits, etc.)

E-30 Taking on a mortgage for a home or business.

E-31 Foreclosure on mortgage or loan.

E-32 Major change in responsibilities at work (e.g., promotion, demotion, lateral transfer)

E-33 Son or daughter leaving home (e.g., marriage, attending college, etc.)

E-34 In-law troubles

E-35 Outstanding personal achievement

E-36 Wife beginning or ceasing work outside the home

E-37 Beginning or ceasing formal schooling

E-38 Major change in living conditions (e.g., building a new home, remodeling, deterioration of home or neighborhood)

E-39 Revision of personal habits (dress, manners, associations, etc.)

E-40 Troubles with boss

E-41 Major change in working hours or conditions

E-42 Change in residence

E-43 Changing to a new school

E-44 Major change in usual type and/or amount of recreation

E-45 Major change in church activities (e.g., a lot more or a lot less than usual)

E-46 Major change in social activities (e.g., clubs, dancing, movies, visiting, etc.)

E-47 Taking on a small mortgage or loan (e.g., purchasing a car, TV, freezer, etc.)

E-48 Major change in sleeping habits (a lot more or a lot less sleep, or a change in part of day when asleep)

E-49 Major change in number of family get-togethers (e.g., a lot more or a lot less than usual)

E-50 Major change in eating habits (e.g., a lot more or a lot less food intake, or very different meal hours or surroundings)

E-51 Vacation

E-52 Christmas

E-53 Minor violations of the law (e.g., traffic tickets, jaywalking, disturbing the peace, etc.)

LIFE EVENT SCALE FOR CHILDREN

E-54 Less than 110 (for age 8–10) or 135 (for age 11–13) Life Change Units

On the LIFE EVENT SCALE FOR CHILDREN, the child's overall

performance is indicative of an individual who has not incurred a significant amount of environmental stress in the last year.

E-55 More than 110 (for age 8–10) or 135 (for age 11–13) Life Change Units
On the LIFE EVENT SCALE FOR CHILDREN, the child's overall performance is indicative of an individual who has incurred a significant number of environmental stresses in the last year, the most significant of which are:

LIFE EVENT SCALE FOR ADOLESCENTS

E-56 Less than 135 (for age 12–13), 170 (for age 14–16), or 200 (for age 17–18)
On the LIFE EVENT SCALE FOR ADOLESCENTS, the individual's overall performance is indicative of an individual who has not incurred a significant amount of stress in the past year, the most significant of which are:

E-57 More than 135 (for age 12–13), 170 (for age 14–16) or 200 (for age 17–18)
On the LIFE EVENT SCALE FOR ADOLESCENTS, the individual's overall performance is indicative of an individual who has incurred a significant number of environmental stresses in the past year, the most significant of which are:

E-58 Loss of job by father or mother

E-59 Major increase in parents' income

E-60 Major decrease in parents' income

E-61 Start of a new problem between parents

E-62 End of a problem between parents

E-63 Change in father's job causing less time at home

E-64 New adult moving into the home

E-65 Mother beginning work outside the home

E-66 Being told you are attractive by a friend

E-67 Going on first date

E-68 Finding a new dating partner

E-69 Breaking up with a boy friend or girl friend

E-70 Being told to break up with a boy friend or girl friend

E-71 Start of a new problem between person and parents

E-72 End of a new problem between person and parents

E-73 Beginning first year of senior high school

E-74 Move to a new school district
E-75 Failure of a grade in school
E-76 Suspension from school
E-77 Graduating from high school
E-78 Being accepted in college of choice
E-79 Recognition for excelling in a sport or other activity
E-80 Getting first driver's license
E-81 Being responsible for an auto accident
E-82 Becoming an adult member of a church
E-83 Being invited to join a social organization
E-84 Being invited by a friend to break the law
E-85 Appearance in juvenile court
E-86 Failing to achieve something really desired
E-87 Getting a summer job
E-88 Getting first permanent job
E-89 Deciding to leave home
E-90 Being sent away from home
E-91 Being hospitalized for injury or illness
E-92 Death of a close friend
E-93 Becoming involved with drugs
E-94 Stopping use of drugs
E-95 Finding an adult who really respects you
E-96 Getting pregnant or fathering a pregnancy
E-97 Getting married
E-98 Outstanding personal achievement (special prize)

CHAPTER SEVENTEEN

Interpretative Statements for the Beck Depression Inventory

The Beck Depression Inventory is a widely used quick, objective assessment of depression. This section presents interpretative statements for the standard form for the Beck Depression Inventory, and provides global statements for the overall depression ratings from the Beck Depression Inventory as well as statements for highlighting major specific symptom areas of depression.

AUTOMATED INTERPRETATIVE STATEMENTS FOR THE BECK DEPRESSION INVENTORY

Beck Depression Inventory has been found useful in measuring the various symptoms often associated with depression. This instrument also gives an overall level of depression score.

X-1 Score 5–12
On the BECK DEPRESSION INVENTORY, the person's overall performance was not indicative of significant depression.

X-2 Score 13–20
On the BECK DEPRESSION INVENTORY, the person's overall performance was indicative of a mildly depressed individual.

X-3 Score 21–25
On the BECK DEPRESSION INVENTORY, the person's overall performance was indicative of a moderately depressed individual.

X-4 Score 26–35
On the BECK DEPRESSION INVENTORY, the person's overall performance was indicative of a severely depressed individual.

X-5 Score of 4 or less
On the BECK DEPRESSON INVENTORY, the person's overall performance was below that usually attained by normals, and may constitute a denial of depression on the part of the individual.

X-6 Score 36+

On the BECK DEPRESSION INVENTORY, the person's overall performance was above that usually attained by severely depressed individuals, and may constitute an exaggeration on the part of the individual. Such exaggeration is most often encountered in persons with histrionic or borderline personality disorders, though a significant minority of those who score in this range are severely depressed.

If a score of 3 is scored on any of the Items X-7 through X-28, print the appropriate statement below:

X-7 Significant symptom areas noted are:

X-8 Sadness

X-9 Pessimism

X-10 Sense of failure

X-11 Dissatisfaction

X-12 Guilt

X-13 Expectation of punishment

X-14 Self-dislike

X-15 Self-accusation

X-16 Suicidal ideas

X-17 Crying

X-18 Irritability

X-19 Social withdrawal

X-20 Indecisiveness

X-21 Body image change

X-22 Work retardation

X-23 Insomnia

X-24 Fatigability

X-25 Anorexia

X-26 Weight loss

X-27 Somatic preoccupation

X-28 Loss of libido

CHAPTER EIGHTEEN

Interpretative Statements for the Vocational Preference Inventory

The Vocational Preference Inventory is Holland's (1985c) initial assessment of his six-factor model of interests. The instrument is currently in its eighth revision, and the following statements are applicable to the eighth edition as well as *all* earlier editions, although some of the earlier editions do not have all of the special scales in addition to the basic RIASEC Codes. The interpretative statements for the Vocational Preference Inventory yield a useful profile that spans the gamut of abilities with regard to the occupations delineated. It should be noted that, because of its brevity, the Vocational Preference Inventory is an ideal scale to read orally to an individual who is handicapped or for some other reason is not up to taking the test in its standard paper and pencil form.

SECTION 1: INVALID PROFILES

Rule 1: Call Invalid (high response):

A.1. If five or more scales have a raw score of 11 or more

or

A.2. The Acquiescence Scale has a raw score of 20 or more

and

B. Over three Vocational Scales (1 through 6) have a raw score of 13 or more.

Use the following only:

V-1 On the Vocational Preference Inventory, the person's overall performance depicts an individual who endorsed an overwhelmingly large number of occupations on the "Like" direction. The test is apt to be invalid and, consequently, the vocational profile is not interpreted. This indiscriminate responding may be associated with a poor attitude, or it may depict an individual who is confused. This type of pattern often occurs in individuals who are still in the fantasy stage of vocational development, or they may feel their choices are some what limited and, consequently, must take whatever may be open to them.

Rule II: *Call Invalid (low response):*

A.1. If five or more scales have a raw score of 3 or less

or

A.2. If the Acquiescence Scale score has a raw score of less than 5

and

B. No Vocational Scales (1 through 6) are above a standard score of 65

C. More than one occupation was chosen

Use the following only:

V-2 On the Vocational Preference Inventory, the person's overall performance depicts an individual who endorsed few occupations on the "Like" direction. The test is apt to be invalid and, consequently, the vocational profile is not interpreted. This may depict an individual who is negative and resistant to testing, who is depressed, or who is committed to an occupation or occupation group to the exclusion of all others. Other possibilities include an individual who is not overly motivated to work, or who is at a virtual loss for an occupational choice and feels ineffectual in doing much of anything.

Rule III Same as Rule II, except only one occupation out of the entire 150 repertoire was chosen. In this case use the following only:

V-3 On the Vocational Preference Inventory, the person's overall performance depicts an individual who endorsed only one occupational choice, to the exclusion of all others. This is usually indicative of a person who is committed to an occupational career and is unwilling to consider vocational alternatives. That one occupation is "______" (insert the one choice here).

Rule IV: If infrequency score is 8 or more, or seven scales have raw scores between 4 and 10, use this paragraph only:

V-4 On the Vocational Preference Inventory, the person's overall performance depicts an individual who is apt to have produced an invalid profile and the probability is that at a level of 80% the profile is a random one. Consequently, the resulting test profile is not interpreted. Possible reasons for this are low intellect, marginal reading ability, poor motivation, or someone is confused or feels quite negative about himself or herself. Assuming the intellectual and academic causes have been ruled out, it may be worthwhile to discuss readministration of the scale with the person.

SECTION II: VALID PROFILE INTERPRETATIONS

Rule I: Begin the interpretation with the Introductory Statement:

V-5 On the Vocational Preference Inventory, the person's overall performance depicts an individual who produced a valid profile and whose interests cluster in the areas of "_____" (pick the three highest occupational scores from the cluster of Realistic, Intellectual, Social, Conventional, Enterprising, and Artistic occupations), using the following rules:

A. If one of the six occupational areas is 25 standard score points above the second highest occupational area, use only the highest occupational area.

B. If the highest two occupational areas are within 25 standard score points of one another, and the third over 25 points below the highest occupational area, use only the two highest occupational areas.

C. If three occupational areas are high and all three are within 25 standard score points of one another, then choose the highest three and list all three. In the case of ties, count from left to right, from Realistic over to Artistic (stated another way, from Occupational Code 1 to occupational Code 6). Add the word "occupations" to the end of the one, two, or three statements so that the sentence ends with the word "occupations"; add *and* if more than one occupation is listed. For example, if the person's interests cluster in the areas of Realistic, Intellectual, and Conventional occupations, then the sentence should read, "On the Vocational Preference Inventory the person's overall performance depicts an individual whose interests cluster in the areas of Realistic, Intellectual, and Conventional occupations."

Rule II: For the same cluster as above, namely, the highest one, two, or three Vocational Scales, Realistic through Artistic (1 through 6), and using the same rules as Rule I, begin the second sentence:

V-6 Such individuals are "_____" (list the following adjectives: for the Realistic Scale, list realistic, practical, mechanical, and technical; for the Intellectual Scale, list scientific, shy, independent, persistent; for the Social Scale, list controlled, conventional, conforming, and orderly; for the Enterprising Scale, list enthusiastic, dominant, adventurous, and impulsive; and for the Artistic Scale, list artistic, expressive, sensitive, and unconventional). NOTE: Be sure to add *and* before the last adjective.

Rule III: On the Self Control Scale, interpret using the following rules:

A. If the person has a raw score of 13 or 14, use the following:

V-7 The person has a large amount of self control and is apt to be cautious, serious, and responsible.

B. If the Self Control Scale is 6 or less, use the following statement:

V-8 The person scored low on the Self Control Scale and the individual is apt to be somewhat impulsive, spontaneous, and hedonistic.

Rule IV: On the Status Scale, interpret using the following rules:

A. If the person has a raw score of 12 or more, use the following:

V-9 The person has a high need for status and is apt to be upwardly mobile, self-confident, and value prestige.

B. If the Status Score is 6 or less, use the following:

V-10 The person has a low need for status and may be somewhat lacking in self-confidence and self-depreciating.

Rule V: If the person has a 3-point Vocational Code (the three highest occupational scores are within 25 points of one another) and the 3-point Vocational Code has a listing of Vocational Code in Section III, Occupations for High Point Codes (below), use the following statement:

V-11 The person's overall vocational interests most closely resemble the following occupations "______" (use out those occupations listed for the 3-point code).

If the 3-point code has no Vocational Code section listed in Section III, Occupations for High Point Codes, go down to the second category and use only the following statement:

V-12 Based on the overall interest profile, suggested occupations are: "______"

Use all occupations where the 3-point code has a 2-point code listed as the first two letters. Do this also where there is only a two high-point code. Two-point codes will list all of the three highest codes in a category that have the 2-point code listed as the first two letters; for instance, if the person's highest interest area was RIA, this would be printed in with the first statement above, followed by the second statement and the other RI interests, which would include the RIS, the RIE, the RIC, and the RIA codes. If only a 2-point code was chosen (such as AS), then only occupations with the first two points of 3-point occupational cluster would be printed out—namely, ASE and ASI. If there is only one high point, that is, that there is a 25-point difference between the highest code and the second highest code, then the only statement used is:

V-13 Based on the overall interest profile, suggested occupations are: "______"

And all codes for that category would be printed out. For instance, if the person chose social occupations to the exclusion of all others and has a valid profile, then all occupations in Section III, Occupations for High Point Codes Section, beginning with an S, would be printed out for that person, namely, SEC, SER, SEI, SCE, SRI, SRE, SIA, SIE, SIC, SIR, SAE, SAC, SAI.

Rule VI: If the person, rather than a professional, is the recipient of the report, add the following statement at the end of the printout:

V-14 The Vocational Preference Inventory is a valid but not perfect or absolute measure of your vocational interests. All things considered, the occupations listed above are apt to reflect most of the occupations most like your interests. Occasionally, an occupation you are interested in may not appear for one reason or another. When that happens, it may be good to try to find out more about it anyway. The occupations this test says you are interested in should serve to broaden your field of occupations to consider as a vocational choice. Please note a wide range of skill levels are presented in the occupational listing section. This test is an interest test, and, to make a wise vocational choice, you will need to consider your scholastic abilities/aptitudes as well as the amount of time you want to spend on education/training in addition to your vocational interests.

SECTION III: OCCUPATIONS FOR HIGH POINT CODES

V-15 RIA
Draftsman/Draftswoman
Dental Laboratory Technician
Decorative Painter
Medical Instrument Maker
Orthopedic Appliance
and Limb Technician

V-16 RIS
Agronomist
Forester
Cook
Baker
Chef
Food Processing Worker
Tool and Die Maker
Powerhouse Repairman
Optician
Powerhouse Electrician
Stationary Engineer
Boiler Operator

V-17 RIE
Civil Engineer
Draftsman
Petroleum Engineer

Well Logging Operator, Mud Analysis
Landscape Artist
Air Traffic Controller
Electroplater
Metal Caster
Instrument Maker
Machinist
Milling Machine Operator
Drill Press Operator
Air Conditioning Mechanic
Machine Operator
Automobile Mechanic
Truck Mechanic
Motor Cycle Mechanic
Aircraft Mechanic
Diesel Mechanic
Maintenance Mechanic
Millwright
Bicycle Repairman
Engraver
Boiler Maker
Automobile-Body Repairman
Lineman
Automatic Equipment Repairman
Telephone Repairman
Electrician
Plumber
Pipe Fitter
Insulation Worker
Floor Layer
Glazer
Roofer
Building Maintenance Man
Gas Plant Operator
Pump Station Operator
Sewage Plant Operator
Tree Trimmer
Shipping and Receiving Clerk
Mail Sorter
Laundry Worker
Soldier
Sailor
Farmer
Rancher
Sandblaster
Enameler
Stillman
Furnace Operator
Steel Worker
Chemical Processing Worker
Paint Mixer
Tire Molder
Chemical operator
Kiln Operator
Concrete Plant Worker
Gunsmith
Bindery Worker
Offset Pressman
Printing Press Operator
Pattern Maker
Sawmill Worker
Woodworking Machine Operator
Lens Grinder
Assembly Press Operator
Leatherworker
Silversmith
Sheet Metal Worker
Bench Assembler
Locksmith
Television Service Repairman
Electronics Assembler
Toy Assembler
Gem Cutter
Stone Cutter
Welder

V-18 RIC

Agricultural Engineer
Marine Engineer
Draftsman
Lineman
Electrical Appliance Salesman
Refrigerator and Air-Conditioning Repairman

Carpenter
Dispatcher
Tow-Truck Operator
Depot Master
Teamster
Oil Driller
Miner
Power Plant Operator

V-19 RAI
Recording Machine Operator
Modelmaker
Printer
Bookbinder

V-20 RSE
Railroad Conductor
Freight Weigher
Housekeeper
Waiter
Butcher
Barber
Security Guard
Jailer
Armored Car Guard
Firefighter
Oven Furnace Operator
Casting Operator
Foundry Worker
Blacksmith
Bus Driver
Taxicab Driver
Service Station Attendant
Parking Lot Attendant
Forklift Truck Operator

V-21 RSC
Bill Collector
Short Order Cook
Bridge Operator
Porter
Janitor
Exterminator
Window Cleaner
Tractor operator
Compress Operator

V-22 RSI
Weaver
Knitting Machiner Operator

V-23 REC
Laundry Worker
Maid
Textile Worker

V-24 REI
Stock Clerk
Parts Clerk
Paper Machine Operator
Air-Conditioning Mechanic
Refrigeration Mechanic
Furnace Installer and Repairman
Construction Worker
Building Wrecker

V-25 RES
Nursemaid and Babysitter
Policeman
Detective
Game Warden
Radio Dispatcher
Fire Inspector
Dog Catcher
Skin Diver
Rancher
Fisherman
Forester
Railroad Brakeman
Locomotive Engineer
Conductor
Airport Serviceman
Freight Expeditor
Packager

V-26 RCI
Surveyor
Yardman
Office Machine Serviceman

Painter
Logger
Motion Picture Projectionist

V-27 RCS
Mail Carrier
Meter Reader
Textile Worker
Upholsterer
Seamstress/Tailor
Alteration Tailor
Seawing Machine Operator
Plasterer
Dry Wall Applicator
Cement Mason
Bulldozer Operator
Power Shovel Operator
Pipe Layer
Paving Machine Operator
Bricklayer
Stone Mason
Longshoreman

V-28 RCE
Truck Driver
Dredge Operator
Crane Operator

V-29 IAR
Astronomer
Physicist
Anthropologist

V-30 ISR
Biological Aid
Osteopath
Medical Technologist
Dental Hygenist
EKG Technician
EEG Technician
X-Ray Technician
Medical Laboratory Assistant
Nuclear Medical Technologist

V-31 ISA
Physician
Surgeon

V-32 IES
Pharmacist

V-33 ICR
Urban Planner
Industrial X-Ray Technician
Handwriting Expert

V-34 IRA
Nuclear Engineer
Test Reactor Operator
Statistician
Programmer
Actuary
Financial Analyst
Chemist
Geologist
Paleontologist
Oceanographer
Meteorologist
Geographer
Laboratory Tester

V-35 IRS
Biochemist
Biologist
Microbiologist
Zoologist
Veterinarian

V-36 IRE
Aircraft Designer
Electrical Engineer
Design Draftsman
Radio Engineer
Electrical Engineer
Ceramic Engineer
Chemical Engineer
Metallurgist
Dentist

V-37 IRC
Airplane Pilot
Helicopter Pilot
Instrument Inspector

V-38 ASE
Drama Teacher

Actor
Dance Instructor
Dancer

V-39 ASI
Art Teacher
Music Teacher
Musician
Singer

V-40 AES
Comedian
Clown
Magician
Puppeteer
Announcer
Camp Counselor
Stuntman
Advertising Executive
Public Relations Man
Model

V-41 AIS
Writer
Editor
News Commentator
Playwright
Reporter
Commercial Artist
Cartoonist
Illustrator
Furrier
Fashion Designer
Sample Maker

V-42 AIE
Display Man
Decorator

V-43 AIR
Architect
Cameraman
Photographer
Painter
Sculptor
Sign Writer
Calligrapher
Layout Person
Sign Painter
Lithographer
Photo Engraver
Xerography Machine Operator
Darkroom Developer
Engraver
Silk Screen Painter

V-44 ASC
Make-Up Artist

V-45 AEI
Film Editor
Set Electrician
Dubbing Machine Operator
Video-Recording Engineer
TV Cameraman

V-46 SEC
Psychologist
Counselor
Personnel Manager
Educational Director
Employment Interviewer
Placement Officer
Kitchen Supervisor
Steward
Bartender
Masseur
Embalmer

V-47 SER
Insurance Claims Adjuster
Retail Salesperson
Commodity Salesperson

V-48 SEI
Historian
Genealogist
Archeological Assistant

V-49 SCE
Public Health Officer
Professional Sports Scout
Institutional Superintendent
Housemother
Funeral Director

Field Representative
Director, Volunteer Services
Director, Nurses Registry
Direct, School Lunch Program
Manager
Motion Picture Producer

V-50 SRI
County Agricultural Agent
Home Economist
Tour Guide
Ambulance Attendant
Nurses Aid
Orderly
Psychiatric Aid
Animal Keeper
Horseshoer
Veterinary-Hospital Attendant

V-51 SRE
Instructor Vocational Training
Education Supervisor
Audiovisual Specialist
Visiting Teacher
Athletic Coach
Adult Education Teacher
Jockey
Umpire
Athlete
Hotel Manager
Housekeeper
Child Care Attendant
Nursery School Teacher

V-52 SIA
Sociologist
Criminologist
Intelligence Specialist
Registered Nurse
Professor
Academic Dean

V-53 SIE
Research Nutritionist
Dietician
Building Inspector
Food and Drug Inspector
Claim Examiner
Customs Inspector

V-54 SIC
Case Worker
Social Worker

V-55 SIR
Audiologist
Chiropractor
Optometrist
Podiatrist
Speech Pathologist
Inhalation Therapist
Occupation Therapist
Dental Assistant
L.V.N.
Physical Therapist
Surgical Technician

V-56 SAE
Principal
Secondary School Teacher

V-57 SAC
Hairdressers
Cosmetologists

V-58 SAI
Political Scientist
Kindergarten Teacher
Elementary School Teacher
Special Education Teacher
Librarian
Curator
Minister
Religious Education Director
Priest
Midwife
First-Aid Assistant
Practical Nurse

V-59 ECI
Economist
Market Research Analyst

V-60 ECS
Broker
Buyer
Purchasing Agent
Title Clerk
Insurance Salesperson
Real Estate Salesperson
Salesperson of Services

V-61 ERI
Construction Inspector
Contractor

V-62 ERC
Mine Foreman
Drilling and Production Superintendent

V-63 EIS
Engineering Supply Salesperson

V-64 EIR
Ship Pilot
Shipmates
Ship Captain
Ship Engineer

V-65 EAS
Lawyer
Judge

V-66 ESC
Sales Manager
Public Relations Person
Labor Relations Specialist
Park Ranger
Underwriter
Production Superintendent
Brewmaster
Television Station Manager
Traffic Manager
Bank Vice President
Controller
Apartment Manager
Customs Agent
Postmaster
Tax Assessor Security Officer
Booking Agent
Business Equipment Salesperson
Grocery Clerk
Telephone Solicitor
Auctioneer
Demonstrator
Model
Carpet Layer

V-67 ESR
Automobile Salesperson
Route Salesperson

V-68 ESI
Safety Engineer
Production Planner
Systems Analyst
Director Quality Control
Store Manager
Wholesaler
Medical Equipment Salesperson

V-69 ESA
Photographic Equipment Salesperson
Musical Instrument Salesperson
Manufacturer's Representative
Automobile Parts Salesperson
Airplane Flight Attendant

V-70 CRI
Duplicating Machine Operator
Dictaphone Typist
Automatic Typewriter Operator
Construction Yard Foreman

V-71 CRS
File Clerk
Addressograph Operator

V-72 CRE
Production Clerk
Mail Clerk
Post Office Clerk

V-73 CIS
Accountant
Auditor
Computer Operator
Keypunch Operator
Data Typist
Payroll Clerk
Billing Clerk
General Office Clerk
Timekeeper
Accounting Clerk

V-74 CIE
Court Reporter
Stenographer
Clerk-Typist

V-75 CIR
Control Clerk
Balance Clerk

V-76 CSE
Secretary
Telephone Operator
Receptionist

V-77 CSI
Insurance Clerk
Bookkeeper
Cashier
Bank Teller

V-78 CSA
Hotel Clerk
Claims Auditor
Survey Worker
Court Clerk
Credit Clerk
Order Clerk

CHAPTER NINETEEN

Interpretative Statements for the Summary and Comments Section

Included in this section is a format for the DSM III multiaxal diagnoses, as well as prepared statements to be used in the Summary and Comments section of the report. Topics covered are general distress of the examinee, as well as anxiety disorders, disassociative disorders, somatization disorders, depressive disorders, psychotic disorders, alcohol and drug problems, adolescent behavior problems, and character disorders. A differential diagnostic statement section is included. Also provided are statements relating to organic brain syndrome, learning disabilities, attention deficit disorders, and mental retardation. Statements relating the person's general IQ and ego level are included. Medical and psychiatric recommendations are included, as are general psychotherapy recommendations and recommendations for marriage and family therapy. Regarding the latter sections of therapy recommendations, the user may wish to refer to the interpretative section for the Diagnostic Inventory of Personality and Symptoms to get the author's own synthesis of which personality types and disorders are most apt to be remedied by which treatment, or the user may wish to make his or her own decisions regarding the use of the statements in this section, or, as always, develop his or her own.

GENERAL DISTRESS

Z-1. The person is currently evidencing a mild amount of reactive emotional distress.

Z-2. The person is currently evidencing a significant amount of reactive emotional distress.

Z-3. The person is currently evidencing a very significant amount of reactive emotional distress.

Z-4. The person is currently evidencing a marked amount of reactive emotional distress.

Z-5. The person is currently evidencing an extreme amount of reactive emotional distress.

NEUROSIS, ANXIETY, DISSOCIATION, AND SOMATIZATION

Z-6. The person appears to be a chronically anxious individual.

Z-7. The person appears to be suffering from what in earlier terminology would be classified as a chronic mixed neurosis.

Z-8. The person appears to be suffering from a mixture of anxiety and somatization.

Z-9. The person is anxious and hypochondriacal.

Z-10. The person appears to be evidencing a post traumatic stress disorder.

Z-11. The person is suffering from phobic anxiety and panic attacks.

Z-12. The person is an anxious, phobic individual.

Z-13. The person is evidencing dissociative phenomena.

Z-14. The person appears to be evidencing psychological factors affecting physical condition.

Z-15. The person appears to be evidencing psychogenic pain.

Z-16. The person appears to meet the criterion for a bona fide somatization disorder, and is evidencing a multiplicity of health complaints.

DEPRESSION

Z-17. The individual is currently evidencing a mild amount of depression.

Z-18. The individual is currently evidencing a significant amount of depression.

Z-19. The individual is currently evidencing a very significant amount of depression.

Z-20. The individual is a severely depressed individual.

Z-21. The person would appear to be a chronically depressed individual who is evidencing a dysthymic disorder.

Z-22. The individual is an anxious, agitated individual.

Z-23. The individual is currently evidencing agitated depression.

Z-24. The individual is currently suffering from an endogenous depression.

PSYCHOSIS

Z-25. The person is a psychotic individual with a thought disorder.

Z-26. The individual is currently psychotic and evidencing a major affective disorder.

Z-27. The individual is currently evidencing a major affective disorder.

Z-28. The individual is currently evidencing a psychotic and paranoid disorder.

ALCOHOL AND DRUG PROBLEMS

Z-29. The person is evidencing episodic alcohol abuse.

Z-30. The person is an alcoholic.

Z-31. The person is an experimental drug user.

Z-32. The person is a chronic substance abuser.

Z-33. The person is dependent on drugs.

Z-34. The person is engaged in very significant poly-drug abuse.

Z-35. The person has engaged in poly-drug abuse.

CHILD AND ADOLESCENT BEHAVIOR PROBLEMS

Z-36. The person is a child who is suffering from significant behavioral and emotional difficulties at present.

Z-37. The person is a child who is currently evidencing mild behavioral-emotional difficulties.

Z-38. The person is a child who is currently evidencing extreme behavioral-emotional problems at present.

Z-39. The person's adolescent behavior problems, if left unattended, are apt to harden into a chronic impulsive characterological stance toward life.

Z-40. Without significant psychotherapeutic intervention at this point in time, the individual's difficulties are apt to harden into a chronic characterological stance toward life.

CHARACTEROLOGICAL

Z-41. The person is an impulsive, unstable individual.

Z-42. The person has difficulty in modulating their emotions.

Z-43. The person is an individual who in earlier terminology would be classified as a psychopath.

Z-44. The person is apt to be anxious and emotionally labile.

Z-45. The person is an emotionally unstable, emotionally labile, over-dramatic individual.

Z-46. The person is a borderline individual who combines the emotional lability and instability of a hysteric with the wariness of others of a schizoid individual.

Z-47. The person is an oversensitive, brittle individual who is wary of others and has a life script of moving against people.

Z-48. The person is a sensitive individual who, while desirous of close interpersonal contact, is nevertheless overly fearful of rejection.

Z-49. The person is a passive, dependent individual who is easy prey for stress.

Z-50. The person is easy prey for stress.

Z-51. The person is a passive person who is desirous of support.

Z-52. The person is an anxious, inhibited individual who is overconscientious and overdutiful.

Z-53. The person is a manipulative individual who is apt to resort to subterfuge in carrying out the letter, but not the spirit, of acts, and has difficulty expressing negative feelings and emotions.

Z-54. Both passive and aggressive features are indicated in the person's personality make-up.

Z-55. The person is an individual who is introverted and is not generally desirous of socialization.

Z-56. The person is a marginal individual who is eccentric and unusual and is wary and fearful of others.

Z-57. The person lacks a viable identity and firm sense of self.

Z-58. The person is apt to be oppositional and negativistic.

Z-59. The person has significant sexual conflicts.

DIFFERENTIAL DIAGNOSTIC STATEMENTS

Z-60. While a case could be made from the test data that the person is suffering from:

Z-61. the data generally favor the above impression.

Z-62. the data favor the above impression.

Z-63. the data strongly favor the above impression.

Z-64. the data slightly favor the above impression.

ORGANIC BRAIN SYNDROME

Z-65. The person's performance on the neuropsychological screening test depicts an individual who is currently suffering from mild organic deficits.

Z-66. The person's performance on the neuropsychological screening tests depict an individual who is currently suffering from mild to moderate organic deficits.

Z-67. The person's performance on the neuropsychological screening tests depict an individual who is currently suffering from moderate organic deficits.

Z-68. The person's performance on the neuropsychological screening tests depicts an individual who is suffering from moderate to severe organic deficits.

Z-69. The person's performance on the neuropsychological screening tests depicts an individual who is suffering from severe organic defects.

Z-70. The person's performance on the neuropsychological screening tests depicts an individual whose performance is equivocal organic deficits.

Z-71. The person's performance on the neuropsychological screening tests depicts an individual who is currently experiencing mild memory deficits.

Z-72. The person's performance on the neuropsychological screening tests depicts an individual who is currently evidencing significant memory impairment.

Z-73. The person's performance on the neuropsychological screening tests depicts an individual who is currently experiencing very significant memory deficits.

Z-74. The person's performance on the neuropsychological screening tests depicts an individual who is currently experiencing marked memory deficits.

OBS RECOMMENDATIONS

Z-75. The person's mild deficits evidenced on the cognitive testing are mild, and the person should generally be able to carry out most of their affairs with minor help and generally remain in independent living.

Z-76. The person's deficits on cognitive testing are moderate and significant, and in all probability the person will need assistance and supervision with the more complex activities of daily living.

Z-77. The person in all probability is going to need a structured and supervised living situation.

Z-78. The person's performance depicts an individual who is in all probability going to require continual ongoing custodial care.

Z-79. The person's performance depicts an individual who in all probability can engage in semi-independent living, but will require some help.

LLD AND ATTENTION DEFICIT DISORDERS

Z-80. The person has a learning disability in the area of reading.

Z-81. The person has a learning disability in the area of math.

Z-82. The person has a learning disability in the areas of reading and math.

Z-83. The person's performance depicts an individual with an attention deficit disorder with hyperactivity.

Z-84. The person's performance depicts an individual with an attention deficit disorder without hyperactivity.

Z-85. The person's academic deficits are in all probability directly related to their impulsive behavioral-emotional difficulties.

Z-86. At this point in time, it is difficult to state whether the person's learning difficulties are the cause of or the result of their emotional difficulties, as the two interact with and affect one another.

MENTAL RETARDATION

Z-87. The person's intellectual ability is in the range of mental retardation, and the person is not competent to handle their everyday affairs without significant assistance.

Z-88. The person is an individual of borderline intellect who will have to be dealt with in a very pragmatic and concrete manner, and whose cognitive deficits impair their ability to function in everyday living.

Z-89. The person is an individual of low intellect who is apt to have difficulty functioning in everyday living and needs to be dealt with in a concrete and behaviorally oriented manner.

GENERAL IQ

Z-90. The person's intellect is a bit below average.

Z-91. The person is an individual of average intelligence.

Z-92. The person is a bright individual.

Z-93. The person is an individual of superior intellect.

Z-94. The person is a genius.

EGO LEVEL

Z-95. The individual's overall level of ego-emotional development is low and at a very primitive and impulsive level.

Z-96. The individual's overall level of ego-conscience development is low.

Z-97. The individual's overall level of ego-conscience development is low, and, while this would be very significant in the case of an adult, in the case of a teenager it is not quite as devastating.

Z-98. The individual's overall level of ego-conscience development appears in transition between hedonism and conformity.

Z-99. The individual's overall level of ego-conscience development is in transition, and, while this is somewhat low in an adult, in an adolescent it is not as aberrant.

Z-100. The individual's overall level of ego-conscience development, though somewhat low, depicts an individual who is not totally devoid of conscience development.

Z-101. The individual's overall level of ego-conscience development is good.

Z-102. The individual's overall level of ego-conscience development is average.

Z-103. The individual's overall level of ego-conscience development is average and, thus, in all probability has some moderating influence on the magnitude of the individual's impulsivity.

Z-104. The individual's overall level of ego-conscience development is above average.

Z-105. The individual's overall level of ego-conscience development is above average and depicts an individual who is apt to be sensitive to their own feelings and the feelings and needs of others.

MEDICAL PSYCHIATRIC RECOMMENDATIONS

Z-106. Medical psychiatric intervention is definitely indicated, and in all probability the person will need outpatient monitoring and follow-up for the indefinite future.

Z-107. Medical psychiatric intervention is indicated, as is supportive therapy.

Z-108. Medical psychiatric intervention should be considered.

PSYCHOTHERAPY RECOMMENDATIONS

Z-109. Psychotherapeutically, the person will probably profit best from a treatment approach that emphasizes developing a more assertive and modulated stance toward life.

Z-110. Psychotherapeutically, the person will probably profit best from a treatment approach that is pragmatic and no-nonsense, and which places the burden of responsibility for their own actions squarely upon their own needs and shoulders.

Z-111. Psychotherapeutically, in addition to abstinence, the person will probably profit best from a treatment approach that emphasizes taking greater responsibility for their own actions, and which reinforces the benefits of long-range, as opposed to short-range, hedonism.

Z-112. Psychotherapeutically, the person will probably profit best from a treatment approach that emphasizes modulating their emotions, thinking things through, and developing a more assertive and balanced stance toward life.

Z-113. Psychotherapeutically, the person will probably profit best from a treatment approach that emphasizes assertive training.

Z-114. Psychotherapeutically, the person will probably profit best from a treatment approach that emphasizes developing an increased repertoire of behavioral-emotional skills.

Z-115. Psychotherapeutically, the person will probably profit best from a treatment approach that emphasizes increasing their overall behavioral-emotional skills and general interpersonal sensitivity.

Z-116. Psychotherapeutically, the person will probably profit best from a treatment approach that is insight-oriented.

Z-117. Psychotherapeutically, the person will probably profit best from a treatment approach that focuses on concrete, here-and-now issues, and on modulating their emotions. Insight Therapy is apt to be contraindicated, as it is apt to cause the person to decompensate.

Z-118. Psychotherapeutically, the person will probably profit best from a treatment approach that emphasizes action and doing, and which de-emphasizes further ruminative introspection.

Z-119. Psychotherapeutically, the person will probably profit from a treatment approach that is concrete and behaviorally-oriented.

Z-120. Psychotherapeutically, due to their low intellect, the person will probably profit best from a treatment approach that is as concrete and behaviorally oriented as possible.

Z-121. Additionally, the person needs to be coaxed back into becoming active again in the business of living.

Z-122. Sick role behavior is to be discouraged.

MARRIAGE AND FAMILY THERAPY

Z-123. Family Therapy should definitely be considered for incorporation into the individual's overall treatment plan.

Z-124. Family Therapy should be considered for incorporation into the individual's overall treatment plan.

Z-125. Family Therapy appears to need to be an integral part of the individual's overall treatment plan.

Z-126. Marital Therapy would appear to be indicated.

Z-127. Marital Therapy should be considered as an adjunct to the individual's overall treatment plan.

Z-128. Marital Therapy *definitely* appears indicated.

Z-129. Marital Therapy should be considered for incorporation into the individual's overall treatment plan.

Z-130. If the individual is to reconcile with their spouse, Marital Therapy is definitely indicated.

References

References Cited in Text

American Psychiatric Association. (1980). *Diagnostic and statistical manual of mental disorders* (3rd. ed.). Washington, DC: Author.

Aronow, E., & Reznikoff, M. (1976). *Rorschach content interpretation.* New York: Grune & Stratton.

Burke, H.R., & Mayer, S. (1985). MMPI and the post-traumatic stress syndrome in Vietnam era veterans. *Journal of Clinical Psychology, 41,* 152–156.

Butcher, J.N., & Owen, P.L. (1978). Objective personality inventories: Recent research on some contemporary issues. In B.B. Wolman (Ed.), *Clinical diagnosis of mental disorders.* New York: Plenum Press.

Chaney, H.S., Williams, S.G., Cohn, C.K., & Vincent, K.R. (1984). MMPI Results: A comparison of trauma victims, psychogenic pain, and patients with organic disease. *Journal of Clinical Psychology, 40,* 1450–1454.

Coddington, R.D. (1981). *Life event scale—Children.* Clairseville, OH: Stress Research.

Davies, A. (1968). The influence of age on trail making test performance. *Journal of Clinical Psychology, 24,* 96–98.

DeHorn, A.B., Lachar, D., & Gdowski, C.L. (1979). Profile of classification strategies for the Personality Inventory for Children. *Journal of Consulting and Clinical Psychology, 47,* 874–881.

Dohrenwend, B.P., Dohrenwend, B.S., Gould, M.S., Link, B., Neugebauer, R., & Wunsch-Hitzig, R. (1980). *Mental illness in the United States.* New York: Praeger.

Erickson, R.C., Caslyn, D.A., & Scheupbach, C.S. (1978). Abbreviating the Halsted-Reitan Neuropsychological Test Battery. *Journal of Clinical Psychology, 34,* 922–926.

Exner, J.E. (1974). *The Rorschach: A comprehensive system.* New York: John Wiley & Sons.

Fairbank, J.A., Keave, T.M., & Malloy, P.F. (1983). Some preliminary data on the psychology characteristics of vietnam veterans with post-traumatic stress disorders. *Journal of Consulting and Clinical Psychology, 51,* 912–919.

Feingold, A. (1982). Validity of the information and vocabulary subtests of the WAIS. *Journal of Clinical Psychology, 38,* 994–997.

Feingold, A. (1983). Entracting maximum validity from the WAIS. *Journal of Clinical Psychology, 39,* 994–997.

Forer, B.R. (1957). *The Forer structured sentence completion test manual.* Los Angeles: Western Psychological Services.

Foy, D.W., Sipprelle, R.C., Rueger, D.B., & Carroll, E.M. (1984). Etiology of post traumatic stress disorder in vietnam veterans. *Journal of Consulting and Clinical Psychology, 52,* 79–87.

Goldberg, P.A. (1965). A review of sentence completion methods in personality measurement. In B.I. Murstein (Ed.), *Handbook of projective techniques.* New York: Basic Books.

Graham, F.K., & Kendall, B.S. (1960). Memory-for-designs test: Revised general manual. *Perceptual and Motor Skills* (Monograph Supplement No. 2-VII), *11*, 147–188.

Gustin, Q.L., Goodpaster, W.A., Sajadi, C., Pitts, W.M., LaBasse, D.L., & Snyder, S. (1983). MMPI characteristics of the DSM-III borderline personality disorder. *Journal of Personality Assessment, 47*, 50–59.

Hain, J.D. (1964). The Bender Gestalt test: A scoring method for identifying brain damage. *Journal Of Consulting Psychology, 28*, 34–40.

Holland, J.L. (1985a). *Vocational preference inventory* (8th ed.). Odessa, FL: Psychological Assessment Resources.

Holland, J.L. (1985b). *Making vocational choices*. Englewood Cliffs, NJ: Prentice-Hall.

Holmes, T.H., & Rahe, R.H. (1967). The Social Readjustment Rating Scale. *Journal of Psychosomatic Research, 11*, 213–218.

Holtzman, W.E. (1975). New developments in Holtzman inkblot technique. In P. McReynolds (Ed.), *Advances in psychological assessment* (Vol. 3). San Francisco, CA: Jossey-Bass.

Kaufman, A.S. (1979). *Intelligent testing with the WISC-R*. New York: John Wiley & Sons.

Lachar, D. (1972). Accuracy and generalizability of an automated MMPI interpretation system. *Journal of Consulting and Clinical Psychology, 42*, 267–273.

Leli, D.A., & Filskov, S.B. (1979). Relationship of intelligence to education and occupation and signs of intellectual deterioration. *Journal of Consulting and Clinical Psychology, 47*, 702–707.

Leli, D.A., & Filskov, S.B. (1981). Clinical-actuarial detection and description of brain damage with the W-B Form 1. *Journal of Clinical Psychology, 37*, 623–629.

Leli, D.A., & Filskov, S.B. (1984). Clinical detection of intellectual deterioration associated with brain damage. *Journal of Clinical Psychology, 40*, 1435–1440.

Loevinger, J., & Wessler, R. (1970). *Measuring ego development, Vol. 1*. San Francisco: Jossey-Bass.

Loevinger, J., Wessler, R., & Redmore, C. (1970). *Measuring ego development, Vol. 2*. San Francisco: Jossey-Bass.

Matarazzo, J.D. (1972). *Wechsler's Measurement and Appraisal of Adult Intelligence*. Baltimore, MD: Williams & Wilkins.

Matarrazo, J.D., & Herman, D.O. (1984). Relationship of education and IQ in the WAIS-R standardization sample. *Journal of Consulting and Clinical Psychology, 52*, 631–634.

McMurrey, A.D., & Vincent, K.R. (1985). Reliability in the psychological inventory of personality and symptoms. *Psychological Reports, 56*, 902.

Meehl, P.E. (1954). *Clinical versus statistical prediction*. Minneapolis, MN: University of Minnesota Press.

Millon, T. (1977). *Millon multiaxial clinical inventory*. Minneapolis, MN: Interpretive Scoring Systems.

Patrick, J. (1984). Characteristics of DSM-III borderline MMPI profiles. *Journal of Clinical Psychology, 40*, 655–658.

Prifitera, A., & Barley, W.D. (1985). Cautions in interpretation of comparisons between the WAIS-R and the Wechsler Memory Scale. *Journal of Consulting and Clinical Psychology, 53*, 464–465.

Sacks, J.M. (1965). The relation effect of projective responses of stimuli referring to the subject and of stimuli referring to other persons. In B.I. Mustein (Ed.), *Handbook of projective techniques*. New York: Basic Books.

Sattler, J.M. (1982). *Assessment of children's intelligence and special abilities* (2nd ed.). Boston: Allyn & Bacon.

Schroeder, D.J., & Piercy, D.C. (1979). A comparison of MMPI two point codes in four alcoholism treatment facilities. *Journal of Clinical Psychology, 35*, 656–663.

Silver, R.J., Isaacs, K., & Mansky, P. (1981). MMPI correlates of affective disorders. *Journal of Clinical Psychology, 37*, 836–839.

United States Department of Labor. (1965). *Dictionary of occupational titles* (Vols. 1–2, 3rd ed.). Washington, DC: Author.

United States Department of Labor. (1967). *Manual for the general aptitude test battery*. Washington, DC: Author.

United States Department of Labor. (1982). *Occupational outlook handbook*. Washington, DC: Author.

Vincent, K.R. (1979). The modified WAIS, an alternative to short forms. *Journal of Clinical Psychology, 35*, 624–625.

Vincent, K.R. (1980a). Semi-automated full battery. *Journal of Clinical Psychology, 36*, 437–446.

Vincent, K.R. (1980b). *MMPI semi-automated interpretative statements*. Houston, TX: Psychometric Press.

Vincent, K.R. (1980c). *The semi-automated full battery*. Houston, TX: Psychometric Press.

Vincent, K.R. (1981). Using a word processor to expedite psychological testing. *Computers In Psychiatry/Psychology*, October, *3*, 8–9.

Vincent, K.R. (1982a). *Vincent biographical inventory*. Richland, WA: Psychological Software Specialists.

Vincent, K.R. (1982b). *Automated interpretative statements for the impression, Vincent biographical inventory, and summary and comments sections of a psychological assessment battery*. Richland, WA: Psychological Software Specialists.

Vincent, K.R. (1983a). The full psychological report via a word processor. In M.D. Schwartz (Ed.), *A guide to small computers in private psychotherapy practice*. New York: Haworth Press.

Vincent, K.R. (1983b). Psychological test analysis and report writing via a word processor. *Innovations in clinical practice* (Vol. 2). Mansfield, PA: Professional Resource Exchange.

Vincent, K.R. (1985a). *Manual for the diagnostic inventory of personality and symptoms (DIPS)*. Richland, WA: Pacific Psychologicals.

Vincent, K.R. (1985b). *Interpretative program for the Diagnostic Inventory of Personality and Symptoms (DIPS)* [Computer program]. Richland, WA: Pacific Psychologicals.

Vincent, K.R. (1985d). Psychological inventory of personality and symptoms (PIPS): A new test of psychopathology based on DSM-III. *The Journal: Houston International Hospital, 3*, 20–27.

Vincent, K.R. (in press). Manual for the Psychological Inventory of Personaltiy and Symptoms (PIPS) and the Diagnostic Inventory of Personality and Symptoms (DIPS). *The Journal: Houston International Hospital*.

Vincent, K.R., & Castillo, I.M. (1984a). Ego development and DSM III Axis II: Personality disorders. *Journal of Clinical Psychology, 40*, 400–403.

Vincent, K.R., & Castillo, I.M. (1984b). Utility on the Pfeiffer (SPMSQ) Scale with non-geriatric populations. *The Journal: Houston International Hospital, 2*, 14–16.

Vincent, K.R., & Castillo, I.M. (1985). MMPI code types and DSM III diagnosis: Some additional code types. *MMPI Review*, 1–5.

Vincent, K.R., Castillo, I., Hauser, R.I., Zapata, J.A., Stuart, H.J., Cohn, C.K., & O'Shanick, G.J. (1983). MMPI code types and DSM III diagnosis. *Journal Of Clinical Psychology, 39*, 829–042.

Vincent, K.R., Castillo, I., Hauser, R.I., Zapata, J.A., Stuart, H.J., Cohn, C.K., & O'Shanick, G.J. (1984). *MMPI-168 codebook*. Norwood, NJ: Ablex.

Vincent, K.R., & Duthie, B. (1983b). *Semi-automated system* (Vol. III). Richland, WA: Psychological Software Specialists.

Vincent, K.R., & Duthie, B. (in press). Factor structure of the Diagnostic Inventory of Personality and Symptoms in a private psychiatric hospital population. *Journal of Clinical Psychology*.

Vincent, L.R., & Vincent, K.R. (1979). Ego Development and psychopathology. *Psychological Reports, 44*, 408–410.

Vincent, K.R., & Williams, W. (1985). Alcohol abuse scale of the Psychological Inventory of Personality and Symptoms (PIPS). *Psychological Reports, 57*, 1077–1078.

Vincent, K.R., Williams, W., Pitts, W.M., & Rodriguez-Garcia, M. (1985). Related clinical utility of the Psychological Inventory of Personality and Symptoms. *Psychological Reports, 56,* 847–850.

Walters, G.D. (1984b). Identifying schizophrenia by mean as of scale 8 Sc of the MMPI. *Journal of Personality Assessment, 48,* 390–391.

Wiggins, J.S. (1973). *Personality and prediction: Principles of personality assessment.* Reading, MA: Addison-Wesley.

Wirt, R.D., & Lachar, D. (1981). The Personality Inventory for Children: Development and applications. In P. McReynolds (Ed.), *Advances in psychological assessment* (Vol. 5). San Francisco: Jossey-Bass.

Additional References

Aronow, E., & Reznikoff, M. (1982). Reliability of Inkblot Content Scales. In C.D. Spielberger & J.N. Buther (Eds.), *Advances in personality assessment, Vol. 1.* Hillsdale, NJ: Erlbaum.

Aronow, E., & Reznikoff, M. (1983). *A Rorschach introduction.* New York: Grune & Stratton.

Baughman, E.E. (1965). A comparative analysis of Rorschach forms with altered stimulus characteristics. In B.I. Mustein (Ed.), *Handbook of projective techniques.* New York: Basic Books.

Beck, A.T. (1967). *Depression.* Philadelphia, PA: University of Pennsylvania Press.

Beck, A.T., Ward, C.H., Mendelson, M., Mock, J., & Erbaugh, J. (1962). An inventory for measuring depression. *Archives of General Psychiatry, 4,* 561–571.

Bumberry, W., Oliver, J.M., & McClure, J.N. (1978). Validation of the Beck Depression Inventory in a university population using psychiatric estimate as the criterion. *Journal of Consulting and Clinical Psychology, 46,* 150–155.

Carlozzi, A.F., Gaa, J.P., & Liberman, D.B. (1983). Empathy and ego development. *Journal of Counseling Psychology, 30,* 113–116.

Castillo, I.M. (1980). Relationship in stressful life events and adolescent's employment. *Psychological Reports, 47,* 1195–1198.

Coddington, R.D. (1972a). The significance of life events as etiologic factors in the diseases of children, I: A survey of professional works. *Journal of Psychosomatic Research, 16,* 7–18.

Coddington, R.D. (1972b). The significance of life events as etiologic factors in the diseases of children, II: A study of a normal population. *Journal of Psychosomatic Research, 16,* 205–213.

Coddington, R.D. (1979). Life events associated with adolescent pregnancies. *Journal of Clinical Psychiatry, 40,* 180–185.

Coddington, R.D. (1983). Measuring the stressfulness of a child's environment. In J.H. Humphrey (Ed.), *Stress in childhood.* New York: AMS Press.

Dahlstrom, W.G., Welsh, G.S., & Dahlstrom, L.E. (1972). *An MMPI handbook, Vol. 1.* Minneapolis, MN: University of Minnesota Press.

Doll, E. (1953). *Measurement of social competence.* Circle Pines, MN: American Guidance Services.

Doll, E. (1965). *Vineland social maturity scale.* Circle Pines, MN: American Guidance Services.

Dunn, L.M., & Markwardt, F.C. (1970). *Peabody individual achievement test manual.* Circle Clines, MN: American Guidance Service.

Duthie, B. (1985). *Adolescent mutiphasic personality inventory.* Richland, WA: Pacific Psychologicals.

Duthie, R.B. (1980). *Psychometric personality classification of community mental health clients in Nome, Alaska.* Nome, AK: Norton Sound Health.

Endicott, N.A. (1972). The Holtzman Inkblot Technique content measures of depression and suspiciousness. *Journal of Personality Assessment, 36,* 424–426.

Exner, J.E. (1969). *The Rorschach systems.* New York: Grune & Stratton.

Exner, J.E. (1978). *The Rorschach: A comprehensive system, Vol. 2.* New York: John Wiley and Sons.

Exner, J.E., & Exner, D.E. (1972). How clinicians use the Rorschach. *Journal of Personality Assessment, 36*, 403–408.

Exner, J.E., & Weiner, J.E. (1982). *The Rorschach: A comprehensive system, Volume 3*. New York: John Wiley & Sons.

Exner, J.E., Thomas, E.A., & Mason, B. (1985). Children's Rorschachs: Description and prediction. *Journal of Personality Assessment, 49*, 13–20.

Fear, R.A. (1958). *The evaluation interview*. New York: McGraw Hill.

Frank, S., & Quinlann, D.M. (1976). Ego development and female delinquency: A cognitive developmental approach. *Journal of Abnormal Psychology, 35*, 505–510.

Friedman, A.M., Kaplan, H.I., & Sadock, B.J. (1972). *Modern synopsis of Comprehensive Textbook of Psychiatry*. Baltimore, MD: Williams & Wilkins.

Giambra, L.M. (1977). Independent dimensions of depression: A factor analysis of three self-report depression measures. *Journal of Clinical Psychology, 33*, 928–935.

Gilbert, J. (1978). *Interpreting psychological test data* (Vols. 1–2). New York: Van Nostrand Reinhold.

Gold, S.N. (1980). Relations between level of ego development and adjustment patterns in adolescents. *Journal of Personality Assessment, 44*, 630–638.

Groth-Marnat, G. (1984). *Handbook of psychological assessment*. New York: Van Nostrand Reinhold.

Hauser, S.T. (1976). Loevinger's model and measure of ego development: A critical review. *Psychological Bulletin, 21*, 195–206.

Hedlund, J.L., Vieweg, B.W., Wood, J.B., Cho, D.W., Evenson, R.C., Hickman, C.W., & Holland, R.A. (1981). *Computers in mental health, A review in annotated bibliography*. Washington, DC: Superintendent of Documents, U.S. Government Printing Office.

Heisel, J.S., Ream, S., Raitz, R., Rappaport, M., & Coddington, R.D. (1973). The significance of life events as contributing factors in the diseases of children, III: A study of pediatric patients. *Journal of Pediatrics, 83*, 119–123.

Hill, E.F. (1972). *The Holtzman Inkblot Technique*. San Francisco: Jossey-Bass.

Holland, J.L. (1966). *The psychology of vocational choice: A theory of personality types and model environments*. Waltham, MS: Blaisdell.

Holland, J.L. (1985). *Making vocational choices: A theory of careers* (2nd ed.). Englewood Cliffs, NJ: Prentice-Hall.

Holmes, T.H. (1984). *Schedule of recent experience manual*. Odessa, FL: Psychological Assessment Resources.

Jastak, J.F., & Jastak, S.R. (1976). *Wide range achievement test manual*. Wilmington, DE: Guidance Associates of Delaware.

Jastak, J.F., & Wilkinson, G.S. (1984). *The wide range achievement test—Revised administration manual*. Wilmington, DE: Jastak Associates.

Kovacs, M., & Beck, A.T. (1978). Maladaptive cognitive structures in depression. *American Journal of Psychiatry, 35*, 525–531.

Lachar, D. (1982). *Personality inventory for Children: Revised format manual supplement*. Los Angeles: Western Psychological Services.

Lachar, D., & Gdowski, C.L. (1979a). *Actuarial assessment of child and adolescent personality*. Los Angeles: Western Psychological Services.

Lachar, D., & Gdowski, C.L. (1979b). Problem-behavior correlates of Personality Inventory for Children profile scales. *Journal of Consulting and Clinical Psychology, 47*, 39–48.

Lachar, D., & Gdowski, C.L., & Snyder, D.K. (1982). Broad-band dimensions of psychopathology: Factor scales for the Personality Inventory for Children. *Journal of Consulting and Clinical Psychology, 50*, 634–642.

Lachar, D., & Gdowski, C.L., & Snyder, D.K. (1984). External validation of the Personality Inventory for Children (PIC) profile and factor scales. *Journal of Consulting and Clinical Psychology, 52*, 255–264.

Lazar, Z.L., & Schwartz, F. (1982). The contaminated Rorschach response: Formal features. *Journal of Clinical Psychology, 38,* 415–419.

Lezaek, M.D. (1976). *Neuropsychological assessment.* New York: Oxford University Press.

Loevinger, J. (1966). The meaning and measurement of ego development. *American Psychologist, 21,* 195–206.

Loevinger, J. (1968). The relationship in adjustment to ego development. In S.S. Salls (Ed.), *The definition and measurement of mental health* (Health Service Publication #183). Washington, DC: U.S. Government Printing Office.

Loevinger, J. (1976). *Ego development: Conceptions and theories.* San Francisco: Jossey-Bass.

Loevinger, J. (1979). Construct validity of the sentence completion test of ego development. *Applied Psychological Measurement, 3,* 281–311.

Lorr, M., & Manning, T.T. (1978a). Measurement of ego development by sentence completion and personality test. *Journal of Clinical Psychology, 34,* 354–360.

Lorr, M., & Manning, T.T. (1978b). Personality correlates of the sex role types. *Journal of Clinical Psychology, 34,* 884–888.

Marks, P.A., Seeman, W., & Haller, D.L. (1974). *The actuarial use of the MMPI with adolescents and adults.* Baltimore, MD: Williams & Wilkins.

Maslow, A.H. (1954). *Motivation and personality.* New York: Harper & Row.

Matarazzo, G.D. (1978). The interview: Its reliability and validity in psychiatric diagnosis. In B.B. Wolman (Ed.), *Clinical diagnosis of mental disorders: A handbook.* New York: Plenum Press.

Mayer, J.M. (1977). Assessment of depression. In P. McReynolds (Ed.), *Advances in psychological assessment* (Vol. 4). San Francisco: Jossey-Bass.

Meyer, R.G. (1983). *The clinician's handbook.* Boston: Allyn & Bacon.

Oakland, T., & Hutchins, S. (1985). A review of the Vineland Adaptive Behavior Scale, Survey Form. *Journal of Counseling and Development, 63,* 585–586.

Ogdon, D.P. (1978). *Psychodiagnostics and personality assessment: A handbook* (2nd ed.). Los Angeles: Western Psychological Services.

Paykel, E.S., Prusoff, B.A., Klerman, G.L., & DiMascio, A. (1972). Self report and clinical interview ratings in depression. *Journal of Nervous and Mental Disease, 56,* 66–82.

Powitsky, R.J. (1976). Ego level and type of federal offense. *Dissertation Abstracts International, 36,* 5768B. (University Microfilms No. 76–1838).

Rapport, D., Gill, M.M., & Schafer, R. (1968). *Diagnostic psychological testing.* New York: International Universities Press.

Reitan, R.M., & Davidson, L.A. (1974). *Clinical neuropsychology.* New York: John Wiley and Sons.

Russell, E.W. (1979). Three patterns of brain damage on the WAIS. *Journal of Clinical Psychology, 35,* 611–620.

Russell, E.W., Neuringer, C., & Goldstein, G. (1970). *Assessment of brain damage.* New York: Wiley-Interscience.

Ryback, R.S. (1974). *The problem oriented record in psychiatry and mental health care.* New York: Grune & Stratton.

Sherman, M.H.G. (1960). *A Rorschach reader.* New York: International Universities Press.

Sparrow, S., Bella, D., & Cicchetti, D. (1984). *Vineland adaptive behavior scales: Survey form manual.* Circle Pines, MN: American Guidance Services.

United States Department of Labor, Bureau of Employment Security. (1967). *College courses and beginning jobs.* Washington, DC: Author.

Viernstein, M.C. (1972). The extension of Holland's occupational classification to all occupations in the Dictionary of Occupational Titles. *Journal of Vocational Behavior, 2,* 107–121.

Vincent, K.R. (1982c). Validation of the interpretive schema for a fully automated inkblot test: The Holtzman Content Analysis Technique. *Computers in Psychiatry and Psychology, 4,* 16–17.

Vincent, K.R. (1982d). The development of a fully automated inkblot test: The Holtzman Content Analysis Technique. *Computers in Psychiatry and Psychology, 4,* 15–17.

Vincent, K.R.(1983c). History and impressions; Summary and recommendations. In B. Duthie & E.G. Allen (Eds.), *Fully automated psychological interpretation system and report writer, System 1* [Computer program]. Richland, WA: Psychological Software Specialists.

Vincent, K.R., & Cox, J.A. (1974). A re-evaluation of Raven's standard progressive matrices. *Journal of Psychology, 88,* 299–303.

Vincent, K.R., & Duthie, B. (1982). *Computerized Holtzman interpretation* [Computer program]. Richland, WA: Psychological Software Specialists.

Vincent, K.R., & Duthie, B. (1983a). *Semi-automated system, System 2* [Computer program]. Richland, WA: Psychological Software Specialists.

Vincent, K.R., & Rosenstock, H.A. (1979). The relationship between stressful life events and hospitalization of adolescent psychiatric patients. *Journal of Clinical Psychiatry, 40,* 28–31.

Vincent, K.R., & Williams, R.E. (1985). Test review of the Loevinger Sentence Completion Test. In D.J. Keyser & R.C. Sweetland (Eds.), *Test critiques* (Vol. 3). Kansas City, MO: Test Corporation of America.

Vincent, K.R., & Williams, R.E. (1985). Test review of the Life Event Scale—Children. In D.J. Keyser & R.C. Sweetland (Eds.), *Test critiques* (Vol. 3). Kansas City, MO: Test Corporation of America.

Vincent, K.R., Wilson, A.L. & Wilson, J.L. (1983a). *Automated administration and interpretative program for the Vincent biographical inventory fully automated form* [Computer program]. Houston, TX: Psychometric Services.

Vincent, K.R., Wilson, A.L., & Wilson, J.L. (1983b). *The automated objective fully psychological battery* [Computer program]. Houston, TX: Psychometric Services.

Watson, R.I. (1978). The sentence completion method. In B.B. Wolman (Ed.), *Clinical diagnosis of mental disorders.* New York: Plenum Press.

Waugh, M.H., & McCaulley, M.H. (1981). Relationship of ego development to type and severity of psychopathology. *Journal of Consulting and Clinical Psychology, 49,* 295–296.

Wechsler, D. (1974). *WISC-R manual.* New York: Psychological Corp.

Wechsler, D. (1981). *WAIS-R manual.* New York: Psychological Corp.

Weiner, I.B., & Exner, J.E. (1978). Rorschach indices of disordered thinking in patient and non-patient adolescents and adults. *Journal of Personality Assessment, 42,* 339–343.

Williams, R.E., & Vincent, K.R. (1985). Test review of the Peabody Individual Achievement Test. In D.J. Keyser & R.C. Sweetland (Eds.), *Test critiques* (Vol. 3). Kansas City, MO: Test Corporation of America.

Wirt, R.D., Lachar, D., Klinedinst, J.K., & Seat, P.D. (1984). *Multidimensional description of child personality: A manual for the Personality Inventory for Children.* Los Angeles: Western Psychological Services.

Workman, E.A., & Stillion, J.M. (1974). The relationship between creativity and ego development. *Journal of Psychology, 88,* 191–195.

Author Index

SUBJECT INDEX

www.ingramcontent.com/pod-product-compliance
Lightning Source LLC
LaVergne TN
LVHW011522200926
848484LV00001B/121